INTERMEDIATE

ILLUSTRATED SERIES™

MICROSOFT® OFFICE 365™

EXCEL® 2016

For Microsoft® Office updates, go to sam.cengage.com

REDING + WERMERS

CENGAGE
Learning®

Australia • Brazil • Mexico • Singapore • United Kingdom • United States

Illustrated Microsoft® Office 365™ &
Excel® 2016—Intermediate
Elizabeth Eisner Reding/Lynn Wermers

SVP, GM Skills & Global Product Management:
    Dawn Gerrain

Product Director: Kathleen McMahon

Senior Product Team Manager: Lauren Murphy

Product Team Manager: Andrea Topping

Associate Product Manager: Melissa Stehler

Senior Director, Development: Marah Bellegarde

Product Development Manager: Leigh Hefferon

Senior Content Developer: Christina Kling-Garrett

Developmental Editor: MT Cozzola

Product Assistant: Erica Chapman

Marketing Director: Michele McTighe

Marketing Manager: Stephanie Albracht

Marketing Coordinator: Cassie Cloutier

Senior Production Director: Wendy Troeger

Production Director: Patty Stephan

Senior Content Project Manager: Stacey Lamodi

Art Director: Diana Graham

Text Designer: Joseph Lee, Black Fish Design

Cover Template Designer: Lisa Kuhn, Curio Press, LLC
    www.curiopress.com

Composition: GEX Publishing Services

Mac users: If you're working through this product using a Mac, some of the
steps may vary. Additional information for Mac users is included with the
Data Files for this product.

Some of the product names and company names used in this book have
been used for identification purposes only and may be trademarks or
registered trademarks of their respective manufacturers and sellers.

Windows® is a registered trademark of Microsoft Corporation. © 2012
Microsoft. Microsoft and the Office logo are either registered trademarks
or trademarks of Microsoft Corporation in the United States and/or other
countries. Cengage Learning is an independent entity from Microsoft
Corporation and not affiliated with Microsoft in any manner. Microsoft
product screenshots used with permission from Microsoft Corporation.
Unless otherwise noted, all clip art is courtesy of openclipart.org.

Disclaimer: Any fictional data related to persons or companies or URLs used
throughout this text is intended for instructional purposes only. At the time
this text was published, any such data was fictional and not belonging to
any real persons or companies.

Disclaimer: The material in this text was written using Microsoft Windows 10
Professional and Office 365 Professional Plus and was Quality Assurance tested
before the publication date. As Microsoft continually updates the Windows 10
operating system and Office 365, your software experience may vary slightly
from what is presented in the printed text.

Library of Congress Control Number: 2016932758
Soft-cover Edition ISBN: 978-1-305-87809-9
Loose-leaf Edition ISBN: 978-1-337-25083-2

Cengage Learning
20 Channel Center Street
Boston, MA 02210
USA

Cengage Learning is a leading provider of customized learning solutions
with employees residing in nearly 40 different countries and sales in more
than 125 countries around the world. Find your local representative at
www.cengage.com.

Cengage Learning products are represented in Canada by
Nelson Education, Ltd.

For your course and learning solutions, visit **www.cengage.com**

Purchase any of our products at your local college store or at our
preferred online store **www.cengagebrain.com**

Printed in the United States of America
Print Number: 02   Print Year: 2016

Brief Contents

Contents

Productivity Apps for School and Work

Corinne Hoisington

Lochlan keeps track of his class notes, football plays, and internship meetings with OneNote.

Zoe is using the annotation features of Microsoft Edge to take and save web notes for her research paper.

Nori is creating a Sway site to highlight this year's activities for the Student Government Association.

Hunter is adding interactive videos and screen recordings to his PowerPoint resume.

© Rawpixel/Shutterstock.com

Being computer literate no longer means mastery of only Word, Excel, PowerPoint, Outlook, and Access. To become technology power users, Hunter, Nori, Zoe, and Lochlan are exploring Microsoft OneNote, Sway, Mix, and Edge in Office 2016 and Windows 10.

Learn to use productivity apps!
Links to companion **Sways**, featuring **videos** with hands-on instructions, are located on www.cengagebrain.com.

Introduction to OneNote 2016

notebook | section tab | To Do tag | screen clipping | note | template | Microsoft OneNote Mobile app | sync | drawing canvas | inked handwriting | Ink to Text

As you glance around any classroom, you invariably see paper notebooks and notepads on each desk. Because deciphering and sharing handwritten notes can be a challenge, Microsoft OneNote 2016 replaces physical notebooks, binders, and paper notes with a searchable, digital notebook. OneNote captures your ideas and schoolwork on any device so you can stay organized, share notes, and work with others on projects. Whether you are a student taking class notes as shown in **Figure 1** or an employee taking notes in company meetings, OneNote is the one place to keep notes for all of your projects.

Figure 1: OneNote 2016 notebook

Each **notebook** is divided into sections, also called **section tabs**, by subject or topic.

Use **To Do tags**, icons that help you keep track of your assignments and other tasks.

Type on a page to add a **note**, a small window that contains text or other types of information.

Personalize a page with a **template**, or stationery.

Write or draw directly on the page using drawing tools.

Pages can include pictures such as **screen clippings**, images from any part of a computer screen.

Attach files and enter equations so you have everything you need in one place.

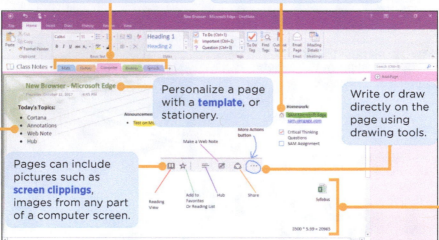

Creating a OneNote Notebook

OneNote is divided into sections similar to those in a spiral-bound notebook. Each OneNote notebook contains sections, pages, and other notebooks. You can use One-Note for school, business, and personal projects. Store information for each type of project in different notebooks to keep your tasks separate, or use any other organization that suits you. OneNote is flexible enough to adapt to the way you want to work.

When you create a notebook, it contains a blank page with a plain white background by default, though you can use templates, or stationery, to apply designs in categories such as Academic, Business, Decorative, and Planners. Start typing or use the buttons on the Insert tab to insert notes, which are small resizable windows that can contain text, equations, tables, on-screen writing, images, audio and video recordings, to-do lists, file attachments, and file printouts. Add as many notes as you need to each page.

Syncing a Notebook to the Cloud

OneNote saves your notes every time you make a change in a notebook. To make sure you can access your notebooks with a laptop, tablet, or smartphone wherever you are, OneNote uses cloud-based storage, such as OneDrive or SharePoint. **Microsoft OneNote Mobile app**, a lightweight version of OneNote 2016 shown in **Figure 2**, is available for free in the Windows Store, Google Play for Android devices, and the AppStore for iOS devices.

If you have a Microsoft account, OneNote saves your notes on OneDrive automatically for all your mobile devices and computers, which is called **syncing**. For example, you can use OneNote to take notes on your laptop during class, and then open OneNote on your phone to study later. To use a notebook stored on your computer with your OneNote Mobile app, move the notebook to OneDrive. You can quickly share notebook content with other people using OneDrive.

Figure 2: Microsoft OneNote Mobile app

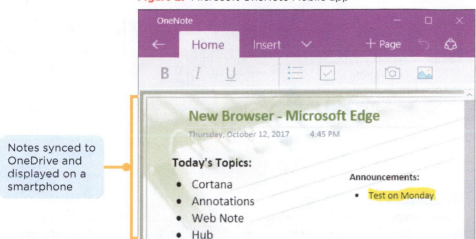

Notes synced to OneDrive and displayed on a smartphone

Taking Notes

Use OneNote pages to organize your notes by class and topic or lecture. Beyond simple typed notes, OneNote stores drawings, converts handwriting to searchable text and mathematical sketches to equations, and records audio and video.

OneNote includes drawing tools that let you sketch freehand drawings such as biological cell diagrams and financial supply-and-demand charts. As shown in **Figure 3**, the Draw tab on the ribbon provides these drawing tools along with shapes so you can insert diagrams and other illustrations to represent your ideas. When you draw on a page, OneNote creates a **drawing canvas**, which is a container for shapes and lines.

Figure 3: Tools on the Draw tab

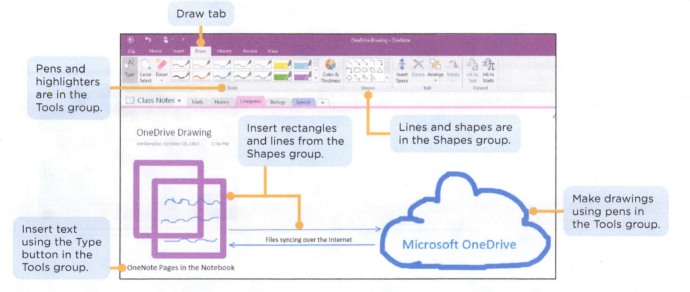

Draw tab

Pens and highlighters are in the Tools group.

Insert rectangles and lines from the Shapes group.

Lines and shapes are in the Shapes group.

Make drawings using pens in the Tools group.

Insert text using the Type button in the Tools group.

Converting Handwriting to Text

When you use a pen tool to write on a notebook page, the text you enter is called **inked handwriting**. OneNote can convert inked handwriting to typed text when you use the **Ink to Text** button in the Convert group on the Draw tab, as shown in **Figure 4**. After OneNote converts the handwriting to text, you can use the Search box to find terms in the converted text or any other note in your notebooks.

Figure 4: Converting handwriting to text

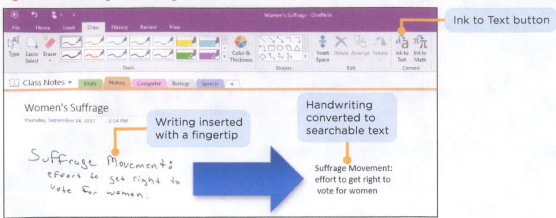

Ink to Text button

Women's Suffrage
Thursday, September 14, 2017   2:14 PM

Writing inserted with a fingertip

Suffrage Movement:
effort to get right to
vote for women.

Handwriting converted to searchable text

Suffrage Movement:
effort to get right to
vote for women

On the Job Now

Use OneNote as a place to brainstorm ongoing work projects. If a notebook contains sensitive material, you can password-protect some or all of the notebook so that only certain people can open it.

Recording a Lecture

If your computer or mobile device has a microphone or camera, OneNote can record the audio or video from a lecture or business meeting as shown in **Figure 5**. When you record a lecture (with your instructor's permission), you can follow along, take regular notes at your own pace, and review the video recording later. You can control the start, pause, and stop motions of the recording when you play back the recording of your notes.

Figure 5: Video inserted in a notebook

Record Video button

Audio & Video Recording tab

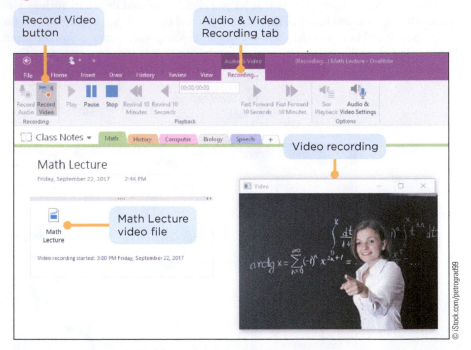

Video recording

Math Lecture
Friday, September 22, 2017   2:44 PM

Math Lecture video file

Video recording started: 3:00 PM Friday, September 22, 2017

Try This Now

Learn to use OneNote!
Links to companion **Sways**, featuring **videos** with hands-on instructions, are located on www.cengagebrain.com.

1: Taking Notes for a Week

As a student, you can get organized by using OneNote to take detailed notes in your classes. Perform the following tasks:

a. Create a new OneNote notebook on your Microsoft OneDrive account (the default location for new notebooks). Name the notebook with your first name followed by "Notes," as in **Caleb Notes**.

b. Create four section tabs, each with a different class name.

c. Take detailed notes in those classes for one week. Be sure to include notes, drawings, and other types of content.

d. Sync your notes with your OneDrive. Submit your assignment in the format specified by your instructor.

2: Using OneNote to Organize a Research Paper

You have a research paper due on the topic of three habits of successful students. Use OneNote to organize your research. Perform the following tasks:

a. Create a new OneNote notebook on your Microsoft OneDrive account. Name the notebook **Success Research**.

b. Create three section tabs with the following names:

- **Take Detailed Notes**
- **Be Respectful in Class**
- **Come to Class Prepared**

c. On the web, research the topics and find three sources for each section. Copy a sentence from each source and paste the sentence into the appropriate section. When you paste the sentence, OneNote inserts it in a note with a link to the source.

d. Sync your notes with your OneDrive. Submit your assignment in the format specified by your instructor.

3: Planning Your Career

Note: This activity requires a webcam or built-in video camera on any type of device.

Consider an occupation that interests you. Using OneNote, examine the responsibilities, education requirements, potential salary, and employment outlook of a specific career. Perform the following tasks:

a. Create a new OneNote notebook on your Microsoft OneDrive account. Name the notebook with your first name followed by a career title, such as **Kara - App Developer**.

b. Create four section tabs with the names **Responsibilities, Education Requirements, Median Salary**, and **Employment Outlook**.

c. Research the responsibilities of your career path. Using OneNote, record a short video (approximately 30 seconds) of yourself explaining the responsibilities of your career path. Place the video in the Responsibilities section.

d. On the web, research the educational requirements for your career path and find two appropriate sources. Copy a paragraph from each source and paste them into the appropriate section. When you paste a paragraph, OneNote inserts it in a note with a link to the source.

e. Research the median salary for a single year for this career. Create a mathematical equation in the Median Salary section that multiplies the amount of the median salary times 20 years to calculate how much you will possibly earn.

f. For the Employment Outlook section, research the outlook for your career path. Take at least four notes about what you find when researching the topic.

g. Sync your notes with your OneDrive. Submit your assignment in the format specified by your instructor.

Introduction to Sway

Sway site | responsive design | Storyline | card | Creative Commons license | animation emphasis effects | Docs.com

Expressing your ideas in a presentation typically means creating PowerPoint slides or a Word document. Microsoft Sway gives you another way to engage an audience. Sway is a free Microsoft tool available at Sway.com or as an app in Office 365. Using Sway, you can combine text, images, videos, and social media in a website called a **Sway site** that you can share and display on any device. To get started, you create a digital story on a web-based canvas without borders, slides, cells, or page breaks. A Sway site organizes the text, images, and video into a **responsive design**, which means your content adapts perfectly to any screen size as shown in **Figure 6**. You store a Sway site in the cloud on OneDrive using a free Microsoft account.

Figure 6: Sway site with responsive design

You can display a Sway presentation in a web browser.

Sway uses responsive design to make sure pages fit perfectly on any device.

© iStock.com/marinello, © iStock.com/marekuliasz

Creating a Sway Presentation

You can use Sway to build a digital flyer, a club newsletter, a vacation blog, an informational site, a digital art portfolio, or a new product rollout. After you select your topic and sign into Sway with your Microsoft account, a **Storyline** opens, providing tools and a work area for composing your digital story. See **Figure 7**. Each story can include text, images, and videos. You create a Sway by adding text and media content into a Storyline section, or **card**. To add pictures, videos, or documents, select a card in the left pane and then select the Insert Content button. The first card in a Sway presentation contains a title and background image.

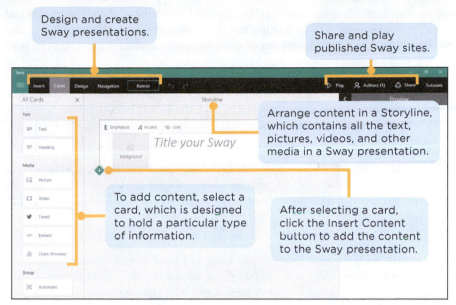

Design and create Sway presentations.

Share and play published Sway sites.

Arrange content in a Storyline, which contains all the text, pictures, videos, and other media in a Sway presentation.

To add content, select a card, which is designed to hold a particular type of information.

After selecting a card, click the Insert Content button to add the content to the Sway presentation.

Adding Content to Build a Story

As you work, Sway searches the Internet to help you find relevant images, videos, tweets, and other content from online sources such as Bing, YouTube, Twitter, and Facebook. You can drag content from the search results right into the Storyline. In addition, you can upload your own images and videos directly in the presentation. For example, if you are creating a Sway presentation about the market for commercial drones, Sway suggests content to incorporate into the presentation by displaying it in the left pane as search results. The search results include drone images tagged with a **Creative Commons license** at online sources as shown in **Figure 8**. A Creative Commons license is a public copyright license that allows the free distribution of an otherwise copyrighted work. In addition, you can specify the source of the media. For example, you can add your own Facebook or OneNote pictures and videos in Sway without leaving the app.

On the Job Now

If you have a Microsoft Word document containing an outline of your business content, drag the outline into Sway to create a card for each topic.

Figure 8: Images in Sway search results

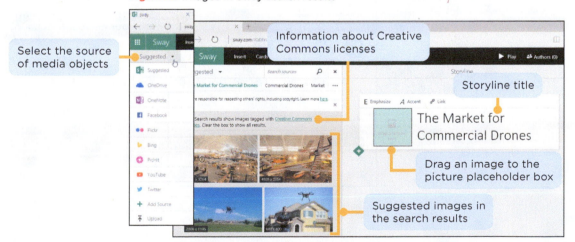

Select the source of media objects

Information about Creative Commons licenses

Storyline title

The Market for Commercial Drones

Drag an image to the picture placeholder box

Suggested images in the search results

Designing a Sway

Sway professionally designs your Storyline content by resizing background images and fonts to fit your display, and by floating text, animating media, embedding video, and removing images as a page scrolls out of view. Sway also evaluates the images in your Storyline and suggests a color palette based on colors that appear in your photos. Use the Design button to display tools including color palettes, font choices, **animation emphasis effects**, and style templates to provide a personality for a Sway presentation. Instead of creating your own design, you can click the Remix button, which randomly selects unique designs for your Sway site.

Publishing a Sway

Use the Play button to display your finished Sway presentation as a website. The Address bar includes a unique web address where others can view your Sway site. As the author, you can edit a published Sway site by clicking the Edit button (pencil icon) on the Sway toolbar.

Sharing a Sway

When you are ready to share your Sway website, you have several options as shown in **Figure 9**. Use the Share slider button to share the Sway site publically or keep it private. If you add the Sway site to the Microsoft **Docs.com** public gallery, anyone worldwide can use Bing, Google, or other search engines to find, view, and share your Sway site. You can also share your Sway site using Facebook, Twitter, Google+, Yammer, and other social media sites. Link your presentation to any webpage or email the link to your audience. Sway can also generate a code for embedding the link within another webpage.

Figure 9: Sharing a Sway site

Share button

Drag the slider button to Just me to keep the Sway site private

Post the Sway site on Docs.com

Options differ depending on your Microsoft account

Send friends a link to the Sway site

> ▷ Play   ⦉ Authors (1)   ⚘ Share
>
> Share ⬤▬ Just me
>
> Share with the world
>   Docs.com - Your public gallery
>
> Share with friends
>   f 🐦 g+ y ⚲ ...
>   https://sway.com/JQDFrUaxmg4lEbbk
>
> ▲ More options
> ☑ Viewers can duplicate this Sway
>   Stop sharing

Try This Now

1: Creating a Sway Resume

Learn to use Sway!
Links to companion **Sways**, featuring **videos** with hands-on instructions, are located on www.cengagebrain.com.

Sway is a digital storytelling app. Create a Sway resume to share the skills, job experiences, and achievements you have that match the requirements of a future job interest. Perform the following tasks:

a. Create a new presentation in Sway to use as a digital resume. Title the Sway Storyline with your full name and then select a background image.

b. Create three separate sections titled **Academic Background, Work Experience**, and **Skills**, and insert text, a picture, and a paragraph or bulleted points in each section. Be sure to include your own picture.

c. Add a fourth section that includes a video about your school that you find online.

d. Customize the design of your presentation.

e. Submit your assignment link in the format specified by your instructor.

2: Creating an Online Sway Newsletter

Newsletters are designed to capture the attention of their target audience. Using Sway, create a newsletter for a club, organization, or your favorite music group. Perform the following tasks:

a. Create a new presentation in Sway to use as a digital newsletter for a club, organization, or your favorite music group. Provide a title for the Sway Storyline and select an appropriate background image.

b. Select three separate sections with appropriate titles, such as Upcoming Events. In each section, insert text, a picture, and a paragraph or bulleted points.

c. Add a fourth section that includes a video about your selected topic.

d. Customize the design of your presentation.

e. Submit your assignment link in the format specified by your instructor.

3: Creating and Sharing a Technology Presentation

To place a Sway presentation in the hands of your entire audience, you can share a link to the Sway presentation. Create a Sway presentation on a new technology and share it with your class. Perform the following tasks:

a. Create a new presentation in Sway about a cutting-edge technology topic. Provide a title for the Sway Storyline and select a background image.

b. Create four separate sections about your topic, and include text, a picture, and a paragraph in each section.

c. Add a fifth section that includes a video about your topic.

d. Customize the design of your presentation.

e. Share the link to your Sway with your classmates and submit your assignment link in the format specified by your instructor.

Introduction to Office Mix

add-in | clip | slide recording | Slide Notes | screen recording | free-response quiz

To enliven business meetings and lectures, Microsoft adds a new dimension to presentations with a powerful toolset called Office Mix, a free add-in for PowerPoint. (An **add-in** is software that works with an installed app to extend its features.) Using Office Mix, you can record yourself on video, capture still and moving images on your desktop, and insert interactive elements such as quizzes and live webpages directly into PowerPoint slides. When you post the finished presentation to OneDrive, Office Mix provides a link you can share with friends and colleagues. Anyone with an Internet connection and a web browser can watch a published Office Mix presentation, such as the one in **Figure 10**, on a computer or mobile device.

Figure 10: Office Mix presentation

Adding Office Mix to PowerPoint

To get started, you create an Office Mix account at the website mix.office.com using an email address or a Facebook or Google account. Next, you download and install the Office Mix add-in (see **Figure 11**). Office Mix appears as a new tab named Mix on the PowerPoint ribbon in versions of Office 2013 and Office 2016 running on personal computers (PCs).

Figure 11: Getting started with Office Mix

Capturing Video Clips

A **clip** is a short segment of audio, such as music, or video. After finishing the content on a PowerPoint slide, you can use Office Mix to add a video clip to animate or illustrate the content. Office Mix creates video clips in two ways: by recording live action on a webcam and by capturing screen images and movements. If your computer has a webcam, you can record yourself and annotate the slide to create a **slide recording** as shown in **Figure 12**.

Figure 12: Making a slide recording

Record your voice; also record video if your computer has a camera.

Use the Slide Notes button to display notes for your narration.

For best results, look directly at your webcam while recording video.

Choose a video and audio device to record images and sound.

Use inking tools to write and draw on the slide as you record.

When you are making a slide recording, you can record your spoken narration at the same time. The **Slide Notes** feature works like a teleprompter to help you focus on your presentation content instead of memorizing your narration. Use the Inking tools to make annotations or add highlighting using different pen types and colors. After finishing a recording, edit the video in PowerPoint to trim the length or set playback options.

The second way to create a video is to capture on-screen images and actions with or without a voiceover. This method is ideal if you want to show how to use your favorite website or demonstrate an app such as OneNote. To share your screen with an audience, select the part of the screen you want to show in the video. Office Mix captures everything that happens in that area to create a **screen recording**, as shown in **Figure 13**. Office Mix inserts the screen recording as a video in the slide.

Figure 13: Making a screen recording

Record the action on the screen within the red dashed outline.

Record audio while capturing your on-screen actions.

Select Area button

Inserting Quizzes, Live Webpages, and Apps

To enhance and assess audience understanding, make your slides interactive by adding quizzes, live webpages, and apps. Quizzes give immediate feedback to the user as shown in **Figure 14**. Office Mix supports several quiz formats, including a **free-response quiz** similar to a short answer quiz, and true/false, multiple-choice, and multiple-response formats.

Figure 14: Creating an interactive quiz

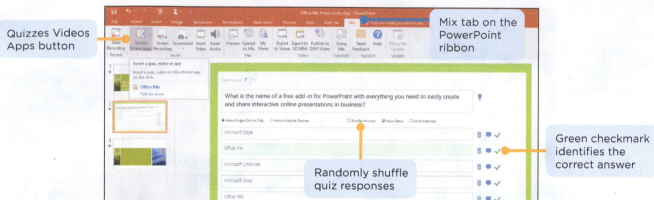

Quizzes Videos Apps button

Mix tab on the PowerPoint ribbon

Green checkmark identifies the correct answer

Randomly shuffle quiz responses

Sharing an Office Mix Presentation

When you complete your work with Office Mix, upload the presentation to your personal Office Mix dashboard as shown in **Figure 15**. Users of PCs, Macs, iOS devices, and Android devices can access and play Office Mix presentations. The Office Mix dashboard displays built-in analytics that include the quiz results and how much time viewers spent on each slide. You can play completed Office Mix presentations online or download them as movies.

Figure 15: Sharing an Office Mix presentation

Office Mix dashboard displays the quiz analytics.

Try This Now

Learn to use Office Mix!
Links to companion **Sways**, featuring **videos** with hands-on instructions, are located on www.cengagebrain.com.

1: Creating an Office Mix Tutorial for OneNote

Note: This activity requires a microphone on your computer.

Office Mix makes it easy to record screens and their contents. Create PowerPoint slides with an Office Mix screen recording to show OneNote 2016 features. Perform the following tasks:

a. Create a PowerPoint presentation with the Ion Boardroom template. Create an opening slide with the title **My Favorite OneNote Features** and enter your name in the subtitle.
b. Create three additional slides, each titled with a new feature of OneNote. Open OneNote and use the Mix tab in PowerPoint to capture three separate screen recordings that teach your favorite features.
c. Add a fifth slide that quizzes the user with a multiple-choice question about OneNote and includes four responses. Be sure to insert a checkmark indicating the correct response.
d. Upload the completed presentation to your Office Mix dashboard and share the link with your instructor.
e. Submit your assignment link in the format specified by your instructor.

2: Teaching Augmented Reality with Office Mix

Note: This activity requires a webcam or built-in video camera on your computer.

A local elementary school has asked you to teach augmented reality to its students using Office Mix. Perform the following tasks:

a. Research augmented reality using your favorite online search tools.
b. Create a PowerPoint presentation with the Frame template. Create an opening slide with the title **Augmented Reality** and enter your name in the subtitle.
c. Create a slide with four bullets summarizing your research of augmented reality. Create a 20-second slide recording of yourself providing a quick overview of augmented reality.
d. Create another slide with a 30-second screen recording of a video about augmented reality from a site such as YouTube or another video-sharing site.
e. Add a final slide that quizzes the user with a true/false question about augmented reality. Be sure to insert a checkmark indicating the correct response.
f. Upload the completed presentation to your Office Mix dashboard and share the link with your instructor.
g. Submit your assignment link in the format specified by your instructor.

3: Marketing a Travel Destination with Office Mix

Note: This activity requires a webcam or built-in video camera on your computer.

To convince your audience to travel to a particular city, create a slide presentation marketing any city in the world using a slide recording, screen recording, and a quiz. Perform the following tasks:

a. Create a PowerPoint presentation with any template. Create an opening slide with the title of the city you are marketing as a travel destination and your name in the subtitle.
b. Create a slide with four bullets about the featured city. Create a 30-second slide recording of yourself explaining why this city is the perfect vacation destination.
c. Create another slide with a 20-second screen recording of a travel video about the city from a site such as YouTube or another video-sharing site.
d. Add a final slide that quizzes the user with a multiple-choice question about the featured city with five responses. Be sure to include a checkmark indicating the correct response.
e. Upload the completed presentation to your Office Mix dashboard and share your link with your instructor.
f. Submit your assignment link in the format specified by your instructor.

Introduction to Microsoft Edge

Reading view | Hub | Cortana | Web Note | Inking | sandbox

Microsoft Edge is the default web browser developed for the Windows 10 operating system as a replacement for Internet Explorer. Unlike its predecessor, Edge lets you write on webpages, read webpages without advertisements and other distractions, and search for information using a virtual personal assistant. The Edge interface is clean and basic, as shown in **Figure 16**, meaning you can pay more attention to the webpage content.

Figure 16: Microsoft Edge tools

Forward button · New tab button · Web address in the Address bar · Add to favorites or reading list button · Back button · Reading view button · More button · Refresh (F5) button · Hub (Favorites, reading list, history, and downloads) button · Share Web Note button · Make a Web Note button

Browsing the Web with Microsoft Edge

One of the fastest browsers available, Edge allows you to type search text directly in the Address bar. As you view the resulting webpage, you can switch to **Reading view**, which is available for most news and research sites, to eliminate distracting advertisements. For example, if you are catching up on technology news online, the webpage might be difficult to read due to a busy layout cluttered with ads. Switch to Reading view to refresh the page and remove the original page formatting, ads, and menu sidebars to read the article distraction-free.

Consider the **Hub** in Microsoft Edge as providing one-stop access to all the things you collect on the web, such as your favorite websites, reading list, surfing history, and downloaded files.

Locating Information with Cortana

Cortana, the Windows 10 virtual assistant, plays an important role in Microsoft Edge. After you turn on Cortana, it appears as an animated circle in the Address bar when you might need assistance, as shown in the restaurant website in **Figure 17**. When you click the Cortana icon, a pane slides in from the right of the browser window to display detailed information about the restaurant, including maps and reviews. Cortana can also assist you in defining words, finding the weather, suggesting coupons for shopping, updating stock market information, and calculating math.

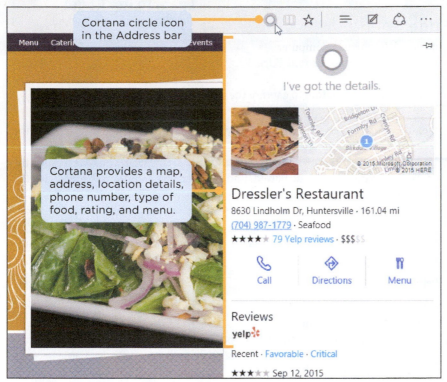

Cortana circle icon in the Address bar

I've got the details.

Cortana provides a map, address, location details, phone number, type of food, rating, and menu.

Dressler's Restaurant

8630 Lindholm Dr, Huntersville · 161.04 mi

(704) 987-1779 · Seafood

★★★★☆ 79 Yelp reviews · $$$$$

Call   Directions   Menu

Reviews

yelp

Recent · Favorable · Critical

★★★☆☆ Sep 12, 2015

Annotating Webpages

One of the most impressive Microsoft Edge features are the **Web Note** tools, which you use to write on a webpage or to highlight text. When you click the Make a Web Note button, an **Inking** toolbar appears, as shown in **Figure 18**, that provides writing and drawing tools. These tools include an eraser, a pen, and a highlighter with different colors. You can also insert a typed note and copy a screen image (called a screen clipping). You can draw with a pointing device, fingertip, or stylus using different pen colors. Whether you add notes to a recipe, annotate sources for a research paper, or select a product while shopping online, the Web Note tools can enhance your productivity. After you complete your notes, click the Save button to save the annotations to OneNote, your Favorites list, or your Reading list. You can share the inked page with others using the Share Web Note button.

On the Job Now

To enhance security, Microsoft Edge runs in a partial sandbox, an arrangement that prevents attackers from gaining control of your computer. Browsing within the **sandbox** protects computer resources and information from hackers.

Figure 18: Web Note tools in Microsoft Edge

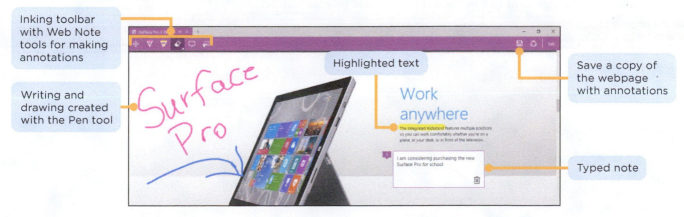

Inking toolbar with Web Note tools for making annotations

Writing and drawing created with the Pen tool

Highlighted text

Work anywhere

Save a copy of the webpage with annotations

Typed note

Try This Now

1: Using Cortana in Microsoft Edge

Learn to use Edge!
Links to companion **Sways**, featuring **videos** with hands-on instructions, are located on www.cengagebrain.com.

Note: This activity requires using Microsoft Edge on a Windows 10 computer.

Cortana can assist you in finding information on a webpage in Microsoft Edge. Perform the following tasks:

a. Create a Word document using the Word Screen Clipping tool to capture the following screenshots.

- Screenshot A—Using Microsoft Edge, open a webpage with a technology news article. Right-click a term in the article and ask Cortana to define it.
- Screenshot B—Using Microsoft Edge, open the website of a fancy restaurant in a city near you. Make sure the Cortana circle icon is displayed in the Address bar. (If it's not displayed, find a different restaurant website.) Click the Cortana circle icon to display a pane with information about the restaurant.
- Screenshot C—Using Microsoft Edge, type **10 USD to Euros** in the Address bar without pressing the Enter key. Cortana converts the U.S. dollars to Euros.
- Screenshot D—Using Microsoft Edge, type **Apple stock** in the Address bar without pressing the Enter key. Cortana displays the current stock quote.

b. Submit your assignment in the format specified by your instructor.

2: Viewing Online News with Reading View

Note: This activity requires using Microsoft Edge on a Windows 10 computer.

Reading view in Microsoft Edge can make a webpage less cluttered with ads and other distractions. Perform the following tasks:

a. Create a Word document using the Word Screen Clipping tool to capture the following screenshots.

- Screenshot A—Using Microsoft Edge, open the website **mashable.com**. Open a technology article. Click the Reading view button to display an ad-free page that uses only basic text formatting.
- Screenshot B—Using Microsoft Edge, open the website **bbc.com**. Open any news article. Click the Reading view button to display an ad-free page that uses only basic text formatting.
- Screenshot C—Make three types of annotations (Pen, Highlighter, and Add a typed note) on the BBC article page displayed in Reading view.

b. Submit your assignment in the format specified by your instructor.

3: Inking with Microsoft Edge

Note: This activity requires using Microsoft Edge on a Windows 10 computer.

Microsoft Edge provides many annotation options to record your ideas. Perform the following tasks:

a. Open the website **wolframalpha.com** in the Microsoft Edge browser. Wolfram Alpha is a well-respected academic search engine. Type **US$100 1965 dollars in 2015** in the Wolfram Alpha search text box and press the Enter key.

b. Click the Make a Web Note button to display the Web Note tools. Using the Pen tool, draw a circle around the result on the webpage. Save the page to OneNote.

c. In the Wolfram Alpha search text box, type the name of the city closest to where you live and press the Enter key. Using the Highlighter tool, highlight at least three interesting results. Add a note and then type a sentence about what you learned about this city. Save the page to OneNote. Share your OneNote notebook with your instructor.

d. Submit your assignment link in the format specified by your instructor.

Getting Started with Microsoft Office 2016

CASE ▶ This module introduces you to the most frequently used programs in Office, as well as common features they all share.

Module Objectives

After completing this module, you will be able to:

- Understand the Office 2016 suite
- Start an Office app
- Identify Office 2016 screen elements
- Create and save a file
- Open a file and save it with a new name
- View and print your work
- Get Help, close a file, and exit an app

Files You Will Need

OF 1-1.xlsx

Understand the Office 2016 Suite

Learning Outcomes
- Identify Office suite components
- Describe the features of each app

Microsoft Office 2016 is a group of programs—which are also called applications or apps—designed to help you create documents, collaborate with coworkers, and track and analyze information. You use different Office programs to accomplish specific tasks, such as writing a letter or producing a presentation, yet all the programs have a similar look and feel. Microsoft Office 2016 apps feature a common, context-sensitive user interface, so you can get up to speed faster and use advanced features with greater ease. The Office apps are bundled together in a group called a **suite**. The Office suite is available in several configurations, but all include Word, Excel, PowerPoint, and OneNote. Some configurations include Access, Outlook, Publisher, Skype, and OneDrive. **CASE** *As part of your job, you need to understand how each Office app is best used to complete specific tasks.*

DETAILS

The Office apps covered in this book include:

- **Microsoft Word 2016**

  When you need to create any kind of text-based document, such as a memo, newsletter, or multipage report, Word is the program to use. You can easily make your documents look great by using formatting tools and inserting eye-catching graphics. The Word document shown in **FIGURE 1-1** contains a company logo and simple formatting.

- **Microsoft Excel 2016**

  Excel is the perfect solution when you need to work with numeric values and make calculations. It puts the power of formulas, functions, charts, and other analytical tools into the hands of every user, so you can analyze sales projections, calculate loan payments, and present your findings in a professional manner. The Excel worksheet shown in **FIGURE 1-1** tracks checkbook transactions. Because Excel automatically recalculates results whenever a value changes, the information is always up to date. A chart illustrates how the monthly expenses are broken down.

- **Microsoft PowerPoint 2016**

  Using PowerPoint, it's easy to create powerful presentations complete with graphics, transitions, and even a soundtrack. Using professionally designed themes and clip art, you can quickly and easily create dynamic slide shows such as the one shown in **FIGURE 1-1**.

- **Microsoft Access 2016**

  Access is a relational database program that helps you keep track of large amounts of quantitative data, such as product inventories or employee records. The form shown in **FIGURE 1-1** can be used to generate reports on customer invoices and tours.

Microsoft Office has benefits beyond the power of each program, including:

- **Note-taking made simple; available on all devices**

  Use OneNote to take notes (organized in tabbed pages) on information that can be accessed on your computer, tablet, or phone. Share the editable results with others. Contents can include text, web page clips (using OneNote Clipper), email contents (directly inserted into a default section), photos (using Office Lens), and web pages.

- **Common user interface: Improving business processes**

  Because the Office suite apps have a similar **interface**, your experience using one app's tools makes it easy to learn those in the other apps. Office documents are **compatible** with one another, so you can easily **integrate**, or combine, elements—for example, you can add an Excel chart to a PowerPoint slide, or an Access table to a Word document.

  Most Office programs include the capability to incorporate feedback—called **online collaboration**—across the Internet or a company network.

FIGURE 1-1: Microsoft Office 2016 documents

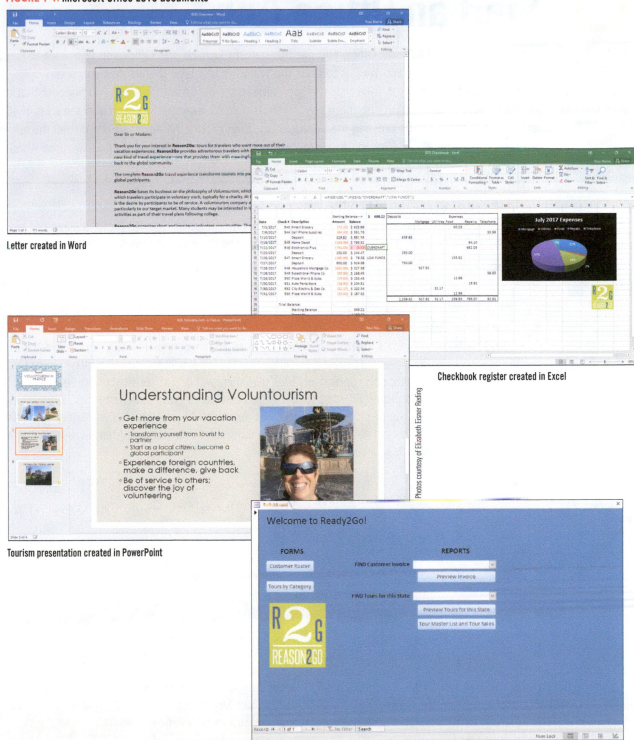

Letter created in Word

Checkbook register created in Excel

Tourism presentation created in PowerPoint

Form created in Access

What is Office 365?

Until recently, most consumers purchased Microsoft Office in a traditional way: by buying a retail package from a store or downloading it from Microsoft.com. You can still purchase Microsoft Office 2016 in this traditional way—but you can also now purchase it as a subscription service called Microsoft Office 365, which is available in a wide variety of configurations.

Depending on which configuration you purchase, you will always have access to the most up-to-date versions of the apps in your package and, in many cases, can install these apps on multiple computers, tablets, and phones. And if you change computers or devices, you can easily uninstall the apps from an old device and install them on a new one.

Start an Office App

To get started using Microsoft Office, you need to start, or **launch**, the Office app you want to use. An easy way to start the app you want is to press the Windows key, type the first few characters of the app name you want to search for, then click the app name In the Best match list. You will discover that there are many ways to accomplish just about any Windows task; for example, you can also see a list of all the apps on your computer by pressing the Windows key, then clicking All Apps. When you see the app you want, click its name. **CASE** *You decide to familiarize yourself with Office by starting Microsoft Word.*

STEPS

1. **Click the Start button ⊞ on the Windows taskbar**

   The Start menu opens, listing the most used apps on your computer. You can locate the app you want to open by clicking the app name if you see it, or you can type the app name to search for it.

2. **Type word**

   Your screen now displays "Word 2016" under "Best match", along with any other app that has "word" as part of its name (such as WordPad). See **FIGURE 1-2**.

3. **Click Word 2016**

   Word 2016 launches, and the Word **start screen** appears, as shown in **FIGURE 1-3**. The start screen is a landing page that appears when you first start an Office app. The left side of this screen displays recent files you have opened. (If you have never opened any files, then there will be no files listed under Recent.) The right side displays images depicting different templates you can use to create different types of documents. A **template** is a file containing professionally designed content and formatting that you can easily customize for your own needs. You can also start from scratch using the Blank Document template, which contains only minimal formatting settings.

Enabling touch mode

If you are using a touch screen with any of the Office 2016 apps, you can enable the touch mode to give the user interface a more spacious look, making it easier to navigate with your fingertips. Enable touch mode by clicking the Quick Access toolbar list arrow, then clicking Touch/Mouse Mode to select it. Then you'll see the Touch Mode button 🔓 in the Quick Access toolbar. Click 🔓, and you'll see the interface spread out.

Using shortcut keys to move between Office programs

You can switch between open apps using a keyboard shortcut. The [Alt][Tab] keyboard combination lets you either switch quickly to the next open program or file or choose one from a gallery. To switch immediately to the next open program or file, press [Alt][Tab]. To choose from all open programs and files, press and hold [Alt], then press and release [Tab] without releasing [Alt]. A gallery opens on screen, displaying the filename and a thumbnail image of each open program and file, as well as of the desktop. Each time you press [Tab] while holding [Alt], the selection cycles to the next open file or location. Release [Alt] when the program, file, or location you want to activate is selected.

FIGURE 1-2: Searching for the Word app

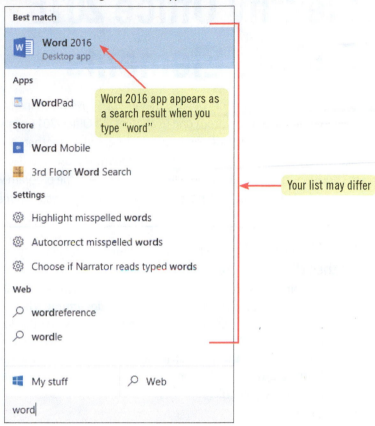

Word 2016 app appears as a search result when you type "word"

Your list may differ

FIGURE 1-3: Word start screen

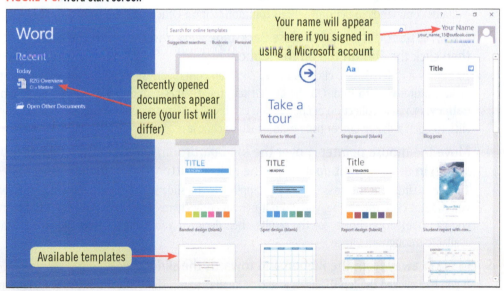

Your name will appear here if you signed in using a Microsoft account

Recently opened documents appear here (your list will differ)

Available templates

Using the Office Clipboard

You can use the Office Clipboard to cut and copy items from one Office program and paste them into others. The Office Clipboard can store a maximum of 24 items. To access it, open the Office Clipboard task pane by clicking the dialog box launcher 📋 in the Clipboard group on the Home tab. Each time you copy a selection, it is saved in the Office Clipboard. Each entry in the Office Clipboard includes an icon that tells you the program it was created in. To paste an entry, click in the document where you want it to appear, then click the item in the Office Clipboard. To delete an item from the Office Clipboard, right-click the item, then click Delete.

Office 2016

Identify Office 2016 Screen Elements

One of the benefits of using Office is that its apps have much in common, making them easy to learn and making it simple to move from one to another. All Office 2016 apps share a similar user interface, so you can use your knowledge of one to get up to speed in another. A **user interface** is a collective term for all the ways you interact with a software program. The user interface in Office 2016 provides intuitive ways to choose commands, work with files, and navigate in the program window. **CASE** *Familiarize yourself with some of the common interface elements in Office by examining the PowerPoint program window.*

STEPS

1. **Click the Start button ⊞ on the Windows taskbar, type pow, click PowerPoint 2016, then click Blank Presentation**

   PowerPoint starts and opens a new file, which contains a blank slide. Refer to **FIGURE 1-4** to identify common elements of the Office user interface. The **document window** occupies most of the screen. At the top of every Office program window is a **title bar** that displays the document name and program name. Below the title bar is the **Ribbon**, which displays commands you're likely to need for the current task. Commands are organized onto **tabs**. The tab names appear at the top of the Ribbon, and the active tab appears in front. The **Share button** in the upper-right corner lets you invite other users to view your cloud-stored Word, Excel, or Powerpoint file.

2. **Click the File tab**

   The File tab opens, displaying **Backstage view**. It is called Backstage view because the commands available here are for working with the files "behind the scenes." The navigation bar on the left side of Backstage view contains commands to perform actions common to most Office programs.

3. **Click the Back button ◀ to close Backstage view and return to the document window, then click the Design tab on the Ribbon**

   To display a different tab, click its name. Each tab contains related commands arranged into **groups** to make features easy to find. On the Design tab, the Themes group displays available design themes in a **gallery**, or visual collection of choices you can browse. Many groups contain a **launcher**, which you can click to open a dialog box or pane from which to choose related commands.

4. **Move the mouse pointer ▷ over the Ion Boardroom theme in the Themes group as shown in FIGURE 1-5, but *do not click* the mouse button**

   The Ion Boardroom theme is temporarily applied to the slide in the document window. However, because you did not click the theme, you did not permanently change the slide. With the **Live Preview** feature, you can point to a choice, see the results, then decide if you want to make the change. Live Preview is available throughout Office.

5. **Move ▷ away from the Ribbon and towards the slide**

   If you had clicked the Ion theme, it would be applied to this slide. Instead, the slide remains unchanged.

6. **Point to the Zoom slider 🔲 on the status bar, then drag to the right until the Zoom level reads 166%**

   The slide display is enlarged. Zoom tools are located on the status bar. You can drag the slider or click the Zoom In or Zoom Out buttons to zoom in or out on an area of interest. **Zooming in** (a higher percentage), makes a document appear bigger on screen but less of it fits on the screen at once; **zooming out** (a lower percentage) lets you see more of the document at a reduced size.

7. **Click the Zoom Out button ▬ on the status bar to the left of the Zoom slider until the Zoom level reads 120%**

FIGURE 1-4: PowerPoint program window

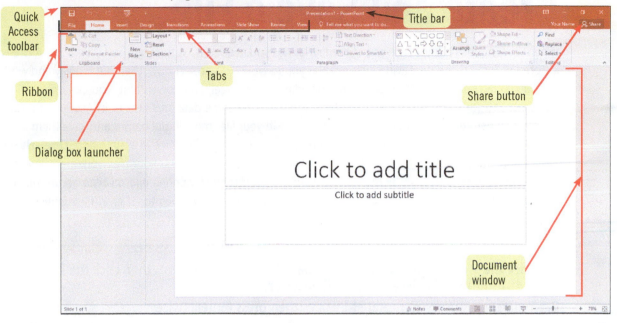

- Quick Access toolbar
- Ribbon
- Dialog box launcher
- Tabs
- Title bar
- Share button
- Document window

Click to add title

Click to add subtitle

FIGURE 1-5: Viewing a theme with Live Preview

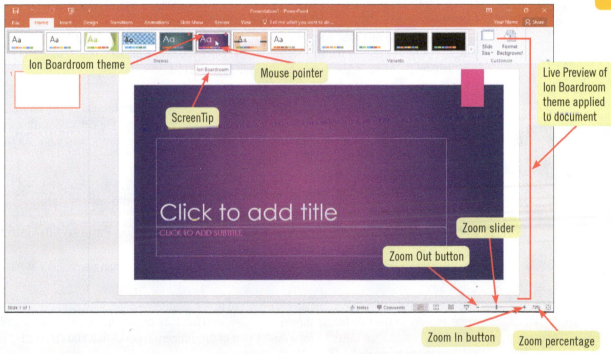

- Ion Boardroom theme
- ScreenTip
- Mouse pointer
- Live Preview of Ion Boardroom theme applied to document
- Zoom slider
- Zoom Out button
- Zoom In button
- Zoom percentage

Click to add title

CLICK TO ADD SUBTITLE

Using Backstage view

Backstage view in each Microsoft Office app offers "one stop shopping" for many commonly performed tasks, such as opening and saving a file, printing and previewing a document, defining document properties, sharing information, and exiting a program. Backstage view opens when you click the File tab in any Office app, and while features such as the Ribbon, Mini toolbar, and Live Preview all help you work *in* your documents, the File tab and Backstage view help you work *with* your documents. You can click commands in the navigation pane to open different places for working with your documents, such as the Open place, the Save place, and so on. You can return to your active document by clicking the Back button.

Create and Save a File

Learning Outcomes
• Create a file
• Save a file
• Explain OneDrive

When working in an Office app, one of the first things you need to do is to create and save a file. A **file** is a stored collection of data. Saving a file enables you to work on a project now, then put it away and work on it again later. In some Office programs, including Word, Excel, and PowerPoint, you can open a new file when you start the app, then all you have to do is enter some data and save it. In Access, you must create a file before you enter any data. You should give your files meaningful names and save them in an appropriate location, such as a folder on your hard drive or OneDrive so they're easy to find. **OneDrive** is a Microsoft cloud storage system that lets you easily save, share, and access your files from anywhere you have Internet access. **CASE** *Use Word to familiarize yourself with creating and saving a document. First you'll type some notes about a possible location for a corporate meeting, then you'll save the information for later use.*

STEPS

1. **Click the Word button** 📄 **on the taskbar, click Blank document, then click the Zoom In button** ➕ **until the level is 120%, if necessary**

2. **Type Locations for Corporate Meeting, then press [Enter] twice**
   The text appears in the document window, and the **insertion point** blinks on a new blank line. The insertion point indicates where the next typed text will appear.

   QUICK TIP
   A filename can be up to 255 characters, including a file extension, and can include upper- or lowercase characters and spaces, but not ?, ", /, \, <, >, *, |, or :.

3. **Type Las Vegas, NV, press [Enter], type Chicago, IL, press [Enter], type Seattle, WA, press [Enter] twice, then type your name**

4. **Click the Save button** 💾 **on the Quick Access toolbar**
   Because this is the first time you are saving this new file, the Save place in Backstage view opens, showing various options for saving the file. See **FIGURE 1-6**. Once you save a file for the first time, clicking 💾 saves any changes to the file *without* opening the Save As dialog box.

5. **Click Browse**
   The Save As dialog box opens, as shown in **FIGURE 1-7**, where you can browse to the location where you want to save the file. The Address bar in the Save As dialog box displays the default location for saving the file, but you can change it to any location. The File name field contains a suggested name for the document based on text in the file, but you can enter a different name.

   QUICK TIP
   Saving a file to the Desktop creates a desktop icon that you can double-click to both launch a program and open a document.

6. **Type OF 1-Possible Corporate Meeting Locations**
   The text you type replaces the highlighted text. (The "OF 1-" in the filename indicates that the file is created in Office Module 1. You will see similar designations throughout this book when files are named.)

7. **In the Save As dialog box, use the Address bar or Navigation Pane to navigate to the location where you store your Data Files**
   You can store files on your computer, a network drive, your OneDrive, or any acceptable storage device.

   QUICK TIP
   To create a new blank file when a file is open, click the File tab, click New on the navigation bar, then choose a template.

8. **Click Save**
   The Save As dialog box closes, the new file is saved to the location you specified, and the name of the document appears in the title bar, as shown in **FIGURE 1-8**. (You may or may not see the file extension ".docx" after the filename.) See **TABLE 1-1** for a description of the different types of files you create in Office, and the file extensions associated with each.

TABLE 1-1: Common filenames and default file extensions

file created in	is called a	and has the default extension
Word	document	.docx
Excel	workbook	.xlsx
PowerPoint	presentation	.pptx
Access	database	.accdb

FIGURE 1-6: Save place in Backstage view

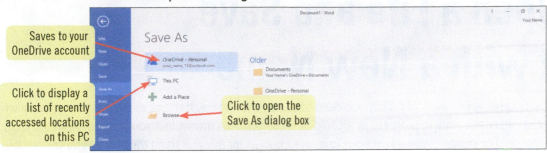

Saves to your OneDrive account

Click to display a list of recently accessed locations on this PC

Click to open the Save As dialog box

FIGURE 1-7: Save As dialog box

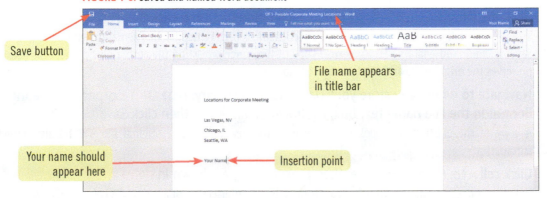

Navigation pane; your links and folders may differ

Address bar; your location may differ

File name field; your computer may not display file extensions

Save as type list

FIGURE 1-8: Saved and named Word document

Save button

File name appears in title bar

Your name should appear here

Insertion point

Office 2016

Saving files to OneDrive

All Office programs include the capability to incorporate feedback—called **online collaboration**—across the Internet or a company network. Using **cloud computing** (work done in a virtual environment), you can store your work in the cloud. Using OneDrive, a file storage service from Microsoft, you and your colleagues can create and store documents in the cloud and make the documents available anywhere there is Internet access to whomever you choose. To use OneDrive, you need a Microsoft Account, which you obtain at onedrive.live.com. Pricing and storage plans vary based on the type of Microsoft account you have. When you are logged into your Microsoft account and you

save a file in any of the Office apps, the first option in the Save As screen is your OneDrive. Double-click your OneDrive option, and the Save As dialog box opens displaying a location in the address bar unique to your OneDrive account. Type a name in the File name text box, then click Save and your file is saved to your OneDrive. To sync your files with OneDrive, you'll need to download and install the OneDrive for Windows app. Then, when you open Explorer, you'll notice a new folder called OneDrive has been added to your folder. In this folder is a sub-folder called Documents. This means if your Internet connection fails, you can work on your files offline.

Learning Outcomes
- Open an existing file
- Save a file with a new name

Open a File and Save It with a New Name

In many cases as you work in Office, you need to use an existing file. It might be a file you or a coworker created earlier as a work in progress, or it could be a complete document that you want to use as the basis for another. For example, you might want to create a budget for this year using the budget you created last year; instead of typing in all the categories and information from scratch, you could open last year's budget, save it with a new name, and just make changes to update it for the current year. By opening the existing file and saving it with the Save As command, you create a duplicate that you can modify to suit your needs, while the original file remains intact. **CASE** ▷ *Use Excel to open an existing workbook file, and save it with a new name so the original remains unchanged.*

STEPS

1. **Click the Start button ⊞ on the Windows taskbar, type exc, click Excel 2016, click Open Other Workbooks, This PC, then click Browse**

   The Open dialog box opens, where you can navigate to any drive or folder accessible to your computer to locate a file.

2. **In the Open dialog box, navigate to the location where you store your Data Files**

   The files available in the current folder are listed, as shown in **FIGURE 1-9**. This folder displays one file.

3. **Click OF 1-1.xlsx, then click Open**

   The dialog box closes, and the file opens in Excel. An Excel file is an electronic spreadsheet, so the new file displays a grid of rows and columns you can use to enter and organize data.

4. **Click the File tab, click Save As on the navigation bar, then click Browse**

   The Save As dialog box opens, and the current filename is highlighted in the File name text box. Using the Save As command enables you to create a copy of the current, existing file with a new name. This action preserves the original file and creates a new file that you can modify.

5. **Navigate to where you store your Data Files if necessary, type OF 1-Corporate Meeting Budget in the File name text box, as shown in FIGURE 1-10, then click Save**

   A copy of the existing workbook is created with the new name. The original file, OF 1-1.xlsx, closes automatically.

6. **Click cell A18, type your name, then press [Enter], as shown in FIGURE 1-11**

   In Excel, you enter data in cells, which are formed by the intersection of a row and a column. Cell A18 is at the intersection of column A and row 18. When you press [Enter], the cell pointer moves to cell A19.

7. **Click the Save button 🖫 on the Quick Access toolbar**

   Your name appears in the workbook, and your changes to the file are saved.

Exploring File Open options

You might have noticed that the Open button in the Open dialog box includes a list arrow to the right of the button. In a dialog box, if a button includes a list arrow you can click the button to invoke the command, or you can click the list arrow to see a list of related commands that you can apply to the currently selected file. The Open list arrow includes several related commands, including Open Read-Only and Open as Copy.

Clicking Open Read-Only opens a file that you can only save with a new name; you cannot make changes to the original file. Clicking Open as Copy creates and opens a copy of the selected file and inserts the word "Copy" in the file's title. Like the Save As command, these commands provide additional ways to use copies of existing files while ensuring that original files do not get changed by mistake.

FIGURE 1-9: Open dialog box

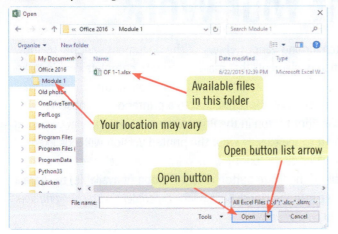

FIGURE 1-10: Save As dialog box

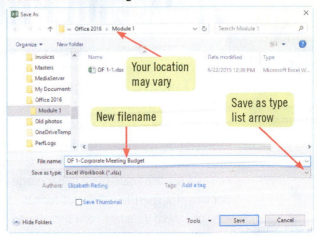

FIGURE 1-11: Your name added to the workbook

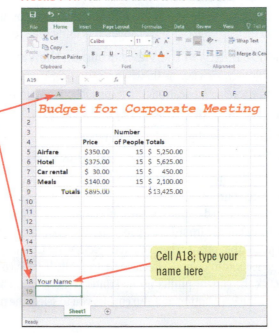

Working in Compatibility Mode

Not everyone upgrades to the newest version of Office. As a general rule, new software versions are **backward compatible**, meaning that documents saved by an older version can be read by newer software. To open documents created in older Office versions, Office 2016 includes a feature called Compatibility Mode. When you use Office 2016 to open a file created in an earlier version of Office, "Compatibility Mode" appears in the title bar, letting you know the file was created in an earlier but usable version of the program. If you are working with someone who may not be using the newest version of the software, you can avoid possible incompatibility problems by saving your file in another, earlier format. To do this in an Office program, click the File tab, click Save As on the navigation bar, then click Browse. In the Save As dialog box, click the Save as type list arrow in the Save As dialog box, then click an option in the list. For example, if you're working in Excel, click Excel 97-2003 Workbook format in the Save as type list to save an Excel file so it can be opened in Excel 97 or Excel 2003.

Office 2016

View and Print Your Work

Each Microsoft Office program lets you switch among various **views** of the document window to show more or fewer details or a different combination of elements that make it easier to complete certain tasks, such as formatting or reading text. Changing your view of a document does not affect the file in any way, it affects only the way it looks on screen. If your computer is connected to a printer or a print server, you can easily print any Office document using the Print button in the Print place in Backstage view. Printing can be as simple as **previewing** the document to see exactly what the printed version will look like and then clicking the Print button. Or, you can customize the print job by printing only selected pages. You can also use the Share place in Backstage view or the Share button on the Ribbon (if available) to share a document, export to a different format, or save it to the cloud. **CASE** *Experiment with changing your view of a Word document, and then preview and print your work.*

STEPS

1. **Click the Word program button** 🔲 **on the taskbar**

   Word becomes active, and the program window fills the screen.

2. **Click the View tab on the Ribbon**

   In most Office programs, the View tab on the Ribbon includes groups and commands for changing your view of the current document. You can also change views using the View buttons on the status bar.

3. **Click the Read Mode button in the Views group on the View tab**

   The view changes to Read Mode view, as shown in **FIGURE 1-12**. This view shows the document in an easy-to-read, distraction-free reading mode. Notice that the Ribbon is no longer visible on screen.

4. **Click the Print Layout button** 🔳 **on the Status bar**

   You return to Print Layout view, the default view in Word.

5. **Click the File tab, then click Print on the navigation bar**

   The Print place opens. The preview pane on the right displays a preview of how your document will look when printed. Compare your screen to **FIGURE 1-13**. Options in the Settings section enable you to change margins, orientation, and related options before printing. To change a setting, click it, and then click a new setting. For instance, to change from Letter paper size to Legal, click Letter in the Settings section, then click Legal on the menu that opens. The document preview updates as you change the settings. You also can use the Settings section to change which pages to print. If your computer is connected to multiple printers, you can click the current printer in the Printer section, then click the one you want to use. The Print section contains the Print button and also enables you to select the number of copies of the document to print.

6. **If your school allows printing, click the Print button in the Print place (otherwise, click the Back button** ⬅ **)**

   If you chose to print, a copy of the document prints, and Backstage view closes.

Customizing the Quick Access toolbar

You can customize the Quick Access toolbar to display your favorite commands. To do so, click the Customize Quick Access Toolbar button 🔽 in the title bar, then click the command you want to add. If you don't see the command in the list, click More Commands to open the Quick Access Toolbar tab of the current program's Options dialog box. In the Options dialog box, use the Choose commands from list to choose a category, click the desired command in the list on the left, click Add to add it to the Quick Access toolbar, then click OK. To remove a button from the toolbar, click the name in the list on the right in the Options dialog box, then click Remove. To add a command to the Quick Access toolbar as you work, simply right-click the button on the Ribbon, then click Add to Quick Access Toolbar on the shortcut menu. To move the Quick Access toolbar below the Ribbon, click the Customize Quick Access Toolbar button, and then click Show Below the Ribbon.

FIGURE 1-12: Read Mode view

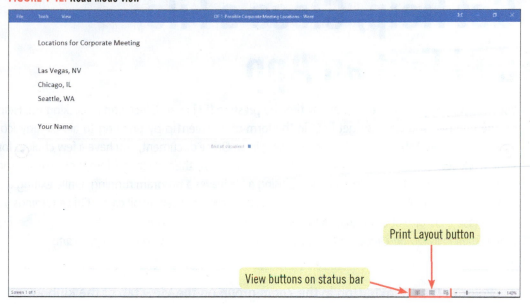

Print Layout button

View buttons on status bar

FIGURE 1-13: Print settings on the File tab

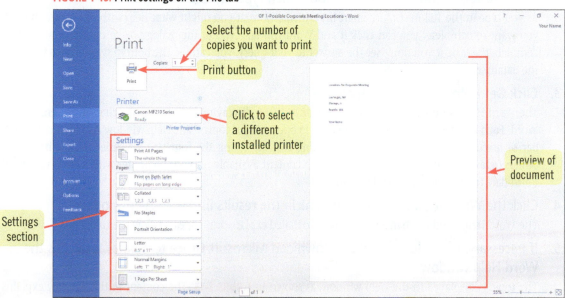

Select the number of copies you want to print

Print button

Click to select a different installed printer

Settings section

Preview of document

Creating a screen capture

A **screen capture** is a digital image of your screen, as if you took a picture of it with a camera. For instance, you might want to take a screen capture if an error message occurs and you want a Technical Support person to see exactly what's on the screen. You can create a screen capture using the Snipping Tool, an accessory designed to capture whole screens or portions of screens. To open the Snipping Tool, click the Start button on the Windows taskbar, type "sni", then click the Snipping Tool when it appears in the left panel. On the Snipping Tool toolbar, click New, then drag the pointer on the screen to select the area of the screen you want to capture. When you release the mouse button, the screen capture opens in the Snipping Tool window, and you can save, copy, or send it in an email. In Word, Excel, and PowerPoint 2016, you can capture screens or portions of screens and insert them in the current document using the Screenshot button in the Illustrations group on the Insert tab. Alternatively, you can create a screen capture by pressing [PrtScn]. (Keyboards differ, but you may find the [PrtScn] button in or near your keyboard's function keys.) Pressing this key places a digital image of your screen in the Windows temporary storage area known as the **Clipboard**. Open the document where you want the screen capture to appear, click the Home tab on the Ribbon (if necessary), then click the Paste button in the Clipboard group on the Home tab. The screen capture is pasted into the document.

Get Help, Close a File, and Exit an App

Learning Outcomes
• Display a ScreenTip
• Use Help
• Close a file
• Exit an app

You can get comprehensive help at any time by pressing [F1] in an Office app or clicking the Help button on the title bar. You can also get help in the form of a ScreenTip by pointing to almost any icon in the program window. When you're finished working in an Office document, you have a few choices for ending your work session. You close a file by clicking the File tab, then clicking Close; you exit a program by clicking the Close button on the title bar. Closing a file leaves a program running, while exiting a program closes all the open files in that program as well as the program itself. In all cases, Office reminds you if you try to close a file or exit a program and your document contains unsaved changes. **CASE** ▶ *Explore the Help system in Microsoft Office, and then close your documents and exit any open programs.*

STEPS

1. **Point to the Zoom button in the Zoom group on the View tab of the Ribbon**
   A ScreenTip appears that describes how the Zoom button works and explains where to find other zoom controls.

QUICK TIP
You can also open Help (in any of the Office apps) by pressing [F1].

2. **Click the Tell me box above the Ribbon, then type Choose a template**
   As you type in the Tell me box, a Smart list anticipates what you might want help with. If you see the task you want to complete, you can click it and Word will take you to the dialog box or options you need to complete the task. If you don't see the answer to your query, you can use the bottom two options to search the database.

QUICK TIP
If you are not connected to the Internet, the Help window displays on the Help content available on your computer.

3. **Click Get Help on "choose a template"**
   The Word Help window opens, as shown in **FIGURE 1-14**, displaying help results for choosing a template in Word. Each entry is a hyperlink you can click to open a list of topics. The Help window also includes a toolbar of useful Help commands such as printing and increasing the font size for easier readability, and a Search field. Office.com supplements the help content available on your computer with a wide variety of up-to-date topics, templates, and training.

4. **Click the Where do I find templates link in the results list Word Help window**
   The Word Help window changes, and a more detailed explanation appears below the topic.

QUICK TIP
You can print the entire current topic by clicking the Print button 🖶 on the Help toolbar, then clicking Print in the Print dialog box.

5. **If necessary, scroll down until the Download Microsoft Office templates topic fills the Word Help window**
   The topic is displayed in the Help window, as shown in **FIGURE 1-15**. The content in the window explains that you can create a wide variety of documents using a template (a pre-formatted document) and that you can get many templates free of charge.

6. **Click the Keep Help on Top button ⊞ in the lower-right corner of the window**
   The Pin Help button rotates so the pin point is pointed towards the bottom of the screen: this allows you to read the Help window while you work on your document.

7. **Click the Word document window, notice the Help window remains visible**

8. **Click a blank area of the Help window, click ⊞ to Unpin Help, click the Close button ✕ in the Help window, then click the Close button ✕ in the Word program window**
   Word closes, and the Excel program window is active.

9. **Click the Close button ✕ in the Excel program window, click the PowerPoint app button ⬚ on the taskbar if necessary, then click the Close button ✕ to exit PowerPoint**
   Excel and PowerPoint both close.

FIGURE 1-14: Word Help window

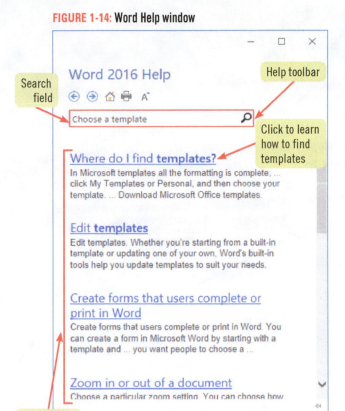

Search field

Help toolbar

Click to learn how to find templates

Help topics are updated frequently; your list may differ

FIGURE 1-15: Create a document Help topic

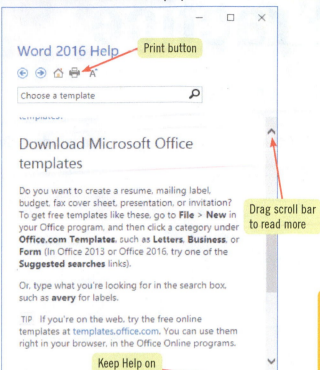

Print button

Drag scroll bar to read more

Keep Help on Top button

Using sharing features and co-authoring capabilities

If you are using Word, Excel, or PowerPoint, you can take advantage of the Share feature, which makes it easy to share your files that have been saved to OneDrive. When you click the Share button, you will be asked to invite others to share the file. To do this, type in the name or email addresses in the Invite people text box. When you invite others, you have the opportunity to give them different levels of permission. You might want some people to have read-only privileges; you might want others to be able to make edits. Also available in Word, Excel, and PowerPoint is real-time co-authoring capabilities for files stored on OneDrive. Once a file on OneDrive is opened and all the users have been given editing privileges, all the users can make edits simultaneously. On first use, each user will be prompted to automatically share their changes.

Recovering a document

Each Office program has a built-in recovery feature that allows you to open and save files that were open at the time of an interruption such as a power failure. When you restart the program(s) after an interruption, the Document Recovery task pane opens on the left side of your screen displaying both original and recovered versions of the files that were open. If you're not sure which file to open (original or recovered), it's usually better to open the recovered file because it will contain the latest information. You can, however, open and review all versions of the file that were recovered and save the best one. Each file listed in the Document Recovery task pane displays a list arrow with options that allow you to open the file, save it as is, delete it, or show repairs made to it during recovery.

Practice

Concepts Review

Label the elements of the program window shown in FIGURE 1-16.

FIGURE 1-16

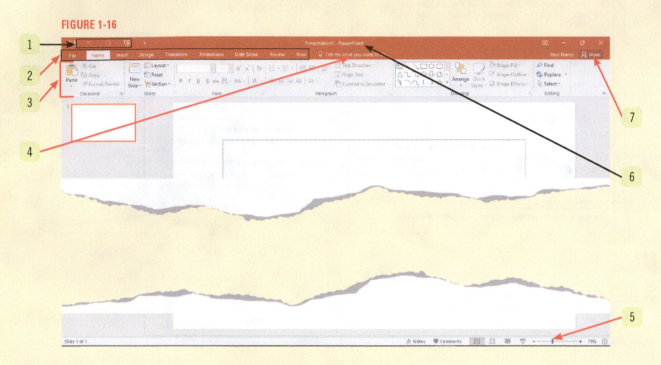

Match each project with the program for which it is best suited.

8. Microsoft PowerPoint   a. Corporate convention budget with expense projections

9. Microsoft Word   b. Presentation for city council meeting

10. Microsoft Excel   c. Business cover letter for a job application

11. Microsoft Access   d. Department store inventory

Independent Challenge 1

You just accepted an administrative position with a local independently owned insurance agent who has recently invested in computers and is now considering purchasing a subscription to Office 365. You have been asked to think of uses for the apps and you put your ideas in a Word document.

    a. Start Word, create a new Blank document, then save the document as **OF 1-Microsoft Office Apps Uses** in the location where you store your Data Files.

    b. Change the zoom factor to 120%, type **Microsoft Access**, press [Enter] twice, type **Microsoft Excel**, press [Enter] twice, type **Microsoft PowerPoint**, press [Enter] twice, type **Microsoft Word**, press [Enter] twice, then type your name.

    c. Click the line beneath each program name, type at least two tasks you can perform using that program (each separated by a comma), then press [Enter].

    d. Save the document, then submit your work to your instructor as directed.

    e. Exit Word.

Getting Started with Excel 2016

CASE ▶ You have been hired as an assistant at Reason2Go (R2G), a company that allows travelers to make a difference in the global community through voluntourism, while having a memorable vacation experience. You report to Yolanda Lee, the vice president of finance. As Yolanda's assistant, you create worksheets to analyze data from various divisions of the company, so you can help her make sound decisions on company expansion, investments, and new voluntourism opportunities.

Module Objectives

After completing this module, you will be able to:

- Understand spreadsheet software
- Identify Excel 2016 window components
- Understand formulas
- Enter labels and values and use the AutoSum button
- Edit cell entries
- Enter and edit a simple formula
- Switch worksheet views
- Choose print options

Files You Will Need

EX 1-1.xlsx   EX 1-4.xlsx
EX 1-2.xlsx   EX 1-5.xlsx
EX 1-3.xlsx

Understand Spreadsheet Software

Learning Outcomes
- Describe the uses of Excel
- Define key spreadsheet terms

Microsoft Excel is the electronic spreadsheet program within the Microsoft Office suite. An **electronic spreadsheet** is an app you use to perform numeric calculations and to analyze and present numeric data. One advantage of a spreadsheet program over pencil and paper is that your calculations are updated automatically, so you can change entries without having to manually recalculate. TABLE 1-1 shows some of the common business tasks people accomplish using Excel. In Excel, the electronic spreadsheet you work in is called a **worksheet**, and it is contained in a file called a **workbook**, which has the file extension .xlsx. **CASE** *At R2G, you use Excel extensively to track finances and manage corporate data.*

DETAILS

When you use Excel, you have the ability to:

QUICK TIP

You can also use the **Quick Analysis tool** to easily create charts and other elements that help you visualize how data is distributed.

- ### Enter data quickly and accurately
  With Excel, you can enter information faster and more accurately than with pencil and paper. FIGURE 1-1 shows a payroll worksheet created using pencil and paper. FIGURE 1-2 shows the same worksheet created using Excel. Equations were added to calculate the hours and pay. You can use Excel to recreate this information for each week by copying the worksheet's structure and the information that doesn't change from week to week, then entering unique data and formulas for each week.

- ### Recalculate data easily
  Fixing typing errors or updating data is easy in Excel. In the payroll example, if you receive updated hours for an employee, you just enter the new hours and Excel recalculates the pay.

QUICK TIP

Power users can perform more complex analysis using **Business Intelligence tools** such as Power Query and new forecasting functions.

- ### Perform what-if analysis
  The ability to change data and quickly view the recalculated results gives you the power to make informed business decisions. For instance, if you're considering raising the hourly rate for an entry-level tour guide from $12.50 to $15.00, you can enter the new value in the worksheet and immediately see the impact on the overall payroll as well as on the individual employee. Any time you use a worksheet to ask the question "What if?" you are performing **what-if analysis**. Excel also includes a Scenario Manager where you can name and save different what-if versions of your worksheet.

- ### Change the appearance of information
  Excel provides powerful features, such as the Quick Analysis tool, for making information visually appealing and easier to understand. Format text and numbers in different fonts, colors, and styles to make it stand out.

- ### Create charts
  Excel makes it easy to create charts based on worksheet information. Charts are updated automatically in Excel whenever data changes. The worksheet in FIGURE 1-2 includes a 3-D pie chart.

QUICK TIP

The **flash fill** feature makes it easy to fill a range of text based on examples that are already in your worksheet. Simply type [Ctrl][E] if Excel correctly matches the information you want, and it will be entered in a cell for you.

- ### Share information
  It's easy for everyone at R2G to collaborate in Excel using the company intranet, the Internet, or a network storage device. For example, you can complete the weekly payroll that your boss, Yolanda Lee, started creating. You can also take advantage of collaboration tools such as shared workbooks so that multiple people can edit a workbook simultaneously.

- ### Build on previous work
  Instead of creating a new worksheet for every project, it's easy to modify an existing Excel worksheet. When you are ready to create next week's payroll, you can open the file for last week's payroll, save it with a new filename, and modify the information as necessary. You can also use predesigned, formatted files called **templates** to create new worksheets quickly. Excel comes with many templates that you can customize.

FIGURE 1-1: Traditional paper worksheet

Reason2Go
Project Leader Divison Payroll Calculator

Name	Hours	O/T Hrs	Hrly Rate	Reg Pay	O/T Pay	Gross Pay
Brucker, Pieter	40	4	16.75	670	134	804
Cucci, Lucia	35	0	12	420	0	420
Klimt, Gustave	40	2	13.25	530	53	583
Lafontaine, Jeanne	29	0	15.25	442.25	0	442.25
Martinez, Juan	37	0	13.2	488.4	0	488.4
Mioshi, Keiko	39	0	21	819	0	819
Shernwood, Burt	40	0	16.75	670	0	670
Strano, Riccardo	40	8	16.25	650	260	910
Wadsworth, Alice	40	5	13.25	530	132.5	662.5
Yamamoto, Johji	38	0	15.5	589	0	589

FIGURE 1-2: Excel worksheet

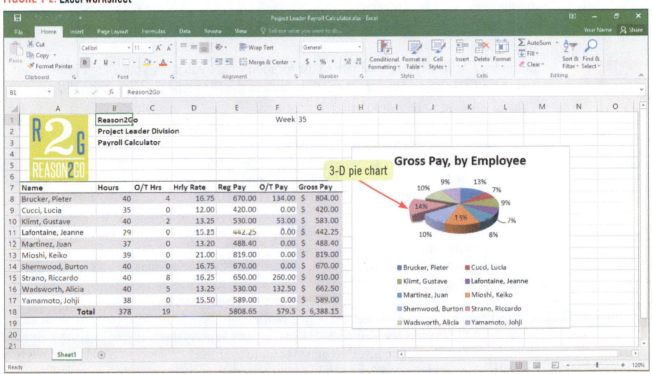

TABLE 1-1: Business tasks you can accomplish using Excel

you can use spreadsheets to	by
Perform calculations	Adding formulas and functions to worksheet data; for example, adding a list of sales results or calculating a car payment
Represent values graphically	Creating charts based on worksheet data; for example, creating a chart that displays expenses
Generate reports	Creating workbooks that combine information from multiple worksheets, such as summarized sales information from multiple stores
Organize data	Sorting data in ascending or descending order; for example, alphabetizing a list of products or customer names, or prioritizing orders by date
Analyze data	Creating data summaries and short lists using PivotTables or AutoFilters; for example, making a list of the top 10 customers based on spending habits
Create what-if data scenarios	Using variable values to investigate and sample different outcomes, such as changing the interest rate or payment schedule on a loan

Identify Excel 2016 Window Components

Learning Outcomes
- Open and save an Excel file
- Identify Excel window elements

To start Excel, Microsoft Windows must be running. Similar to starting any app in Office, you can use the Start button on the Windows taskbar, the Start button on your keyboard, or you may have a shortcut on your desktop you prefer to use. If you need additional assistance, ask your instructor or technical support person. **CASE** ▶ *You decide to start Excel and familiarize yourself with the worksheet window.*

STEPS

1. **Start Excel, click Open Other Workbooks on the navigation bar, click This PC, then click Browse to open the Open dialog box**

2. **In the Open dialog box, navigate to the location where you store your Data Files, click EX 1-1.xlsx, then click Open**

   The file opens in the Excel window.

3. **Click the File tab, click Save As on the navigation bar, then click Browse to open the Save As dialog box**

4. **In the Save As dialog box, navigate to the location where you store your Data Files if necessary, type EX 1-Project Leader Payroll Calculator in the File name text box, then click Save**

   Using **FIGURE 1-3** as a guide, identify the following items:

   - The **Name box** displays the active cell address. "A1" appears in the Name box.
   - The **formula bar** allows you to enter or edit data in the worksheet.
   - The **worksheet window** contains a grid of columns and rows. Columns are labeled alphabetically and rows are labeled numerically. The worksheet window can contain a total of 1,048,576 rows and 16,384 columns. The intersection of a column and a row is called a **cell**. Cells can contain text, numbers, formulas, or a combination of all three. Every cell has its own unique location or **cell address**, which is identified by the coordinates of the intersecting column and row. The column and row indicators are shaded to make identifying the cell address easy.
   - The **cell pointer** is a dark rectangle that outlines the cell you are working in. This cell is called the **active cell**. In **FIGURE 1-3**, the cell pointer outlines cell A1, so A1 is the active cell. The column and row headings for the active cell are highlighted, making it easier to locate.
   - **Sheet tabs** below the worksheet grid let you switch from sheet to sheet in a workbook. By default, a workbook file contains one worksheet—but you can have as many sheets as your computer's memory allows, in a workbook. The New sheet button to the right of Sheet 1 allows you to add worksheets to a workbook. **Sheet tab scrolling buttons** let you navigate to additional sheet tabs when available.
   - You can use the **scroll bars** to move around in a worksheet that is too large to fit on the screen at once.
   - The **status bar** is located at the bottom of the Excel window. It provides a brief description of the active command or task in progress. **The mode indicator** in the lower-left corner of the status bar provides additional information about certain tasks.

5. **Click cell A4**

   Cell A4 becomes the active cell. To activate a different cell, you can click the cell or press the arrow keys on your keyboard to move to it.

6. **Click cell B5, press and hold the mouse button, drag ✛ to cell B14, then release the mouse button**

   You selected a group of cells and they are highlighted, as shown in **FIGURE 1-4**. A selection of two or more cells such as B5:B14 is called a **range**; you select a range when you want to perform an action on a group of cells at once, such as moving them or formatting them. When you select a range, the status bar displays the average, count (or number of items selected), and sum of the selected cells as a quick reference.

FIGURE 1-3: Open workbook

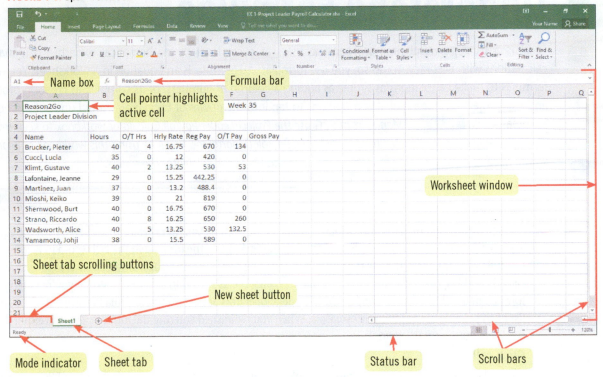

- Name box
- Formula bar
- Cell pointer highlights active cell
- Worksheet window
- Sheet tab scrolling buttons
- New sheet button
- Mode indicator
- Sheet tab
- Status bar
- Scroll bars

FIGURE 1-4: Selected range

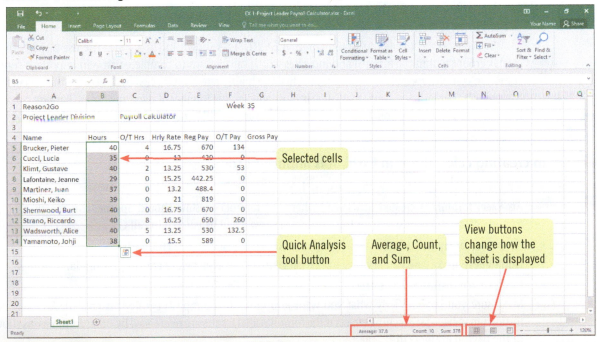

- Selected cells
- Quick Analysis tool button
- Average, Count, and Sum
- View buttons change how the sheet is displayed

Using OneDrive and Office Online

If you have a Microsoft account, you can save your Excel files and photos in OneDrive, a cloud-based service from Microsoft. When you save files in OneDrive, you can access them on other devices—such as a tablet or smartphone. OneDrive is available as an app on smartphones and tablets, making access simple. You can open files to view them on any device, and you can even make edits to them using **Office Online**, which includes simplified versions of the apps found in the Office 2016 suite. Because Office Online is web-based, the apps take up no computer disk space and you can use them on any Internet-connected device.

Understand Formulas

Learning
Outcomes
• Explain how a
  formula works
• Identify Excel
  arithmetic operators

Excel is a truly powerful program because users at every level of mathematical expertise can make calculations with accuracy. To do so, you use formulas. A **formula** is an equation in a worksheet. You use formulas to make calculations as simple as adding a column of numbers, or as complex as creating profit-and-loss projections for a global corporation. To tap into the power of Excel, you should understand how formulas work. **CASE** *Managers at R2G use the Project Leader Payroll Calculator workbook to keep track of employee hours prior to submitting them to the Payroll Department. You'll be using this workbook regularly, so you need to understand the formulas it contains and how Excel calculates the results.*

STEPS

1. **Click cell E5**

   The active cell contains a formula, which appears on the formula bar. All Excel formulas begin with the equal sign (=). If you want a cell to show the result of adding 4 plus 2, the formula in the cell would look like this: =4+2. If you want a cell to show the result of multiplying two values in your worksheet, such as the values in cells B5 and D5, the formula would look like this: =B5*D5, as shown in **FIGURE 1-5**. While you're entering a formula in a cell, the cell references and arithmetic operators appear on the formula bar. See **TABLE 1-2** for a list of commonly used arithmetic operators. When you're finished entering the formula, you can either click the Enter button on the formula bar or press [Enter].

2. **Click cell F5**

   This cell contains an example of a more complex formula, which calculates overtime pay. At R2G, overtime pay is calculated at twice the regular hourly rate times the number of overtime hours. The formula used to calculate overtime pay for the employee in row 5 is:

   O/T Hrs times (2 times Hrly Rate)

   In the worksheet cell, you would enter: =C5*(2*D5), as shown in **FIGURE 1-6**. The use of parentheses creates groups within the formula and indicates which calculations to complete first—an important consideration in complex formulas. In this formula, first the hourly rate is multiplied by 2, because that calculation is within the parentheses. Next, that value is multiplied by the number of overtime hours. Because overtime is calculated at twice the hourly rate, managers are aware that they need to closely watch this expense.

DETAILS

In creating calculations in Excel, it is important to:

• **Know where the formulas should be**

  An Excel formula is created in the cell where the formula's results should appear. This means that the formula calculating Gross Pay for the employee in row 5 will be entered in cell G5.

• **Know exactly what cells and arithmetic operations are needed**

  Don't guess; make sure you know exactly what cells are involved before creating a formula.

• **Create formulas with care**

  Make sure you know exactly what you want a formula to accomplish before it is created. An inaccurate formula may have far-reaching effects if the formula or its results are referenced by other formulas, as shown in the payroll example in **FIGURE 1-6**.

• **Use cell references rather than values**

  The beauty of Excel is that whenever you change a value in a cell, any formula containing a reference to that cell is automatically updated. For this reason, it's important that you use cell references in formulas, rather than actual values, whenever possible.

• **Determine what calculations will be needed**

  Sometimes it's difficult to predict what data will be needed within a worksheet, but you should try to anticipate what statistical information may be required. For example, if there are columns of numbers, chances are good that both column and row totals should be present.

FIGURE 1-5: Viewing a formula

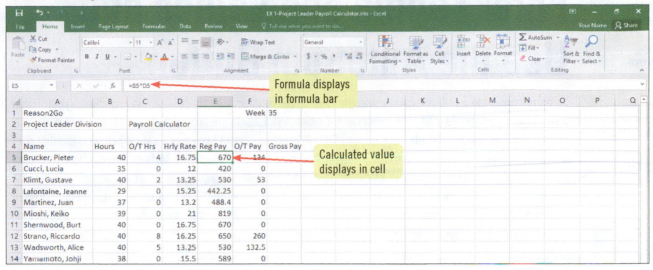

Formula displays in formula bar

Calculated value displays in cell

FIGURE 1-6: Formula with multiple operators

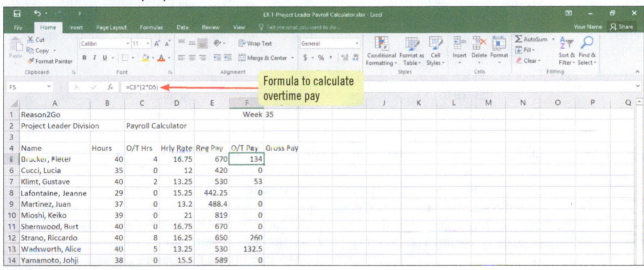

Formula to calculate overtime pay

TABLE 1-2: Excel arithmetic operators

operator	purpose	example
+	Addition	=A5+A7
-	Subtraction or negation	=A5-10
*	Multiplication	=A5*A7
/	Division	=A5/A7
%	Percent	=35%
^ (caret)	Exponent	=6^2 (same as 6^2)

Enter Labels and Values and Use the AutoSum Button

Learning Outcomes
- Build formulas with the AutoSum button
- Copy formulas with the fill handle

To enter content in a cell, you can type in the formula bar or directly in the cell itself. When entering content in a worksheet, you should start by entering all the labels first. **Labels** are entries that contain text and numerical information not used in calculations, such as "2019 Sales" or "Travel Expenses". Labels help you identify data in worksheet rows and columns, making your worksheet easier to understand. **Values** are numbers, formulas, and functions that can be used in calculations. To enter a calculation, you type an equal sign (=) plus the formula for the calculation; some examples of an Excel calculation are "=2+2" and "=C5+C6". Functions are built-in formulas; you learn more about them in the next module. **CASE** ▸ *You want to enter some information in the Project Leader Payroll Calculator workbook and use a very simple function to total a range of cells.*

STEPS

1. **Click cell A15, then click in the formula bar**

   Notice that the **mode indicator** on the status bar now reads "Edit," indicating you are in Edit mode. You are in Edit mode any time you are entering or changing the contents of a cell.

   > **QUICK TIP**
   > If you change your mind and want to cancel an entry in the formula bar, click the Cancel button ☒ on the formula bar.

2. **Type Totals, then click the Enter button ✓ on the formula bar**

   Clicking the Enter button accepts the entry. The new text is left-aligned in the cell. Labels are left-aligned by default, and values are right-aligned by default. Excel recognizes an entry as a value if it is a number or it begins with one of these symbols: +, -, =, @, #, or $. When a cell contains both text and numbers, Excel recognizes it as a label.

3. **Click cell B15**

   You want this cell to total the hours worked by all the trip advisors. You might think you need to create a formula that looks like this: =B5+B6+B7+B8+B9+B10+B11+B12+B13+B14. However, there's an easier way to achieve this result.

   > **QUICK TIP**
   > The AutoSum button is also referred to as the Sum button because clicking it inserts the SUM function.

4. **Click the AutoSum button Σ in the Editing group on the Home tab on the Ribbon**

   The SUM function is inserted in the cell, and a suggested range appears in parentheses, as shown in **FIGURE 1-7**. A **function** is a built-in formula; it includes the **arguments** (the information necessary to calculate an answer) as well as cell references and other unique information. Clicking the AutoSum button sums the adjacent range (that is, the cells next to the active cell) above or to the left, although you can adjust the range if necessary by selecting a different range before accepting the cell entry. Using the SUM function is quicker than entering a formula, and using the range B5:B14 is more efficient than entering individual cell references.

   > **QUICK TIP**
   > You can create formulas in a cell even before you enter the values to be calculated.

5. **Click ✓ on the formula bar**

   Excel calculates the total contained in cells B5:B14 and displays the result, 378, in cell B15. The cell actually contains the formula =SUM(B5:B14), and the result is displayed.

6. **Click cell C13, type 6, then press [Enter]**

   The number 6 replaces the cell's contents, the cell pointer moves to cell C14, and the value in cell F13 changes.

   > **QUICK TIP**
   > You can also press [Tab] to complete a cell entry and move the cell pointer to the right.

7. **Click cell C18, type Average Gross Pay, then press [Enter]**

   The new label is entered in cell C18. The contents appear to spill into the empty cells to the right.

8. **Click cell B15, position the pointer on the lower-right corner of the cell (the fill handle) so that the pointer changes to ✛, drag ✛ to cell G15, then release the mouse button**

   Dragging the fill handle across a range of cells copies the contents of the first cell into the other cells in the range. In the range B15:G15, each filled cell now contains a function that sums the range of cells above, as shown in **FIGURE 1-8**.

9. **Save your work**

FIGURE 1-7: Creating a formula using the AutoSum button

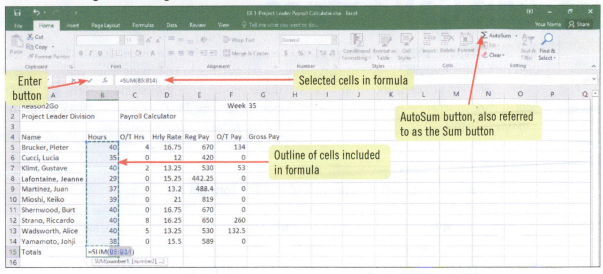

FIGURE 1-8: Results of copied SUM functions

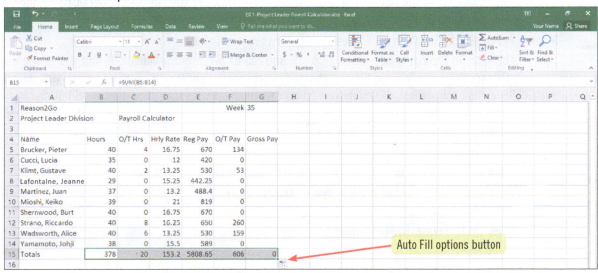

Navigating a worksheet

With over a million cells available in a worksheet, it is important to know how to move around in, or **navigate**, a worksheet. You can use the arrow keys on the keyboard ↑, ↓, →, or ← to move one cell at a time, or press [Page Up] or [Page Down] to move one screen at a time. To move one screen to the left, press [Alt][Page Up]; to move one screen to the right, press

[Alt][Page Down]. You can also use the mouse pointer to click the desired cell. If the desired cell is not visible in the worksheet window, use the scroll bars or use the Go To command by clicking the Find & Select button in the Editing group on the Home tab on the Ribbon. To quickly jump to the first cell in a worksheet, press [Ctrl][Home]; to jump to the last cell, press [Ctrl][End].

Excel 2016

Edit Cell Entries

Learning Outcomes
• Edit cell entries in the formula bar
• Edit cell entries in the cell

You can change, or **edit**, the contents of an active cell at any time. To do so, double-click the cell, and then click in the formula bar or just start typing. Excel switches to Edit mode when you are making cell entries. Different pointers, shown in **TABLE 1-3**, guide you through the editing process. **CASE** *You noticed some errors in the worksheet and want to make corrections. The first error is in cell A5, which contains a misspelled name.*

STEPS

1. **Click cell A5, then click to the right of P in the formula bar**

    As soon as you click in the formula bar, a blinking vertical line called the **insertion point** appears on the formula bar at the location where new text will be inserted. See **FIGURE 1-9**. The mouse pointer changes to I when you point anywhere in the formula bar.

2. **Press [Delete], then click the Enter button ✓ on the formula bar**

    Clicking the Enter button accepts the edit, and the spelling of the employee's first name is corrected. You can also press [Enter] or [Tab] to accept an edit. Pressing [Enter] to accept an edit moves the cell pointer down one cell, and pressing [Tab] to accept an edit moves the cell pointer one cell to the right.

    > **QUICK TIP**
    > On some keyboards, you might need to press an [F-Lock] key to enable the function keys.

3. **Click cell B6, then press [F2]**

    Excel switches to Edit mode, and the insertion point blinks in the cell. Pressing [F2] activates the cell for editing directly in the cell instead of the formula bar. Whether you edit in the cell or the formula bar is simply a matter of preference; the results in the worksheet are the same.

    > **QUICK TIP**
    > The Undo button allows you to reverse up to 100 previous actions, one at a time.

4. **Press [Backspace], type 8, then press [Enter]**

    The value in the cell changes from 35 to 38, and cell B7 becomes the active cell. Did you notice that the calculations in cells B15 and E15 also changed? That's because those cells contain formulas that include cell B6 in their calculations. If you make a mistake when editing, you can click the Cancel button ☒ on the formula bar *before* pressing [Enter] to confirm the cell entry. The Enter and Cancel buttons appear only when you're in Edit mode. If you notice the mistake *after* you have confirmed the cell entry, click the Undo button ↺▾ on the Quick Access toolbar.

    > **QUICK TIP**
    > You can use the keyboard to select all cell contents by clicking to the right of the cell contents in the cell or formula bar, pressing and holding [Shift], then pressing [Home].

5. **Click cell A9, then double-click the word Juan in the formula bar**

    Double-clicking a word in a cell selects it. When you selected the word, the Mini toolbar automatically displayed.

6. **Type Javier, then press [Enter]**

    When text is selected, typing deletes it and replaces it with the new text.

7. **Double-click cell C12, press [Delete], type 4, then click ✓**

    Double-clicking a cell activates it for editing directly in the cell. Compare your screen to **FIGURE 1-10**.

8. **Save your work**

Recovering unsaved changes to a workbook file

You can use Excel's AutoRecover feature to automatically save (Autosave) your work as often as you want. This means that if you suddenly lose power or if Excel closes unexpectedly while you're working, you can recover all or some of the changes you made since you saved it last. (Of course, this is no substitute for regularly saving your work: this is just added insurance.) To customize the AutoRecover settings, click the File tab, click Options, then click

Save. AutoRecover lets you decide how often and into which location it should Autosave files. When you restart Excel after losing power, a Document Recovery pane opens and provides access to the saved and Autosaved versions of the files that were open when Excel closed. You can also click the File tab, click Open on the navigation bar, then click any file in the Recover Unsaved Workbooks list to open Autosaved workbooks.

FIGURE 1-9: Worksheet in Edit mode

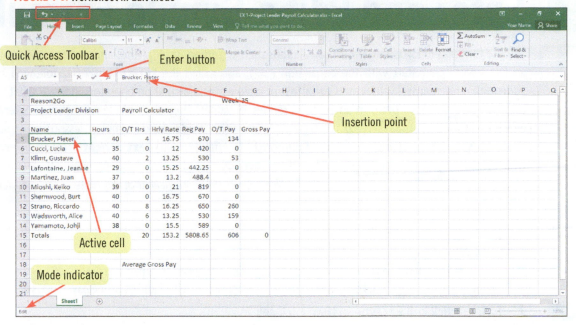

FIGURE 1-10: Edited worksheet

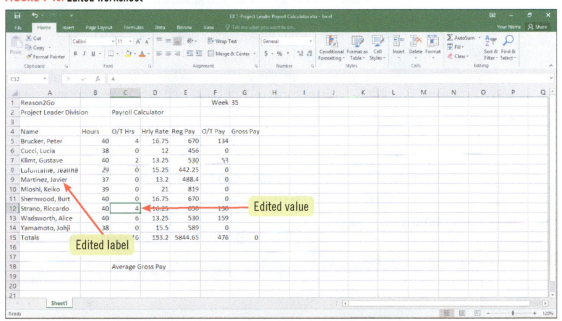

TABLE 1-3: Common pointers in Excel

name	pointer	use to	visible over the
Normal		Select a cell or range; indicates Ready mode	Active worksheet
Fill handle		Copy cell contents to adjacent cells	Lower right corner of the active cell or range
I-beam	I	Edit cell contents in active cell or formula bar	Active cell in Edit mode or over the formula bar
Move		Change the location of the selected cell(s)	Perimeter of the active cell(s)
Copy		Create a duplicate of the selected cell(s)	Perimeter of the active cell(s) when [Ctrl] is pressed
Column resize		Change the width of a column	Border between column heading indicators

Enter and Edit a Simple Formula

You use formulas in Excel to perform calculations such as adding, multiplying, and averaging. Formulas in an Excel worksheet start with the equal sign (=), also called the **formula prefix**, followed by cell addresses, range names, values, and **calculation operators**. Calculation operators indicate what type of calculation you want to perform on the cells, ranges, or values. They can include **arithmetic operators**, which perform mathematical calculations (see TABLE 1-2 in the "Understand Formulas" lesson); **comparison operators**, which compare values for the purpose of true/false results; **text concatenation operators**, which join strings of text in different cells; and **reference operators**, which enable you to use ranges in calculations. **CASE** ➤ *You want to create a formula in the worksheet that calculates gross pay for each employee.*

STEPS

1. **Click cell G5**

   This is the first cell where you want to insert the formula. To calculate gross pay, you need to add regular pay and overtime pay. For employee Peter Brucker, regular pay appears in cell E5 and overtime pay appears in cell F5.

2. **Type =, click cell E5, type +, then click cell F5**

   Compare your formula bar to **FIGURE 1-11**. The blue and red cell references in cell G5 correspond to the colored cell outlines. When entering a formula, it's a good idea to use cell references instead of values whenever you can. That way, if you later change a value in a cell (if, for example, Peter's regular pay changes to 690), any formula that includes this information reflects accurate, up-to-date results.

3. **Click the Enter button ✓ on the formula bar**

   The result of the formula =E5+F5, 804, appears in cell G5. This same value appears in cell G15 because cell G15 contains a formula that totals the values in cells G5:G14, and there are no other values at this time.

4. **Click cell F5**

   The formula in this cell calculates overtime pay by multiplying overtime hours (C5) times twice the regular hourly rate (2*D5). You want to edit this formula to reflect a new overtime pay rate.

5. **Click to the right of 2 in the formula bar, then type .5 as shown in FIGURE 1-12**

   The formula that calculates overtime pay has been edited.

6. **Click ✓ on the formula bar**

   Compare your screen to **FIGURE 1-13**. Notice that the calculated values in cells G5, F15, and G15 have all changed to reflect your edits to cell F5.

7. **Save your work**

Understanding named ranges

It can be difficult to remember the cell locations of critical information in a worksheet, but using cell names can make this task much easier. You can name a single cell or range of contiguous, or touching, cells. For example, you might name a cell that contains data on average gross pay "AVG_GP" instead of trying to remember the cell address C18. A named range must begin with a letter or an underscore. It cannot contain any spaces or be the same as a built-in name, such as a function or another object (such as a different named range) in the workbook. To name a range, select the cell(s) you want to name, click the Name box in the formula bar, type the name you want to use, then press [Enter]. You can also name a range by clicking the Formulas tab, then clicking the Define Name button in the Defined Names group. Type the new range name in the Name text box in the New Name dialog box, verify the selected range, then click OK. When you use a named range in a formula, the named range appears instead of the cell address. You can also create a named range using the contents of a cell already in the range. Select the range containing the text you want to use as a name, then click the Create from Selection button in the Defined Names group. The Create Names from Selection dialog box opens. Choose the location of the name you want to use, then click OK.

FIGURE 1-11: Simple formula in a worksheet

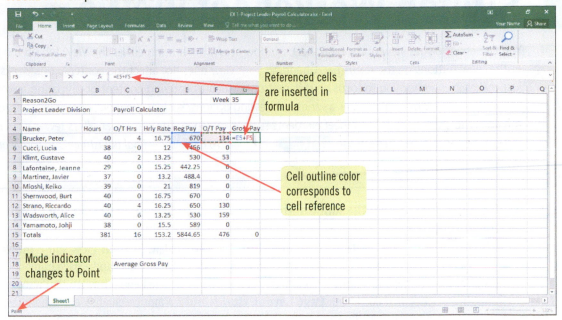

FIGURE 1-12: Edited formula in a worksheet

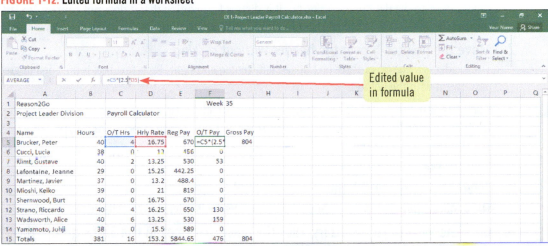

FIGURE 1-13: Edited formula with changes

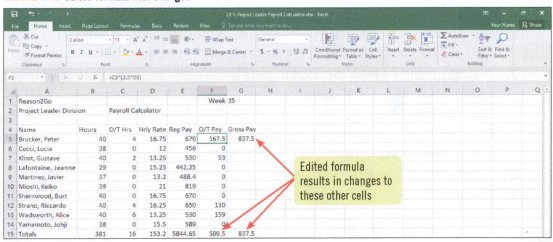

Switch Worksheet Views

Learning Outcomes
- Change worksheet views
- Create a header/footer
- Select a range

You can change your view of the worksheet window at any time, using either the View tab on the Ribbon or the View buttons on the status bar. Changing your view does not affect the contents of a worksheet; it just makes it easier for you to focus on different tasks, such as entering content or preparing a worksheet for printing. The View tab includes a variety of viewing options, such as View buttons, zoom controls, and the ability to show or hide worksheet elements such as gridlines. The status bar offers fewer View options but can be more convenient to use. **CASE** *You want to make some final adjustments to your worksheet, including adding a header so the document looks more polished.*

STEPS

QUICK TIP

Although a worksheet can contain more than a million rows and thousands of columns, the current document contains only as many pages as necessary for the current project.

1. **Click the View tab on the Ribbon, then click the Page Layout button in the Workbook Views group**

   The view switches from the default view, Normal, to Page Layout view. **Normal view** shows the worksheet without including certain details like headers and footers, or tools like rulers and a page number indicator; it's great for creating and editing a worksheet, but may not be detailed enough when you want to put the finishing touches on a document. **Page Layout view** provides a more accurate view of how a worksheet will look when printed, as shown in **FIGURE 1-14**. The margins of the page are displayed, along with a text box for the header. A footer text box appears at the bottom of the page, but your screen may not be large enough to view it without scrolling. Above and to the left of the page are rulers. Part of an additional page appears to the right of this page, but it is dimmed, indicating that it does not contain any data. A page number indicator on the status bar tells you the current page and the total number of pages in this worksheet.

2. **Move the pointer over the header** *without clicking*

   The header is made up of three text boxes: left, center, and right. Each text box is outlined in green as you pass over it with the pointer.

QUICK TIP

You can change header and footer information using the Header & Footer Tools Design tab that opens on the Ribbon when a header or footer is active. For example, you can insert the date by clicking the Current Date button in the Header & Footer Elements group, or insert the time by clicking the Current Time button.

3. **Click the left header text box, type Reason2Go, click the center header text box, type Project Leader Payroll Calculator, click the right header text box, then type Week 35**

   The new text appears in the text boxes, as shown in **FIGURE 1-15**. You can also press the [Tab] key to advance from one header box to the next.

4. **Select the range A1:G2, then press [Delete]**

   The duplicate information you just entered in the header is deleted from cells in the worksheet.

5. **Click the View tab if necessary, click the Ruler check box in the Show group, then click the Gridlines check box in the Show group**

   The rulers and the gridlines are hidden. By default, gridlines in a worksheet do not print, so hiding them gives you a more accurate image of your final document.

6. **Click the Page Break Preview button on the status bar**

   Your view changes to Page Break Preview, which displays a reduced view of each page of your worksheet, along with page break indicators that you can drag to include more or less information on a page.

QUICK TIP

Once you view a worksheet in Page Break Preview, the page break indicators appear as dotted lines after you switch back to Normal view or Page Layout view.

7. **Drag the pointer from the bottom page break indicator to the bottom of row 20**

   See **FIGURE 1-16**. When you're working on a large worksheet with multiple pages, sometimes you need to adjust where pages break; in this worksheet, however, the information all fits comfortably on one page.

8. **Click the Page Layout button in the Workbook Views group, click the Ruler check box in the Show group, then click the Gridlines check box in the Show group**

   The rulers and gridlines are no longer hidden. You can show or hide View tab items in any view.

9. **Save your work**

FIGURE 1-14: Page Layout view

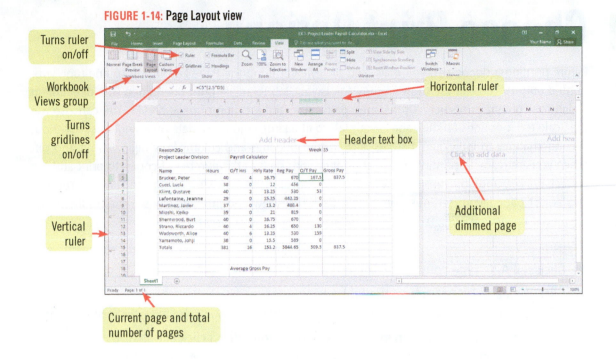

Turns ruler on/off

Workbook Views group

Turns gridlines on/off

Horizontal ruler

Header text box

Additional dimmed page

Vertical ruler

Current page and total number of pages

FIGURE 1-15: Header text entered

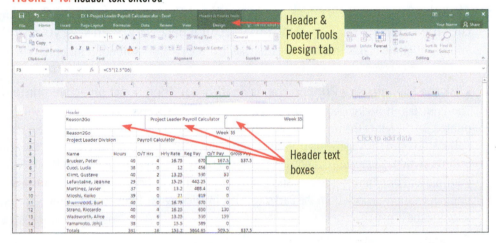

Header & Footer Tools Design tab

Header text boxes

FIGURE 1-16: Page Break Preview

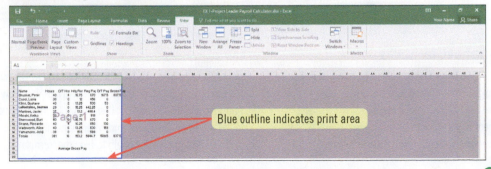

Blue outline indicates print area

Excel 2016

Choose Print Options

Learning Outcomes
• Change the page orientation
• Hide/view gridlines when printing
• Preview and print a worksheet

Before printing a document, you may want to review it using the Page Layout tab to fine-tune your printed output. You can use tools on the Page Layout tab to adjust print orientation (the direction in which the content prints across the page), paper size, and location of page breaks. You can also use the Scale to Fit options on the Page Layout tab to fit a large amount of data on a single page without making changes to individual margins, and to turn gridlines and column/row headings on and off. When you are ready to print, you can set print options such as the number of copies to print and the correct printer, and you can preview your document in Backstage view using the File tab. You can also adjust page layout settings from within Backstage view and immediately see the results in the document preview. **CASE** ▶ *You are ready to prepare your worksheet for printing.*

STEPS

1. **Click cell A20, type your name, then click** ✓

2. **Click the Page Layout tab on the Ribbon**

   Compare your screen to FIGURE 1-17. The solid outline indicates the default **print area**, the area to be printed.

3. **Click the Orientation button in the Page Setup group, then click Landscape**

   The paper orientation changes to **landscape**, so the contents will print across the length of the page instead of across the width. Notice how the margins of the worksheet adjust.

4. **Click the Orientation button in the Page Setup group, then click Portrait**

   The orientation returns to **portrait**, so the contents will print across the width of the page.

5. **Click the Gridlines View check box in the Sheet Options group on the Page Layout tab, click the Gridlines Print check box to select it if necessary, then save your work**

   Printing gridlines makes the data easier to read, but the gridlines will not print unless the Gridlines Print check box is checked.

6. **Click the File tab, click Print on the navigation bar, then select an active printer if necessary**

   The Print tab in Backstage view displays a preview of your worksheet exactly as it will look when it is printed. To the left of the worksheet preview, you can also change a number of document settings and print options. To open the Page Setup dialog box and adjust page layout options, click the Page Setup link in the Settings section. Compare your preview screen to FIGURE 1-18. You can print from this view by clicking the Print button, or return to the worksheet without printing by clicking the Back button ⬅. You can also print an entire workbook from the Backstage view by clicking the Print button in the Settings section, then selecting the active sheet or entire workbook.

7. **Compare your settings to FIGURE 1-18, then click the Print button**

   One copy of the worksheet prints.

8. **Submit your work to your instructor as directed, then exit Excel**

Printing worksheet formulas

Sometimes you need to keep a record of all the formulas in a worksheet. You might want to do this to see exactly how you came up with a complex calculation, so you can explain it to others. To prepare a worksheet to show formulas rather than results when printed, open the workbook containing the formulas you want to print. Click the Formulas tab, then click the Show Formulas button in the Formula Auditing group to select it. When the Show Formulas button is selected, formulas rather than resulting values are displayed in the worksheet on screen and when printed. (The Show Formulas button is a toggle: click it again to hide the formulas.)

FIGURE 1-17: Worksheet with Portrait orientation

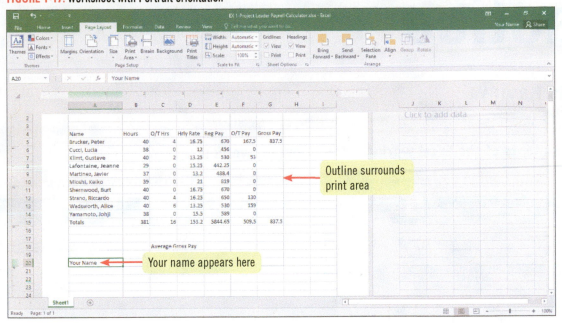

Outline surrounds print area

Your name appears here

FIGURE 1-18: Worksheet in Backstage view

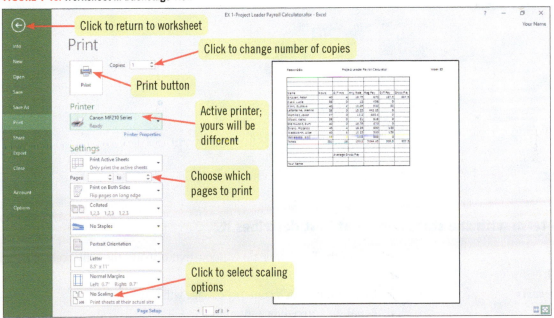

Click to return to worksheet

Click to change number of copies

Print button

Active printer; yours will be different

Choose which pages to print

Click to select scaling options

Scaling to fit

If you have a large amount of data that you want to fit to a single sheet of paper, but you don't want to spend a lot of time trying to adjust the margins and other settings, you have several options. You can easily print your work on a single sheet by clicking the No Scaling list arrow in the Settings section on the Print place in Backstage view, then clicking Fit Sheet in One Page. Another method for fitting worksheet content onto one page is to click the Page Layout tab, then change the Width and Height settings in the Scale to Fit group each to 1 Page. You can also use the Fit to option in the Page Setup dialog box to fit a worksheet on one page. To open the Page Setup dialog box, click the dialog box launcher in the Scale to Fit group on the Page Layout tab, or click the Page Setup link in the Print place in Backstage view. Make sure the Page tab is selected in the Page Setup dialog box, then click the Fit to option button.

Practice

Concepts Review

Label the elements of the Excel worksheet window shown in FIGURE 1-19.

FIGURE 1-19

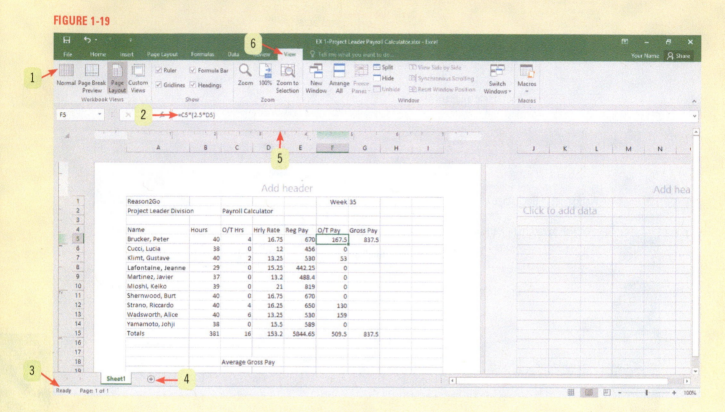

Match each term with the statement that best describes it.

7. Name box
8. Workbook
9. Formula prefix
10. Orientation
11. Cell
12. Normal view

a. Part of the Excel program window that displays the active cell address
b. Default view in Excel
c. Direction in which contents of page will print
d. Equal sign preceding a formula
e. File consisting of one or more worksheets
f. Intersection of a column and a row

Select the best answer from the list of choices.

13. **Which feature could be used to print a very long worksheet on a single sheet of paper?**
    a. Show Formulas
    b. Scale to Fit
    c. Page Break Preview
    d. Named Ranges

14. **In which area can you see a preview of your worksheet?**
    a. Page Setup
    b. Backstage view
    c. Printer Setup
    d. View tab

15. **A selection of multiple cells is called a:**
    a. Group.
    b. Range.
    c. Reference.
    d. Package.

16. **Using a cell address in a formula is known as:**
    a. Formularizing.
    b. Prefixing.
    c. Cell referencing.
    d. Cell mathematics.

17. **Which worksheet view shows how your worksheet will look when printed?**
    a. Page Layout
    b. Data
    c. Review
    d. View

18. **Which key can you press to switch to Edit mode?**
    a. [F1]
    b. [F2]
    c. [F4]
    d. [F6]

19. **In which view can you see the header and footer areas of a worksheet?**
    a. Normal view
    b. Page Layout view
    c. Page Break Preview
    d. Header/Footer view

20. **Which view shows you a reduced view of each page of your worksheet?**
    a. Normal
    b. Page Layout
    c. Thumbnail
    d. Page Break Preview

21. **The maximum number of worksheets you can include in a workbook is:**
    a. 3.
    b. 250.
    c. 255.
    d. Unlimited.

Skills Review

1. **Understand spreadsheet software.**
   a. What is the difference between a workbook and a worksheet?
   b. Identify five common business uses for electronic spreadsheets.
   c. What is what-if analysis?

2. **Identify Excel 2016 window components.**
   a. Start Excel.
   b. Open EX 1-2.xlsx from the location where you store your Data Files, then save it as **EX 1-Weather Data**.
   c. Locate the formula bar, the Sheet tabs, the mode indicator, and the cell pointer.

3. **Understand formulas.**
   a. What is the average high temperature of the listed cities? (*Hint*: Select the range B5:G5 and use the status bar.)
   b. What formula would you create to calculate the difference in altitude between Atlanta and Dallas? Enter your answer (as an equation) in cell D13.

4. Enter labels and values and use the AutoSum button.

   a. Click cell H8, then use the AutoSum button to calculate the total snowfall.

   b. Click cell H7, then use the AutoSum button to calculate the total rainfall.

   c. Save your changes to the file.

5. Edit cell entries.

   a. Use [F2] to correct the spelling of SanteFe in cell G3 (the correct spelling is Santa Fe).

   b. Click cell A17, then type your name.

   c. Save your changes.

6. Enter and edit a simple formula.

   a. Change the value 41 in cell C8 to **52**.

   b. Change the value 37 in cell D6 to **35.4**.

   c. Select cell J4, then use the fill handle to copy the formula in cell J4 to cells J5:J8.

   d. Save your changes.

7. Switch worksheet views.

   a. Click the View tab on the Ribbon, then switch to Page Layout view.

   b. Add the header **Average Annual Weather Data** to the center header text box.

   c. Add your name to the right header box.

   d. Delete the contents of cell A17.

   e. Delete the contents of cell A1.

   f. Save your changes.

8. Choose print options.

   a. Use the Page Layout tab to change the orientation to Portrait.

   b. Turn off gridlines by deselecting both the Gridlines View and Gridlines Print check boxes (if necessary) in the Sheet Options group.

   c. Scale the worksheet so all the information fits on one page. If necessary, scale the worksheet so all the information fits on one page. (*Hint*: Click the Width list arrow in the Scale to Fit group, click 1 page, click the Height list arrow in the Scale to Fit group, then click 1 page.) Compare your screen to **FIGURE 1-20**.

   d. Preview the worksheet in Backstage view, then print the worksheet.

   e. Save your changes, submit your work to your instructor as directed, then close the workbook and exit Excel.

FIGURE 1-20

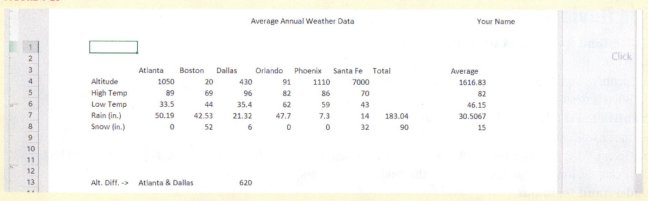

Independent Challenge 1

A real estate development company has hired you to help them make the transition to using Excel in their office. They would like to list properties they are interested in acquiring in a workbook. You've started a worksheet for this project that contains labels but no data.

a. Open the file EX 1-3.xlsx from the location where you store your Data Files, then save it as **EX 1-Real Estate Acquisitions**.

b. Enter the data shown in **TABLE 1-4** in columns A, C, D, and E (the property address information should spill into column B).

TABLE 1-4

Property Address	Price	Bedrooms	Bathrooms	Area
1507 Pinon Lane	575000	4	2.5	NE
32 Zanzibar Way	429000	3	4	SE
60 Pottery Lane	526500	2	2	NE
902 Excelsior Drive	315000	4	3	NW

c. Use Page Layout view to create a header with the following components: the title **Real Estate Acquisitions** in the center and your name on the right.

d. Create formulas for totals in cells C6:E6.

e. Save your changes, then compare your worksheet to **FIGURE 1-21**.

f. Submit your work to your instructor as directed.

g. Close the worksheet and exit Excel.

FIGURE 1-21

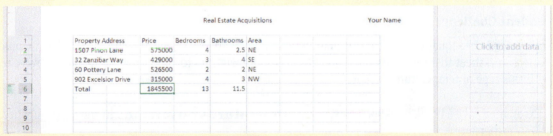

Independent Challenge 2

You are the general manager for Luxury Motors, a high-end auto reseller. Although the company is just five years old, it is expanding rapidly, and you are continually looking for ways to save time. You recently began using Excel to manage and maintain data on inventory and sales, which has greatly helped you to track information accurately and efficiently.

a. Start Excel.

b. Save a new workbook as **EX 1-Luxury Motors** in the location where you store your Data Files.

c. Switch to an appropriate view, then add a header that contains your name in the left header text box and the title **Luxury Motors** in the center header text box.

Independent Challenge 2 (continued)

d. Using **FIGURE 1-22** as a guide, create labels for at least seven car manufacturers and sales for three months. Include other labels as appropriate. The car make should be in column A and the months should be in columns B, C, and D. A Total row should be beneath the data, and a Total column should be in column E.

FIGURE 1-22

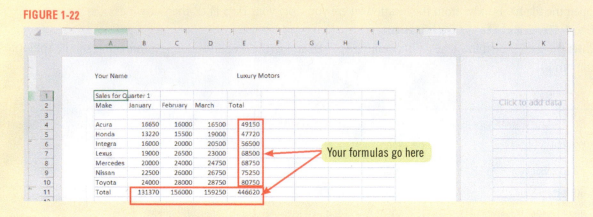

e. Enter values of your choice for the monthly sales for each make.

f. Add formulas in the Total column to calculate total quarterly sales for each make. Add formulas at the bottom of each column of values to calculate the total for that column. Remember that you can use the AutoSum button and the fill handle to save time.

g. Save your changes, preview the worksheet in Backstage view, then submit your work to your instructor as directed.

h. Close the workbook and exit Excel.

Independent Challenge 3

This Independent Challenge requires an Internet connection.

Your company, which is headquartered in Paris, is planning to open an office in New York City. You think it would be helpful to create a worksheet that can be used to convert Celsius temperatures to Fahrenheit, to help employees who are unfamiliar with this type of temperature measurement.

a. Start Excel, then save a blank workbook as **EX 1-Temperature Conversions** in the location where you store your Data Files.

b. Create column headings using **FIGURE 1-23** as a guide. (*Hint*: You can widen column B by clicking cell B1, clicking the Format button in the Cells group on the Home tab, then clicking AutoFit Column Width.)

FIGURE 1-23

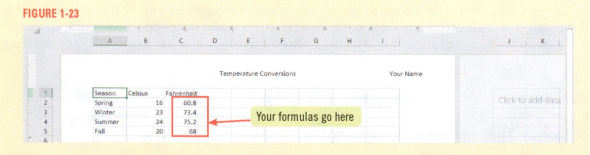

c. Create row labels for each of the seasons.

d. In the appropriate cells, enter what you determine to be a reasonable indoor temperature for each season.

e. Use your web browser to find out the conversion rate for Fahrenheit to Celsius. (*Hint*: Use your favorite search engine to search on a term such as **temperature conversion formula**.)

Independent Challenge 3 (continued)

f. In the appropriate cells, create a formula that calculates the conversion of the Fahrenheit temperature you entered into a Celsius temperature.

g. In Page Layout View, add your name and the title **Temperature Conversions** to the header.

h. Save your work, then submit your work to your instructor as directed.

i. Close the file, then exit Excel.

Independent Challenge 4: Explore

You've been asked to take over a project started by a co-worker whose Excel skills are not as good as your own. The assignment was to create a sample invoice for an existing client. The invoice will include personnel hours, supplies, and sales tax. Your predecessor started the project, including layout and initial calculations, but she has not made good use of Excel features and has made errors in her calculations. Complete the worksheet by correcting the errors and improving the design. Be prepared to discuss what is wrong with each of the items in the worksheet that you change.

a. Start Excel, open the file EX 1-4.xlsx from the location where you store your Data Files, then save it as **EX 1-Improved Invoice**.

b. There is an error in cell E5: please use the Help feature to find out what is wrong. If you need additional assistance, search Help on *overview of formulas*.

c. Correct the error in the formula in cell E5, then copy the corrected formula into cells E6:E7.

d. Correct the error in the formula in cell E11, then copy the corrected formula into cells E12 and E13.

e. Cells E8 and E14 also contain incorrect formulas. Cell E8 should contain a formula that calculates the total personnel expense, and cell E14 should calculate the total supplies used.

f. Cell G17 should contain a formula that adds the Invoice subtotal (total personnel and total supplies).

g. Cell G18 should calculate the sales tax by multiplying the Subtotal (G17) and the sales tax (cell G18).

h. The Invoice Total (cell G19) should contain a formula that adds the Invoice subtotal (cell G17) and Sales tax (cell G18).

i. Add the following to cell A21: **Terms**, then add the following to cell B21: **Net 10**.

j. Switch to Page Layout view and make the following changes to the Header: Improved Invoice for Week 22 (in the left header box), Client ABC (in the center header box), and your name (in the right header box).

k. Delete the contents of A1:A2, switch to Normal view, then compare your worksheet to FIGURE 1-24.

l. Save your work.

FIGURE 1-24

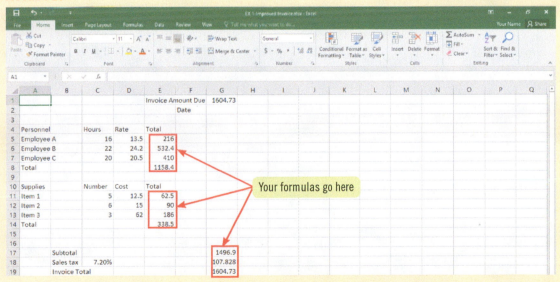

Visual Workshop

Open the file EX 1-5.xlsx from the location where you store your Data Files, then save it as **EX 1-Project Tools**. Using the skills you learned in this module, modify your worksheet so it matches FIGURE 1-25. Enter formulas in cells D4 through D13 and in cells B14 and C14. Use the AutoSum button and fill handle to make entering your formulas easier. Add your name in the left header text box, then print one copy of the worksheet with the formulas displayed.

FIGURE 1-25

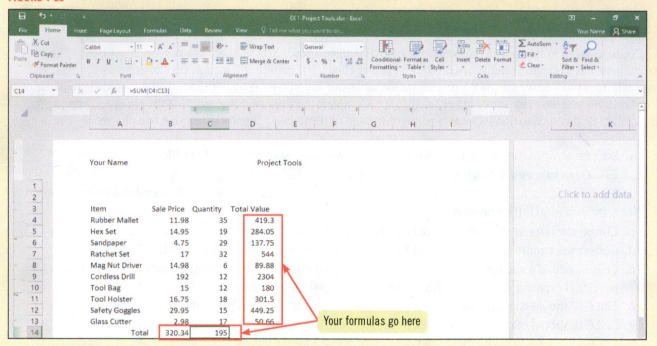

Working with Formulas and Functions

CASE ▶ Yolanda Lee, the vice president of finance at Reason2Go, needs to analyze tour expenses for the current year. She has asked you to prepare a worksheet that summarizes this expense data and includes some statistical analysis. She would also like you to perform some what-if analysis, to see what quarterly expenses would look like with various projected increases.

Module Objectives

After completing this module, you will be able to:

- Create a complex formula
- Insert a function
- Type a function
- Copy and move cell entries
- Understand relative and absolute cell references

- Copy formulas with relative cell references
- Copy formulas with absolute cell references
- Round a value with a function

Files You Will Need

EX 2-1.xlsx EX 2-3.xlsx
EX 2-2.xlsx EX 2-4.xlsx

Create a Complex Formula

Learning Outcomes:
- Create a complex formula by pointing
- Use the fill handle and Auto Fill

A **complex formula** is one that uses more than one arithmetic operator. You might, for example, need to create a formula that uses addition and multiplication. In formulas containing more than one arithmetic operator, Excel uses the standard **order of precedence** rules to determine which operation to perform first. You can change the order of precedence in a formula by using parentheses around the part you want to calculate first. For example, the formula =4+2*5 equals 14, because the order of precedence dictates that multiplication is performed before addition. However, the formula =(4+2)*5 equals 30, because the parentheses cause 4+2 to be calculated first. **CASE** *You want to create a formula that calculates a 20% increase in tour expenses.*

STEPS

1. **Start Excel, open the file EX 2-1.xlsx from the location where you store your Data Files, then save it as EX 2-R2G Tour Expense Analysis**

2. **Select the range B4:B11, click the Quick Analysis tool** [icon] **that appears below the selection, then click the Totals tab**

   The Totals tab in the Quick Analysis tool displays commonly used functions, as seen in **FIGURE 2-1**.

3. **Click the AutoSum button** Σ **in the Quick Analysis tool**

   The newly calculated value displays in cell B12 and has bold formatting automatically applied, helping to set it off as a sum. This shading is temporary, and will not appear after you click a cell.

4. **Click cell B12, then drag the fill handle to cell E12**

   The formula in cell B12, as well as the bold formatting, is copied to cells C12:E12.

QUICK TIP

When the mode indicator on the status bar says "Point," cells you click are added to the formula.

5. **Click cell B14, type =, click cell B12, then type +**

   In this first part of the formula, you are inserting a reference to the cell that contains total expenses for Quarter 1.

6. **Click cell B12, then type *.2**

   The second part of this formula adds a 20% increase (B12*.2) to the original value of the cell (the total expenses for Quarter 1).

7. **Click the Enter button** [icon] **on the formula bar**

   The result, 42749.58, appears in cell B14.

QUICK TIP

You can also copy the formulas by selecting the range C14:E14, clicking the Fill button [icon] in the Editing group on the Home tab, then clicking Right.

8. **Press [Tab], type =, click cell C12, type +, click cell C12, type *.2, then click** [icon]

   The result, 42323.712, appears in cell C14.

9. **Drag the fill handle from cell C14 to cell E14, then save your work**

   The calculated values appear in the selected range, as shown in **FIGURE 2-2**. Dragging the fill handle on a cell copies the cell's contents or continues a series of data (such as Quarter 1, Quarter 2, etc.) into adjacent cells. This option is called **Auto Fill**.

Using Add-ins to improve worksheet functionality

Excel has more functionality than simple and complex math computations. Using the My Add-ins feature (found in the Add-ins group in the Insert tab), you can insert an add-in into your worksheet that accesses the web and adds functionality. Many of the add-ins are free or available for a small fee and can be used to create an email, appointment, meeting, contact, or task, or be a reference source, such as the Mini Calendar or Date Picker. When you click the My Add-ins button list arrow, you'll see any Recently Used Add-ins. Click See All to display the featured Add-ins for Office and to go to the Store to view available add-ins. When you find one you want, make sure you're logged in to Office.com, click the add-in, click Trust It, and the add-in will be installed. Click the My Add-ins button and your add-in should display under Recently Used Add-ins. Click it, then click Insert. The add-in will display in the Recently Used Add-ins pane when you click the My Add-ins button.

FIGURE 2-1: Totals tab in the Quick Analysis tool

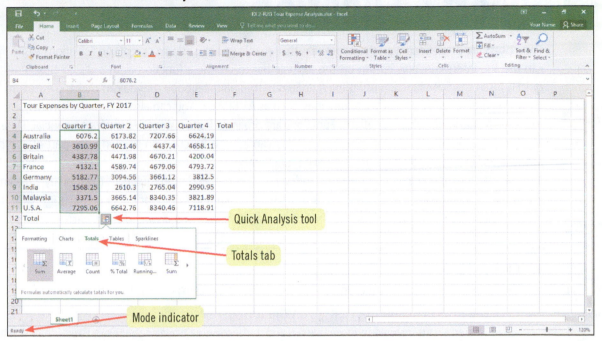

FIGURE 2-2: Results of copied formulas

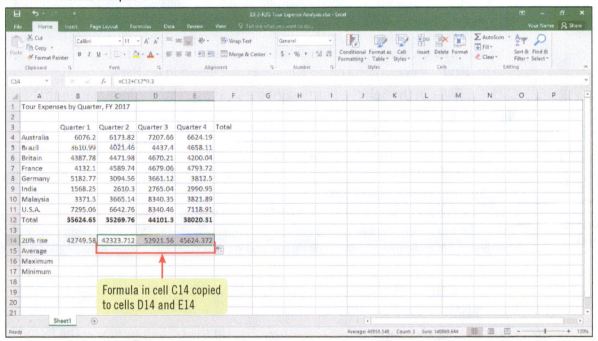

Formula in cell C14 copied to cells D14 and E14

Reviewing the order of precedence

When you work with formulas that contain more than one operator, the order of precedence is very important because it affects the final value. If a formula contains two or more operators, such as 4+.55/4000*25, Excel performs the calculations in a particular sequence based on the following rules: Operations inside parentheses are calculated before any other operations. Reference operators (such as ranges) are calculated first. Exponents are calculated next, then any multiplication and division—progressing from left to right. Finally, addition and subtraction are calculated from left to right. In the example 4+.55/4000*25, Excel performs the arithmetic operations by first dividing .55 by 4000, then multiplying the result by 25, then adding 4. You can change the order of calculations by using parentheses. For example, in the formula (4+.55)/4000*25, Excel would first add 4 and .55, then divide that amount by 4000, then finally multiply by 25.

Working with Formulas and Functions

Insert a Function

Functions are predefined worksheet formulas that enable you to perform complex calculations easily. You can use the Insert Function button on the formula bar to choose a function from a dialog box. You can quickly insert the SUM function using the AutoSum button on the Ribbon, or you can click the AutoSum list arrow to enter other frequently used functions, such as **AVERAGE**. You can also use the Quick Analysis tool to calculate commonly used functions. Functions are organized into categories, such as Financial, Date & Time, and Statistical, based on their purposes. You can insert a function on its own or as part of another formula. For example, you have used the SUM function on its own to add a range of cells. You could also use the SUM function within a formula that adds a range of cells and then multiplies the total by a decimal. If you use a function alone, it always begins with an equal sign (=) as the formula prefix. **CASE** *You need to calculate the average expenses for the first quarter of the year and decide to use a function to do so.*

STEPS

1. **Click cell B15**

   This is the cell where you want to enter a calculation that averages expenses per country for the first quarter.

2. **Click the Insert Function button 𝑓𝑥 on the formula bar**

   An equal sign (=) is inserted in the active cell and in the formula bar, and the Insert Function dialog box opens, as shown in **FIGURE 2-3**. In this dialog box, you specify the function you want to use by clicking it in the Select a function list. The Select a function list initially displays recently used functions. If you don't see the function you want, you can click the Or select a category list arrow to choose the desired category. If you're not sure which category to choose, you can type the function name or a description in the Search for a function field. The AVERAGE function is a statistical function, but you don't need to open the Statistical category because this function already appears in the Most Recently Used category.

3. **Click AVERAGE in the Select a function list if necessary, read the information that appears under the list, then click OK**

   The Function Arguments dialog box opens, in which you define the range of cells you want to average.

4. **Click the Collapse button 🖼 in the Number1 field of the Function Arguments dialog box, select the range B4:B11 in the worksheet, then click the Expand button 🖼 in the Function Arguments dialog box**

   Clicking the Collapse button minimizes the dialog box so that you can select cells in the worksheet. When you click the Expand button, the dialog box is restored, as shown in **FIGURE 2-4**. You can also begin dragging in the worksheet to automatically minimize the dialog box; after you select the desired range, the dialog box is restored.

5. **Click OK**

   The Function Arguments dialog box closes, and the calculated value is displayed in cell B15. The average expenses per country for Quarter 1 is 4453.0813.

6. **Click cell C15, click the AutoSum list arrow Σ ⌄ in the Editing group on the Home tab, then click Average**

   A ScreenTip beneath cell C15 displays the arguments needed to complete the function. The text "number1" is in boldface, telling you that the next step is to supply the first cell in the group you want to average.

7. **Select the range C4:C11 in the worksheet, then click the Enter button ✔ on the formula bar**

   The average expenses per country for the second quarter appear in cell C15.

8. **Drag the fill handle from cell C15 to cell E15**

   The formula in cell C15 is copied to the rest of the selected range, as shown in **FIGURE 2-5**.

9. **Save your work**

FIGURE 2-3: Insert Function dialog box

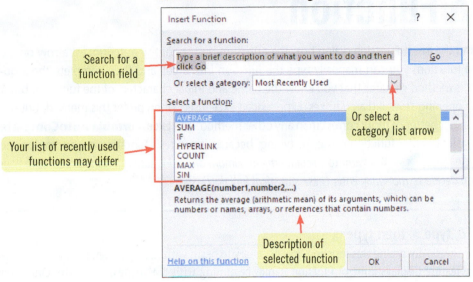

Search for a function field

Your list of recently used functions may differ

Or select a category list arrow

Description of selected function

FIGURE 2-4: Expanded Function Arguments dialog box

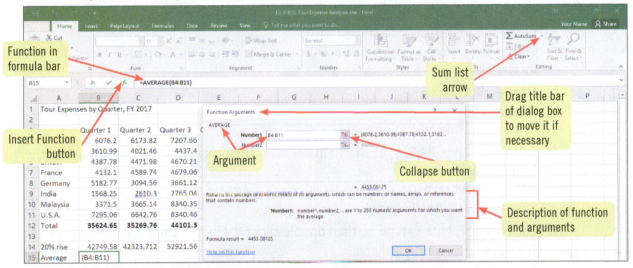

Function in formula bar

Insert Function button

Argument

Sum list arrow

Drag title bar of dialog box to move it if necessary

Collapse button

Description of function and arguments

FIGURE 2-5: Average functions used in worksheet

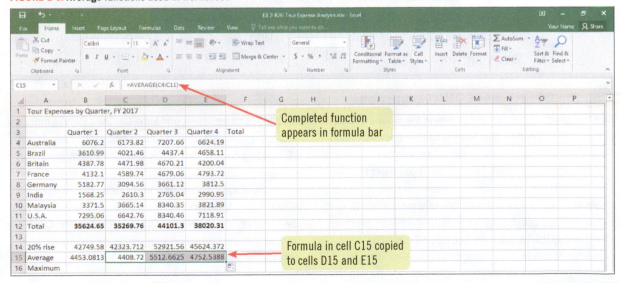

Completed function appears in formula bar

Formula in cell C15 copied to cells D15 and E15

Type a Function

Learning
Outcomes
• Select a function
  by typing
• Use AutoComplete
  to copy formulas

In addition to using the Insert Function dialog box, the AutoSum button, or the AutoSum list arrow on the Ribbon to enter a function, you can manually type the function into a cell and then complete the arguments needed. This method requires that you know the name and initial characters of the function, but it can be faster than opening several dialog boxes. Experienced Excel users often prefer this method, but it is only an alternative, not better or more correct than any other method. The Excel **Formula AutoComplete** feature makes it easier to enter function names by typing, because it suggests functions depending on the first letters you type. **CASE** ▶ *You want to calculate the maximum and minimum quarterly expenses in your worksheet, and you decide to manually enter these statistical functions.*

STEPS

1. **Click cell B16, type =, then type m**

   Because you are manually typing this function, it is necessary to begin with the equal sign (=). The Formula AutoComplete feature displays a list of function names beginning with "M" beneath cell B16. Once you type an equal sign in a cell, each letter you type acts as a trigger to activate the Formula AutoComplete feature. This feature minimizes the amount of typing you need to do to enter a function and reduces typing and syntax errors.

2. **Click MAX in the list**

   Clicking any function in the Formula AutoComplete list opens a ScreenTip next to the list that describes the function.

3. **Double-click MAX**

   The function is inserted in the cell, and a ScreenTip appears beneath the cell to help you complete the formula. See **FIGURE 2-6**.

4. **Select the range B4:B11, as shown in FIGURE 2-7, then click the Enter button ☑ on the formula bar**

   The result, 7295.06, appears in cell B16. When you completed the entry, the closing parenthesis was automatically added to the formula.

5. **Click cell B17, type =, type m, then double-click MIN in the list of function names**

   The MIN function appears in the cell.

6. **Select the range B4:B11, then press [Enter]**

   The result, 1568.25, appears in cell B17.

7. **Select the range B16:B17, then drag the fill handle from cell B17 to cell E17**

   The maximum and minimum values for all of the quarters appear in the selected range, as shown in **FIGURE 2-8**.

8. **Save your work**

Using the COUNT and COUNTA functions

When you select a range, a count of cells in the range that are not blank appears in the status bar. You can use this information to determine things such as how many team members entered project hours in a worksheet. For example, if you select the range A1:A5 and only cells A1, A4, and A5 contain data, the status bar displays "Count: 3." To count nonblank cells more precisely, or to incorporate these calculations in a worksheet, you can use the COUNT and COUNTA functions. The COUNT function returns the number of cells in a range that contain numeric data, including numbers, dates, and formulas. The COUNTA function returns the number of cells in a range that contain any data at all, including numeric data, labels, and even a blank space. For example, the formula =COUNT(A1:A5) returns the number of cells in the range that contain numeric data, and the formula =COUNTA(A1:A5) returns the number of cells in the range that are not empty. If you use the COUNT functions in the Quick Analysis tool, the calculation is entered in the cell immediately beneath the selected range.

FIGURE 2-6: MAX function in progress

FIGURE 2-6: MAX function in progress

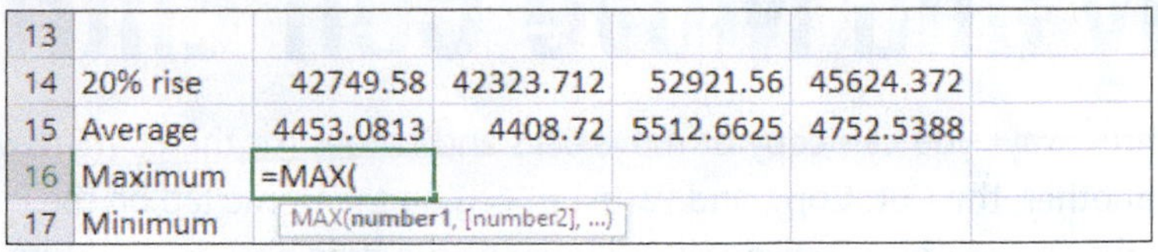

13					
14	20% rise	42749.58	42323.712	52921.56	45624.372
15	Average	4453.0813	4408.72	5512.6625	4752.5388
16	Maximum	=MAX(			
17	Minimum	MAX(**number1**, [number2], ...)			

FIGURE 2-7: Completing the MAX function

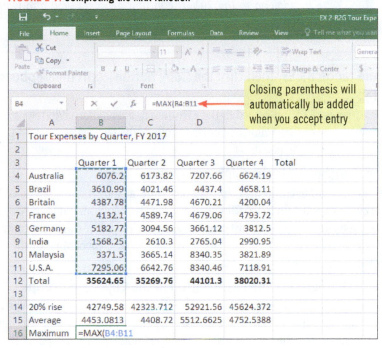

FIGURE 2-8: Completed MAX and MIN functions

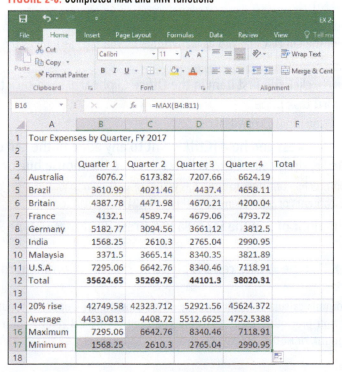

Copy and Move Cell Entries

Learning Outcomes
- Copy a range to the Clipboard
- Paste a Clipboard entry
- Empty cell contents
- Copy cell contents

There are three ways you can copy or move cells and ranges (or the contents within them) from one location to another: the Cut, Copy, and Paste buttons on the Home tab on the Ribbon; the fill handle in the lower-right corner of the active cell or range; or the drag-and-drop feature. When you copy cells, the original data remains in the original location; when you cut or move cells, the original data is deleted from its original location. You can also cut, copy, and paste cells or ranges from one worksheet to another. **CASE** ▶ *In addition to the 20% rise in tour expenses, you also want to show a 30% rise. Rather than retype this information, you copy and move selected cells.*

STEPS

QUICK TIP
To cut or copy selected cell contents, activate the cell, then select the characters within the cell that you want to cut or copy.

1. **Select the range B3:E3, then click the Copy button 📋 in the Clipboard group on the Home tab**

    The selected range (B3:E3) is copied to the **Clipboard**, a temporary Windows storage area that holds the selections you copy or cut. A moving border surrounds the selected range until you press [Esc] or copy an additional item to the Clipboard.

2. **Click the launcher 🔽 in the Clipboard group**

    The Office Clipboard opens in the Clipboard task pane, as shown in **FIGURE 2-9**. When you copy or cut an item, it is cut or copied both to the Clipboard provided by Windows and to the Office Clipboard. Unlike the Windows Clipboard, which holds just one item at a time, the Office Clipboard contains up to 24 of the most recently cut or copied items from any Office program. Your Clipboard task pane may contain more items than shown in the figure.

QUICK TIP
Once the Office Clipboard contains 24 items, the oldest existing item is automatically deleted each time you add an item.

3. **Click cell B19, then click the Paste button in the Clipboard group**

    A copy of the contents of range B3:E3 is pasted into the range B19:E19. When pasting an item from the Office Clipboard or Clipboard into a worksheet, you only need to specify the upper left cell of the range where you want to paste the selection. Notice that the information you copied remains in the original range B3:E3; if you had cut instead of copied, the information would have been deleted from its original location once it was pasted.

4. **Press [Delete]**

    The selected cells are empty. You have decided to paste the cells in a different row. You can repeatedly paste an item from the Office Clipboard as many times as you like, as long as the item remains in the Office Clipboard.

QUICK TIP
You can also close the Office Clipboard pane by clicking the launcher in the Clipboard group.

5. **Click cell B20, click the first item in the Office Clipboard, then click the Close button ✕ on the Clipboard task pane**

    Cells B20:E20 contain the copied labels.

6. **Click cell A14, press and hold [Ctrl], point to any edge of the cell until the pointer changes to ⤢, drag cell A14 to cell A21, release the mouse button, then release [Ctrl]**

    The copy pointer ⤢ continues to appear as you drag, as shown in **FIGURE 2-10**. When you release the mouse button, the contents of cell A14 are copied to cell A21.

7. **Click to the right of 2 in the formula bar, press [Backspace], type 3, then click the Enter button ✓**

8. **Click cell B21, type =, click cell B12, type *1.3, click ✓ on the formula bar, then save your work**

    This new formula calculates a 30% increase of the expenses for Quarter 1, though using a different method from what you previously used. Anything you multiply by 1.3 returns an amount that is 130% of the original amount, or a 30% increase. Compare your screen to **FIGURE 2-11**.

FIGURE 2-9: Copied data in Office Clipboard

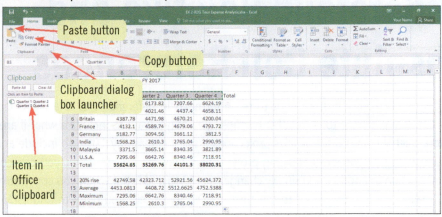

FIGURE 2-10: Copying cell contents with drag-and-drop

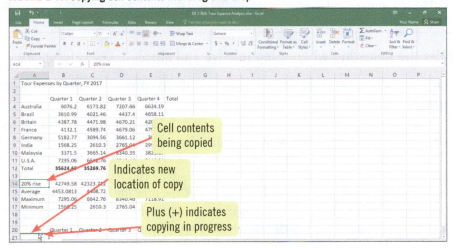

FIGURE 2-11: Formula entered to calculate a 30% increase

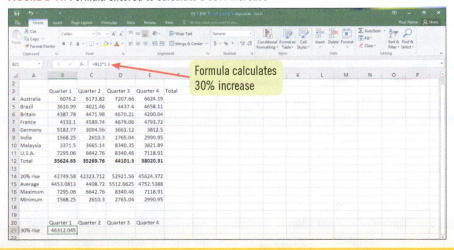

Inserting and deleting selected cells

As you add formulas to your workbook, you may need to insert or delete cells. When you do this, Excel automatically adjusts cell references to reflect their new locations. To insert cells, click the Insert list arrow in the Cells group on the Home tab, then click Insert Cells. The Insert dialog box opens, asking if you want to insert a cell and move the current active cell down or to the right of the new one. To delete one or more selected cells, click the Delete list arrow in the Cells group, click Delete Cells, and in the Delete dialog box, indicate which way you want to move the adjacent cells. When using this option, be careful not to disturb row or column alignment that may be necessary to maintain the accuracy of cell references in the worksheet. Click the Insert button or Delete button in the Cells group to insert or delete a single cell.

Working with Formulas and Functions

Understand Relative and Absolute Cell References

Learning Outcomes
- Identify cell referencing
- Identify when to use absolute or relative cell references

As you work in Excel, you may want to reuse formulas in different parts of a worksheet to reduce the amount of data you have to retype. For example, you might want to include a what-if analysis in one part of a worksheet showing a set of sales projections if sales increase by 10%. To include another analysis in another part of the worksheet showing projections if sales increase by 50%, you can copy the formulas from one section to another and simply change the "1" to a "5". But when you copy formulas, it is important to make sure that they refer to the correct cells. To do this, you need to understand the difference between relative and absolute cell references. **CASE** ▶ *You plan to reuse formulas in different parts of your worksheets, so you want to understand relative and absolute cell references.*

DETAILS

Consider the following when using relative and absolute cell references:

- **Use relative references when you want to preserve the relationship to the formula location**

  When you create a formula that references another cell, Excel normally does not "record" the exact cell address for the cell being referenced in the formula. Instead, it looks at the relationship that cell has to the cell containing the formula. For example, in **FIGURE 2-12**, cell F5 contains the formula: =SUM(B5:E5). When Excel retrieves values to calculate the formula in cell F5, it actually looks for "the four cells to the left of the formula," which in this case is cells B5:E5. This way, if you copy the cell to a new location, such as cell F6, the results will reflect the new formula location and will automatically retrieve the values in cells B6, C6, D6, and E6. These are **relative cell references**, because Excel is recording the input cells *in relation to* or *relative to* the formula cell.

  In most cases, you want to use relative cell references when copying or moving, so this is the Excel default. In **FIGURE 2-12**, the formulas in cells F5:F12 and cells B13:F13 contain relative cell references. They total the "four cells to the left of" or the "eight cells above" the formulas.

- **Use absolute cell references when you want to preserve the exact cell address in a formula**

  There are times when you want Excel to retrieve formula information from a specific cell, and you don't want the cell address in the formula to change when you copy it to a new location. For example, you might have a price in a specific cell that you want to use in all formulas, regardless of their location. If you use relative cell referencing, the formula results would be incorrect, because the formula would reference a different cell every time you copy it. Therefore, you need to use an **absolute cell reference**, which is a reference that does not change when you copy the formula.

  You create an absolute cell reference by placing a $ (dollar sign) in front of both the column letter and the row number of the cell address. You can either type the dollar sign when typing the cell address in a formula (for example, "=C12*$B$16") or you can select a cell address on the formula bar and then press [F4], and the dollar signs are added automatically. **FIGURE 2-13** shows formulas containing both absolute and relative references. The formulas in cells B19 to E26 use absolute cell references to refer to a potential sales increase of 50%, shown in cell B16.

FIGURE 2-12: Formulas containing relative references

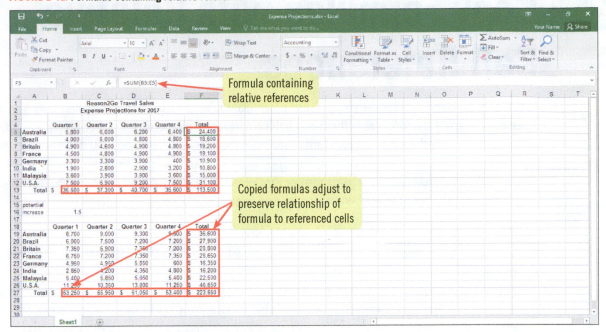

Formula containing relative references

Copied formulas adjust to preserve relationship of formula to referenced cells

FIGURE 2-13: Formulas containing absolute and relative references

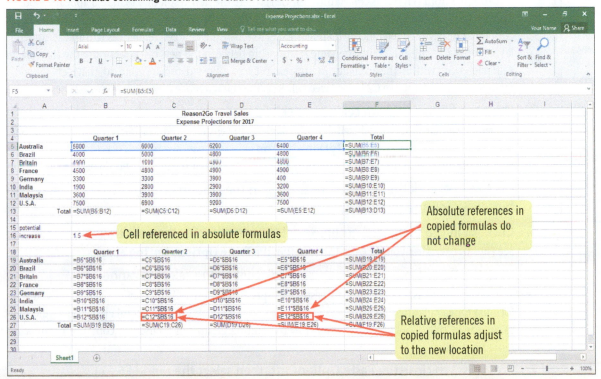

Cell referenced in absolute formulas

Absolute references in copied formulas do not change

Relative references in copied formulas adjust to the new location

Using a mixed reference

Sometimes when you copy a formula, you want to change the row reference, but keep the column reference the same. This type of cell referencing combines elements of both absolute and relative referencing and is called a **mixed reference**. For example, when copied, a formula containing the mixed reference C$14 would change the column letter relative to its new location, but not the row number. In the mixed reference $C14, the column letter would not change, but the row number would be updated relative to its location. Like an absolute reference, a mixed reference can be created by pressing the [F4] function key with the cell reference selected. With each press of the [F4] key, you cycle through all the possible combinations of relative, absolute, and mixed references (C14, $C$14, C$14, and $C14).

Excel 2016

Copy Formulas with Relative Cell References

Copying and moving a cell allow you to reuse a formula you've already created. Copying cells is usually faster than retyping the formulas in them and helps to prevent typing errors. If the cells you are copying contain relative cell references and you want to maintain the relative referencing, you don't need to make any changes to the cells before copying them. **CASE** ➤ *You want to copy the formula in cell B21, which calculates the 30% increase in quarterly expenses for Quarter 1, to cells C21 through E21. You also want to create formulas to calculate total expenses for each tour country.*

STEPS

1. **Click cell B21 if necessary, then click the Copy button 📋 in the Clipboard group on the Home tab**

   The formula for calculating the 30% expense increase during Quarter 1 is copied to the Clipboard. Notice that the formula =B12*1.3 appears in the formula bar, and a moving border surrounds the active cell.

2. **Click cell C21, then click the Paste button 📋** *(not the list arrow)* **in the Clipboard group**

   The formula from cell B21 is copied into cell C21, where the new result of 45850.688 appears. Notice in the formula bar that the cell references have changed so that cell C12 is referenced instead of B12. This formula contains a relative cell reference, which tells Excel to substitute new cell references within the copied formulas as necessary. This maintains the same relationship between the new cell containing the formula and the cell references within the formula. In this case, Excel adjusted the formula so that cell C12—the cell reference nine rows above C21—replaced cell B12, the cell reference nine rows above B21.

3. **Drag the fill handle from cell C21 to cell E21**

   A formula similar to the one in cell C21 now appears in cells D21 and E21. After you use the fill handle to copy cell contents, the **Auto Fill Options button** appears, as shown in **FIGURE 2-14**. You can use the Auto Fill Options button to fill the cells with only specific elements of the copied cell if you wish.

4. **Click cell F4, click the AutoSum button Σ in the Editing group, then click the Enter button ✓ on the formula bar**

5. **Click 📋 in the Clipboard group, select the range F5:F6, then click 📋**

   See **FIGURE 2-15**. After you click the Paste button, the **Paste Options button** appears.

6. **Click the Paste Options button 📋 (Ctrl) ▾ adjacent to the selected range**

   You can use the Paste options list to paste only specific elements of the copied selection if you wish. The formula for calculating total expenses for tours in Britain appears in the formula bar. You would like totals to appear in cells F7:F11. The Fill button in the Editing group can be used to copy the formula into the remaining cells.

7. **Press [Esc] to close the Paste Options list, then select the range F6:F11**

8. **Click the Fill button 🔽 in the Editing group, then click Down**

   The formulas containing relative references are copied to each cell. Compare your worksheet to **FIGURE 2-16**.

9. **Save your work**

FIGURE 2-14: Formula copied using the fill handle

FIGURE 2-15: Formulas pasted in the range F5:F6

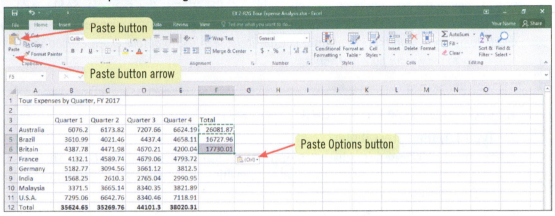

FIGURE 2-16: Formula copied using Fill Down

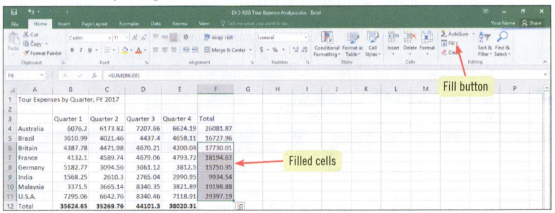

Using Paste Preview

You can selectively copy formulas, values, or other choices using the Paste list arrow, and you can see how the pasted contents will look using the Paste Preview feature. When you click the Paste list arrow, a gallery of paste option icons opens. When you point to an icon, a preview of how the content will be pasted using that option is shown in the worksheet. Options include pasting values only, pasting values with number formatting, pasting formulas only, pasting formatting only, pasting transposed data so that column data appears in rows and row data appears in columns, and pasting with no borders (to remove any borders around pasted cells).

Copy Formulas with Absolute Cell References

When copying cells, you might want one or more cell references in a formula to remain unchanged. In such an instance, you need to apply an absolute cell reference before copying the formula to preserve the specific cell address when the formula is copied. You create an absolute reference by placing a dollar sign ($) before the column letter and row number of the address (for example, $A$1). **CASE** ▶ *You need to do some what-if analysis to see how various percentage increases might affect total expenses. You decide to add a column that calculates a possible increase in the total tour expenses, and then change the percentage to see various potential results.*

STEPS

1. **Click cell G1, type Change, then press [Enter]**

2. **Type 1.1, then press [Enter]**

   You store the increase factor that will be used in the what-if analysis in this cell (G2). The value 1.1 can be used to calculate a 10% increase: anything you multiply by 1.1 returns an amount that is 110% of the original amount.

3. **Click cell H3, type What if?, then press [Enter]**

4. **In cell H4, type =, click cell F4, type *, click cell G2, then click the Enter button ☑ on the formula bar**

   The result, 28690.1, appears in cell H4. This value represents the total annual expenses for Australia if there is a 10% increase. You want to perform a what-if analysis for all the tour countries.

5. **Drag the fill handle from cell H4 to cell H11**

   The resulting values in the range H5:H11 are all zeros, which is not the result you wanted. Because you used relative cell addressing in cell H4, the copied formula adjusted so that the formula in cell H5 is =F5*G3; because there is no value in cell G3, the result is 0, an error. You need to use an absolute reference in the formula to keep the formula from adjusting itself. That way, it will always reference cell G2.

6. **Click cell H4, press [F2] to change to Edit mode, then press [F4]**

   When you press [F2], the range finder outlines the arguments of the equation in blue and red. The insertion point appears next to the G2 cell reference in cell H4. When you press [F4], dollar signs are inserted in the G2 cell reference, making it an absolute reference. See **FIGURE 2-17**.

7. **Click ☑, then drag the fill handle from cell H4 to cell H11**

   Because the formula correctly contains an absolute cell reference, the correct values for a 10% increase appear in cells H4:H11. You now want to see what a 20% increase in expenses looks like.

8. **Click cell G2, type 1.2, then click ☑**

   The values in the range H4:H11 change to reflect the 20% increase. Compare your worksheet to **FIGURE 2-18**.

9. **Save your work**

Working with Formulas and Functions

FIGURE 2-17: Absolute reference created in formula

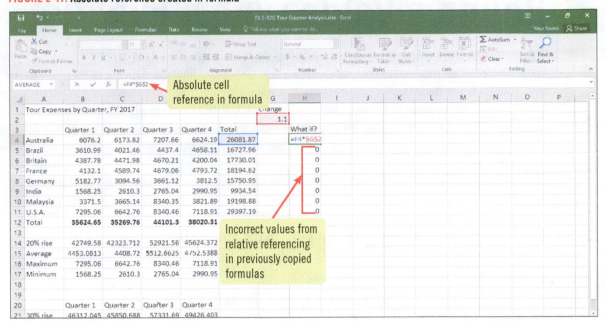

FIGURE 2-18: What-if analysis with modified change factor

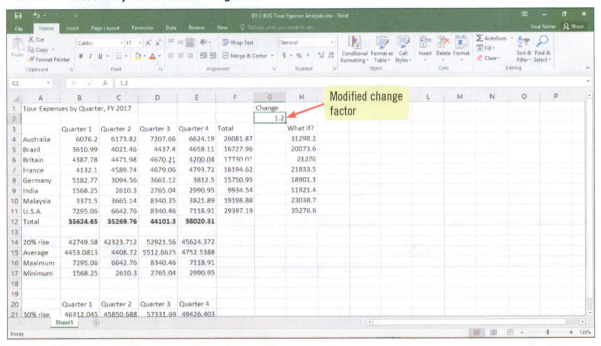

Using the fill handle for sequential text or values

Often, you need to fill cells with sequential text: months of the year, days of the week, years, or text plus a number (Quarter 1, Quarter 2,...). For example, you might want to create a worksheet that calculates data for every month of the year. Using the fill handle, you can quickly and easily create labels for the months of the year just by typing "January" in a cell. Drag the fill handle from the cell containing "January" until you have all the monthly labels you need. You can also easily fill cells with a date sequence by dragging the fill handle on a single cell containing a date. You can fill cells with a number sequence (such as 1, 2, 3,...) by dragging the fill handle on a selection of two or more cells that contain the sequence. To create a number sequence using the value in a single cell, press and hold [Ctrl] as you drag the fill handle of the cell. As you drag the fill handle, Excel automatically extends the existing sequence into the additional cells. (The content of the last filled cell appears in the ScreenTip.) To choose from all the fill series options for the current selection, click the Fill button in the Editing group on the Home tab, then click Series to open the Series dialog box.

Excel 2016

Round a Value with a Function

Learning
Outcomes
• Use Formula
AutoComplete to
insert a function
• Copy an edited
formula

The more you explore features and tools in Excel, the more ways you'll find to simplify your work and convey information more efficiently. For example, cells containing financial data are often easier to read if they contain fewer decimal places than those that appear by default. You can round a value or formula result to a specific number of decimal places by using the ROUND function. **CASE** *In your worksheet, you'd like to round the cells showing the 20% rise in expenses to show fewer digits; after all, it's not important to show cents in the projections, only whole dollars. You want Excel to round the calculated value to the nearest integer. You decide to edit cell B14 so it includes the ROUND function, and then copy the edited formula into the other formulas in this row.*

STEPS

1. **Click cell B14, then click to the right of = in the formula bar**

   You want to position the function at the beginning of the formula, before any values or arguments.

2. **Type RO**

   Formula AutoComplete displays a list of functions beginning with RO beneath the formula bar.

3. **Double-click ROUND in the functions list**

   The new function and an opening parenthesis are added to the formula, as shown in **FIGURE 2-19**. A few additional modifications are needed to complete your edit of the formula. You need to indicate the number of decimal places to which the function should round numbers, and you also need to add a closing parenthesis around the set of arguments that comes after the ROUND function.

4. **Press [END], type ,0), then click the Enter button ✓ on the formula bar**

   The comma separates the arguments within the formula, and 0 indicates that you don't want any decimal places to appear in the calculated value. When you complete the edit, the parentheses at either end of the formula briefly become bold, indicating that the formula has the correct number of open and closed parentheses and is balanced.

5. **Drag the fill handle from cell B14 to cell E14**

   The formula in cell B14 is copied to the range C14:E14. All the values are rounded to display no decimal places. Compare your worksheet to **FIGURE 2-20**.

6. **Scroll down so row 25 is visible, click cell A25, type your name, then click ✓**

7. **Save your work, preview the worksheet in the Print place in Backstage view, then submit your work to your Instructor as directed**

8. **Exit Excel**

Using Auto Fill options

When you use the fill handle to copy cells, the Auto Fill Options button appears. Auto Fill options differ depending on what you are copying. If you had selected cells containing a series (such as "Monday" and "Tuesday") and then used the fill handle, you would see options for continuing the series (such as "Wednesday" and "Thursday") or for simply pasting the copied cells. Clicking the Auto Fill Options button opens a list that lets you choose from the following options: Copy Cells, Fill Series (if applicable), Fill Formatting Only, Fill Without Formatting, or Flash Fill. Choosing Copy Cells means that the cell's contents and its formatting will be copied. The Fill Formatting Only option copies only the formatting attributes, but not cell contents. The Fill Without Formatting option copies the cell contents, but no formatting attributes. Copy Cells is the default option when using the fill handle to copy a cell, so if you want to copy the cell's contents and its formatting, you can ignore the Auto Fill Options button. The Flash Fill option allows you to create customized fill ranges on the fly, such as 2, 4, 6, 8, 10, by entering at least two values in a pattern: Excel automatically senses the pattern.

FIGURE 2-19: ROUND function added to an existing formula

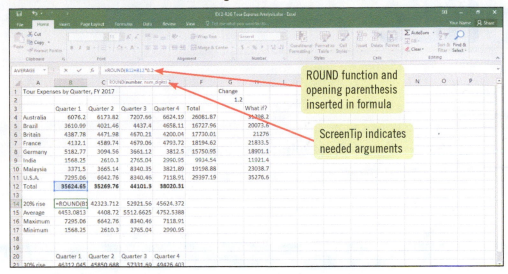

ROUND function and opening parenthesis inserted in formula

ScreenTip indicates needed arguments

FIGURE 2-20: Completed worksheet

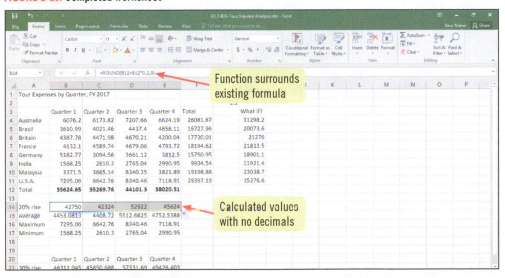

Function surrounds existing formula

Calculated values with no decimals

Creating a new workbook using a template

Excel **templates** are predesigned workbook files intended to save time when you create common documents such as balance sheets, budgets, or time cards. Templates contain labels, values, formulas, and formatting, so all you have to do is customize them with your own information. Excel comes with many templates, and you can also create your own or find additional templates on the web. Unlike a typical workbook, which has the file extension .xlsx, a template has the extension .xltx. To create a workbook using a template, click the File tab, then click New on the navigation bar. The New place in Backstage view displays thumbnails of some of the many templates available. The Blank workbook template is selected by default and is used to create a blank workbook with no content or special formatting. To select a different template, click one of the selections in the New place, view the preview, then click Create. **FIGURE 2-21** shows an example. (Your available templates may differ.) When you click

Create, a new workbook is created based on the template; when you save the new file in the default format, it has the regular .xlsx extension. To save a workbook of your own as a template, open the Save As dialog box, click the Save as type list arrow, then change the file type to Excel Template.

FIGURE 2-21: Previewing the Budget Planner template

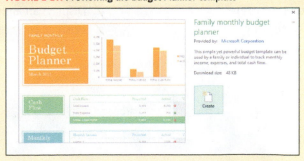

Practice

Concepts Review

Label each element of the Excel worksheet window shown in FIGURE 2-22.

FIGURE 2-22

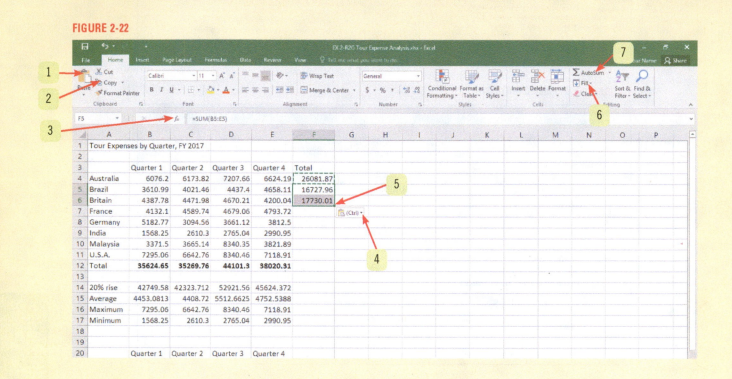

Match each term or button with the statement that best describes it.

8. **Launcher**
9. **Fill handle**
10. **Drag-and-drop method**
11. **Formula AutoComplete**
12. **[Delete] key**

a. Clears the contents of selected cells

b. Item on the Ribbon that opens a dialog box or task pane

c. Lets you move or copy data from one cell to another without using the Clipboard

d. Displays an alphabetical list of functions from which you can choose

e. Lets you copy cell contents or continue a series of data into a range of selected cells

Select the best answer from the list of choices.

13. You can use any of the following features to enter a new function *except*:

    a. Insert Function button.

    b. Formula AutoComplete.

    c. AutoSum list arrow.

    d. Clipboard.

14. Which key do you press and hold to copy while dragging and dropping selected cells?

    a. [Alt]

    b. [Ctrl]

    c. [F2]

    d. [Tab]

15. What type of cell reference is C$19?

    a. Relative

    b. Absolute

    c. Mixed

    d. Certain

16. Which key do you press to convert a relative cell reference to an absolute cell reference?

    a. [F2]

    b. [F4]

    c. [F5]

    d. [F6]

17. What type of cell reference changes when it is copied?

    a. Circular

    b. Absolute

    c. Relative

    d. Specified

Skills Review

1. Create a complex formula.

    a. Open EX 2-2.xlsx from the location where you store your Data Files, then save it as **EX 2-Construction Supply Company Inventory**.

    b. Select the range B4:B8, click the Totals tab in the Quick Analysis tool, then click the AutoSum button.

    c. Use the fill handle to copy the formula in cell B9 to cells C9:E9.

    d. In cell B11, create a complex formula that calculates a 30% decrease in the total number of cases of pylons.

    e. Use the fill handle to copy this formula into cell C11 through cell E11.

    f. Save your work.

2. Insert a function.

    a. Use the AutoSum list arrow to create a formula in cell B13 that averages the number of cases of pylons in each storage area.

    b. Use the Insert Function button to create a formula in cell B14 that calculates the maximum number of cases of pylons in a storage area.

    c. Use the AutoSum list arrow to create a formula in cell B15 that calculates the minimum number of cases of pylons in a storage area.

    d. Save your work.

3. Type a function.

   a. In cell C13, type a formula that includes a function to average the number of cases of bricks in each storage area. (*Hint*: Use Formula AutoComplete to enter the function.)

   b. In cell C14, type a formula that includes a function to calculate the maximum number of cases of bricks in a storage area.

   c. In cell C15, type a formula that includes a function to calculate the minimum number of cases of bricks in a storage area.

   d. Save your work.

4. Copy and move cell entries.

   a. Select the range B3:F3.

   b. Copy the selection to the Clipboard.

   c. Open the Clipboard task pane, then paste the selection into cell B17.

   d. Close the Clipboard task pane, then select the range A4:A9.

   e. Use the drag-and-drop method to copy the selection to cell A18. (*Hint*: The results should fill the range A18:A23.)

   f. Save your work.

5. Understand relative and absolute cell references.

   a. Write a brief description of the difference between relative and absolute references.

   b. List at least three situations in which you think a business might use an absolute reference in its calculations. Examples can include calculations for different types of worksheets, such as time cards, invoices, and budgets.

6. Copy formulas with relative cell references.

   a. Calculate the total in cell F4.

   b. Use the Fill button to copy the formula in cell F4 down to cells F5:F8.

   c. Select the range C13:C15.

   d. Use the fill handle to copy these cells to the range D13:F15.

   e. Save your work.

7. Copy formulas with absolute cell references.

   a. In cell H1, change the existing value to **1.575**.

   b. In cell H4, create a formula that multiplies F4 and an absolute reference to cell H1.

   c. Use the fill handle to copy the formula in cell H4 to cells H5 and H6.

   d. Use the Copy and Paste buttons to copy the formula in cell H4 to cells H7 and H8.

   e. Change the amount in cell H1 to **2.5**.

   f. Save your work.

Skills Review (continued)

8. **Round a value with a function.**
   a. Click cell H4.
   b. Edit this formula to include the ROUND function showing zero decimal places.
   c. Use the fill handle to copy the formula in cell H4 to the range H5:H8.
   d. Enter your name in cell A25, then compare your work to FIGURE 2-23.
   e. Save your work, preview the worksheet in Backstage view, then submit your work to your instructor as directed.
   f. Close the workbook, then exit Excel.

FIGURE 2-23

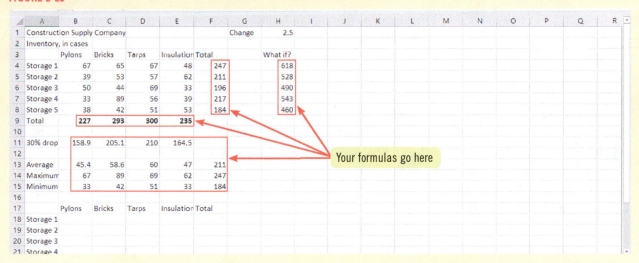

Independent Challenge 1

You are thinking of starting a small coffee shop where locals can gather. Before you begin, you need to evaluate what you think your monthly expenses will be. You've started a workbook, but need to complete the entries and add formulas.

a. Open EX 2-3.xlsx from the location where you store your Data Files, then save it as **EX 2-Coffee Shop Expenses**.

b. Make up your own expense data, and enter it in cells B4:B10. (Monthly sales are already included in the worksheet.)

c. Create a formula in cell C4 that calculates the annual rent.

d. Copy the formula in cell C4 to the range C5:C10.

e. Move the label in cell A15 to cell A14.

f. Create formulas in cells B11 and C11 that total the monthly and annual expenses.

g. Create a formula in cell C13 that calculates annual sales.

h. Create a formula in cell B14 that determines whether you will make a profit or loss, then copy the formula into cell C14.

i. Copy the labels in cells B3:C3 to cells E3:F3.

j. Type **Projected Increase** in cell G1, then type **.2** in cell H2.

k. Create a formula in cell E4 that calculates an increase in the monthly rent by the amount in cell H2. You will be copying this formula to other cells, so you'll need to use an absolute reference.

l. Create a formula in cell F4 that calculates the increased annual rent expense based on the calculation in cell E4.

m. Copy the formulas in cells E4:F4 into cells E5:F10 to calculate the remaining monthly and annual expenses.

n. Create a formula in cell E11 that calculates the total monthly expenses, then copy that formula to cell F11.

o. Copy the contents of cells B13:C13 into cells E13:F13.

p. Create formulas in cells E14 and F14 that calculate profit/loss based on the projected increase in monthly and annual expenses.

q. Change the projected increase to **.17**, then compare your work to the sample in FIGURE 2-24.

r. Enter your name in a cell in the worksheet.

s. Save your work, preview the worksheet in Backstage view, submit your work to your instructor as directed, close the workbook, and exit Excel.

FIGURE 2-24

	A	B	C	D	E	F	G	H	I
1	Estim	Your formulas go here (your formula results will differ)	enses				Projected Increase		
2								0.17	
3		Monthly	Annually		Monthly	Annually			
4	Rent	2500	30000		2925	35100			
5	Supplies	1600	19200		1872	22464			
6	Milk	3600	43200		4212	50544			
7	Sugar	1300	15600		1521	18252			
8	Pastries	850	10200		994.5	11934			
9	Coffee	600	7200		702	8424			
10	Utilities	750	9000		877.5	10530			
11	Total	11200	134400		13104	157248			
12									
13	Sales	24500	294000		23000	276000			
14	Profit/Loss	13300	159600		9896	118752			

Independent Challenge 2

The Office Specialists Center is a small, growing business that rents small companies space and provides limited business services. They have hired you to organize their accounting records using Excel. The owners want you to track the company's expenses. Before you were hired, one of the bookkeepers began entering last year's expenses in a workbook, but the analysis was never completed.

a. Start Excel, open EX 2-4.xlsx from the location where you store your Data Files, then save it as **EX 2-Office Specialists Center Finances**. The worksheet includes labels for functions such as the average, maximum, and minimum amounts of each of the expenses in the worksheet.

b. Think about what information would be important for the bookkeeping staff to know.

c. Using the Quick Analysis tool, create a formula in the Quarter 1 column that uses the SUM function, then copy that formula into the Total row for the remaining quarters.

d. Use the SUM function to create formulas for each expense in the Total column.

e. Create formulas for each expense and each quarter in the Average, Maximum, and Minimum columns and rows using the method of your choice.

f. Compare your worksheet to the sample shown in **FIGURE 2-25**.

g. Enter your name in cell A25, then save your work.

h. Preview the worksheet, then submit your work to your instructor as directed.

i. Close the workbook and exit Excel.

FIGURE 2-25

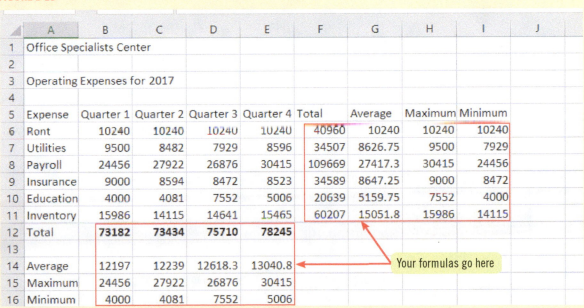

	A	B	C	D	E	F	G	H	I	J
1	Office Specialists Center									
2										
3	Operating Expenses for 2017									
4										
5	Expense	Quarter 1	Quarter 2	Quarter 3	Quarter 4	Total	Average	Maximum	Minimum	
6	Rent	10240	10240	10240	10240	40960	10240	10240	10240	
7	Utilities	9500	8482	7929	8596	34507	8626.75	9500	7929	
8	Payroll	24456	27922	26876	30415	109669	27417.3	30415	24456	
9	Insurance	9000	8594	8472	8523	34589	8647.25	9000	8472	
10	Education	4000	4081	7552	5006	20639	5159.75	7552	4000	
11	Inventory	15986	14115	14641	15465	60207	15051.8	15986	14115	
12	Total	73182	73434	75710	78245					
13										
14	Average	12197	12239	12618.3	13040.8					
15	Maximum	24456	27922	26876	30415					
16	Minimum	4000	4081	7552	5006					

Your formulas go here

Independent Challenge 3

As the accounting manager of a locally owned food co-op with multiple locations, it is your responsibility to calculate accrued sales tax payments on a monthly basis and then submit the payments to the state government. You've decided to use an Excel workbook to make these calculations.

a. Start Excel, then save a new, blank workbook to the drive and folder where you store your Data Files as **EX 2-Food Co-op Sales Tax Calculations**.

b. Decide on the layout for all columns and rows. The worksheet will contain data for six stores, which you can name by store number, neighborhood, or another method of your choice. For each store, you will calculate total sales tax based on the local sales tax rate. You'll also calculate total tax owed for all six locations.

c. Make up sales data for all six stores.

d. Enter the rate to be used to calculate the sales tax, using your own local rate.

e. Create formulas to calculate the sales tax owed for each location. If you don't know the local tax rate, use **6.5%**.

f. Create a formula to total all the accrued sales tax.

g. Use the ROUND function to eliminate any decimal places in the sales tax figures for each location and in the total due.

h. Add your name to the header, then compare your work to the sample shown in **FIGURE 2-26**.

i. Save your work, preview the worksheet, and submit your work to your instructor as directed.

j. Close the workbook and exit Excel.

FIGURE 2-26

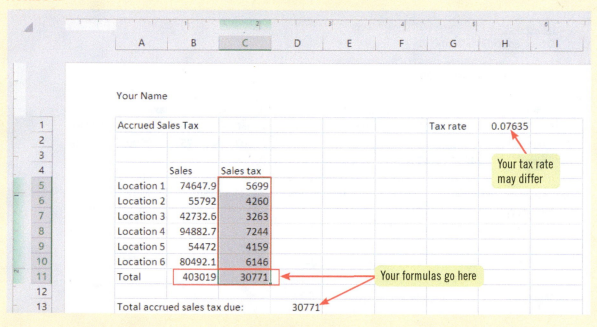

Independent Challenge 4: Explore

So many friends have come to you for help in understanding the various fees associated with purchasing a home that you've decided to create a business that specializes in helping first-time home-buyers. Your first task is to create a worksheet that clearly shows all the information a home buyer will need. Some fees are based on a percentage of the purchase price, and others are a flat fee; overall, they seem to represent a substantial amount above the purchase prices you see listed. A client has seen five houses so far that interest her; one is easily affordable, and the remaining four are all nice, but increasingly more expensive. You decide to create an Excel workbook to help her figure out the real cost of each home.

a. Find out the typical cost or percentage rate of at least three fees that are usually charged when buying a home and taking out a mortgage. (*Hint:* If you have access to the Internet, you can research the topic of home buying on the web, or you can ask friends about standard rates or percentages for items such as title insurance, credit reports, and inspection fees.)

b. Start Excel, then save a new, blank workbook to the location where you store your Data Files as **EX 2-Home Purchase Fees Worksheet**.

c. Create labels and enter data for at least five homes. If you enter this information across the columns in your worksheet, you should have one column for each house, with the purchase price in the cell below each label. Be sure to enter a different purchase price for each house.

d. Create labels for the Fees column and for an Amount or Rate column. Enter the information for each of the fees you have researched.

e. In each house column, enter formulas that calculate the fee for each item. The formulas (and use of absolute or relative referencing) will vary depending on whether the charges are a flat fee or based on a percentage of the purchase price. Make sure that the formulas for items that are based on a percentage of the purchase price (such as the fees for the Title Insurance Policy, Loan Origination, and Underwriter) contain absolute references. A sample of what your workbook might look like is shown in **FIGURE 2-27**.

f. Total the fees for each house, then create formulas that add the total fees to the purchase price.

g. Enter a title for the worksheet and include your client's name (or use Client 1) in the header.

h. Enter your name in the header, save your work, preview the worksheet, then submit your work to your instructor as directed.

i. Close the file and exit Excel.

FIGURE 2-27

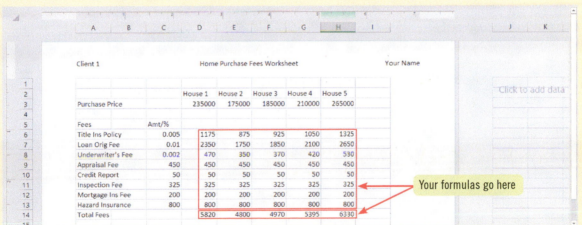

Visual Workshop

Create the worksheet shown in **FIGURE 2-28** using the skills you learned in this module. Save the workbook as **EX 2-Monthly Expenses** to the location where you store your Data Files. Enter your name and worksheet title in the header as shown, hide the gridlines, preview the worksheet, and then submit your work to your instructor as directed. (*Hint:* Change the Zoom factor to 90% by using the Zoom out button.)

FIGURE 2-28

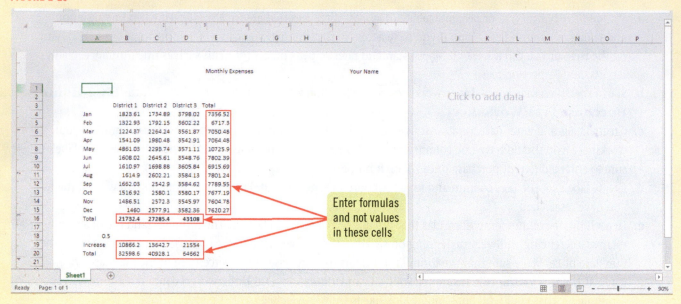

Working with Formulas and Functions

Formatting a Worksheet

CASE ▶ The marketing managers at Reason2Go have requested data from all R2G locations for advertising expenses incurred during the first quarter of this year. Mary Watson has created a worksheet listing this information. She asks you to format the worksheet to make it easier to read and to call attention to important data.

Module Objectives

After completing this module, you will be able to:

- Format values
- Change font and font size
- Change font styles and alignment
- Adjust column width
- Insert and delete rows and columns
- Apply colors, patterns, and borders
- Apply conditional formatting
- Rename and move a worksheet
- Check spelling

Files You Will Need

EX 3-1.xlsx	EX 3-4.xlsx
EX 3-2.xlsx	EX 3-5.xlsx
EX 3-3.xlsx	

Format Values

The **format** of a cell determines how the labels and values look—for example, whether the contents appear boldfaced, italicized, or with dollar signs and commas. Formatting changes only the appearance of a value or label; it does not alter the actual data in any way. To format a cell or range, first you select it, then you apply the formatting using the Ribbon, Mini toolbar, or a keyboard shortcut. You can apply formatting before or after you enter data in a cell or range. **CASE** *Mary has provided you with a worksheet that details advertising expenses, and you're ready to improve its appearance and readability. You start by formatting some of the values so they are displayed as currency, percentages, and dates.*

STEPS

1. **Start Excel, open the file EX 3-1.xlsx from the location where you store your Data Files, then save it as EX 3-R2G Advertising Expenses**

   This worksheet is difficult to interpret because all the information is crowded and looks the same. In some columns, the contents appear cut off because there is too much data to fit given the current column width. You decide not to widen the columns yet, because the other changes you plan to make might affect column width and row height. The first thing you want to do is format the data showing the cost of each ad.

2. **Select the range D4:D32, then click the Accounting Number Format button $ in the Number group on the Home tab**

   The default Accounting **number format** adds dollar signs and two decimal places to the data, as shown in **FIGURE 3-1**. Formatting this data in Accounting format makes it clear that its values are monetary values. Excel automatically resizes the column to display the new formatting. The Accounting and Currency number formats are both used for monetary values, but the Accounting format aligns currency symbols and decimal points of numbers in a column.

3. **Select the range F4:H32, then click the Comma Style button , in the Number group**

   The values in columns F, G, and H display the Comma Style format, which does not include a dollar sign but can be useful for some types of accounting data.

4. **Select the range J4:J32, click the Number Format list arrow, click Percentage, then click the Increase Decimal button in the Number group**

   The data in the % of Total column is now formatted with a percent sign (%) and three decimal places. The Number Format list arrow lets you choose from popular number formats and shows an example of what the selected cell or cells would look like in each format (when multiple cells are selected, the example is based on the first cell in the range). Each time you click the Increase Decimal button, you add one decimal place; clicking the button twice would add two decimal places.

5. **Click the Decrease Decimal button in the Number group twice**

   Two decimal places are removed from the percentage values in column J.

6. **Select the range B4:B31, then click the launcher in the Number group**

   The Format Cells dialog box opens with the Date category already selected on the Number tab.

7. **Select the first 14-Mar-12 format in the Type list box as shown in FIGURE 3-2, then click OK**

   The dates in column B appear in the 14-Mar-12 format. The second 14-Mar-12 format in the list (visible if you scroll down the list) displays all days in two digits (it adds a leading zero if the day is only a single-digit number), while the one you chose displays single-digit days without a leading zero.

8. **Select the range C4:C31, right-click the range, click Format Cells on the shortcut menu, click 14-Mar in the Type list box in the Format Cells dialog box, then click OK**

   Compare your worksheet to **FIGURE 3-3**.

9. **Press [Ctrl][Home], then save your work**

FIGURE 3-1: Accounting number format applied to range

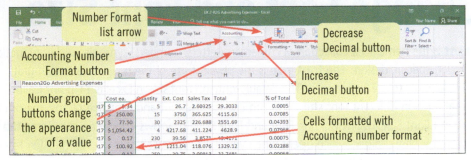

FIGURE 3-2: Format Cells dialog box

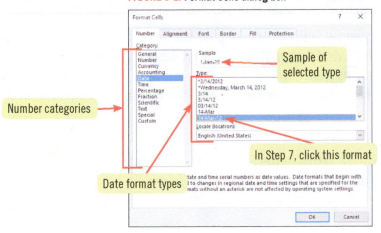

FIGURE 3-3: Worksheet with formatted values

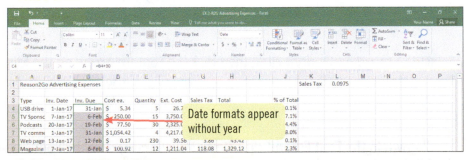

Formatting as a table

Excel includes 60 predefined **table styles** to make it easy to format selected worksheet cells as a table. You can apply table styles to any range of cells that you want to format quickly, or even to an entire worksheet, but they're especially useful for those ranges with labels in the left column and top row, and totals in the bottom row or right column. To apply a table style, select the data to be formatted or click anywhere within the intended range (Excel can automatically detect a range of cells filled with data), click the Format as Table button in the Styles group on the Home tab, then click a style in the gallery, as shown in **FIGURE 3-4**. Table styles are organized in three categories: Light, Medium, and Dark. Once you click a style, Excel asks you to confirm the range selection, then applies the style. Once you have formatted a range as a table, you can use Live Preview to preview the table in other styles by pointing to any style in the Table Styles gallery.

FIGURE 3-4: Table Styles gallery

Formatting a Worksheet

Change Font and Font Size

Learning Outcomes
• Change a font
• Change a font size
• Use the Mini toolbar

A **font** is the name for a collection of characters (letters, numbers, symbols, and punctuation marks) with a similar, specific design. The **font size** is the physical size of the text, measured in units called points. A **point** is equal to 1/72 of an inch. The default font and font size in Excel is 11-point Calibri. **TABLE 3-1** shows several fonts in different font sizes. You can change the font and font size of any cell or range using the Font and Font Size list arrows. The Font and Font Size list arrows appear on the Home tab on the Ribbon and on the Mini toolbar, which opens when you right-click a cell or range. **CASE** ▶ *You want to change the font and font size of the labels and the worksheet title so that they stand out more from the data.*

STEPS

QUICK TIP
When you point to an option in the Font or Font Size list, Live Preview shows the selected cells with the option temporarily applied.

1. **Click the** Font list arrow **in the Font group on the Home tab, scroll down in the Font list to see an alphabetical listing of the fonts available on your computer, then click** Times New Roman, **as shown in FIGURE 3-5**

   The font in cell A1 changes to Times New Roman. Notice that the font names on the list are displayed in the font they represent.

QUICK TIP
You can format an entire row by clicking the row indicator button to select the row before formatting (or select an entire column by clicking the column indicator button before formatting).

2. **Click the** Font Size list arrow **in the Font group, then click** 20

   The worksheet title appears in 20-point Times New Roman, and the Font and Font Size list boxes on the Home tab display the new font and font size information.

3. **Click the** Increase Font Size button [A˄] **in the Font group twice**

   The font size of the title increases to 24 point.

4. **Select the range** A3:J3, **right-click, then click the** Font list arrow **on the Mini toolbar**

   The Mini toolbar includes the most commonly used formatting tools, so it's great for making quick formatting changes.

QUICK TIP
To quickly move to a font in the Font list, type the first few characters of its name.

5. **Scroll down in the Font list and click** Times New Roman, **click the** Font Size list arrow **on the Mini toolbar, then click** 14

   The Mini toolbar closes when you move the pointer away from the selection. Compare your worksheet to **FIGURE 3-6**. Notice that some of the column labels are now too wide to appear fully in the column. Excel does not automatically adjust column widths to accommodate cell formatting; you have to adjust column widths manually. You'll learn to do this in a later lesson.

6. **Save your work**

TABLE 3-1: Examples of fonts and font sizes

font	12 point	24 point
Calibri	Excel	Excel
Playbill	Excel	Excel
Comic Sans MS	Excel	Excel
Times New Roman	Excel	Excel

FIGURE 3-5: Font list

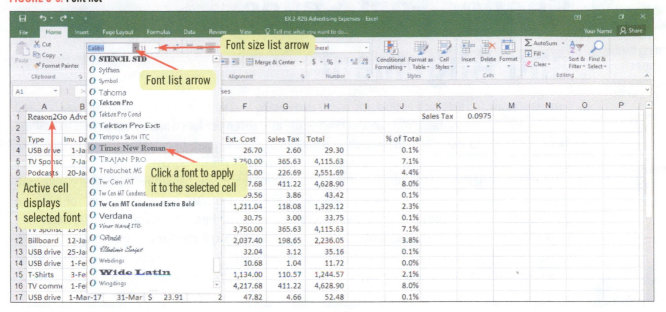

FIGURE 3-6: Worksheet with formatted title and column labels

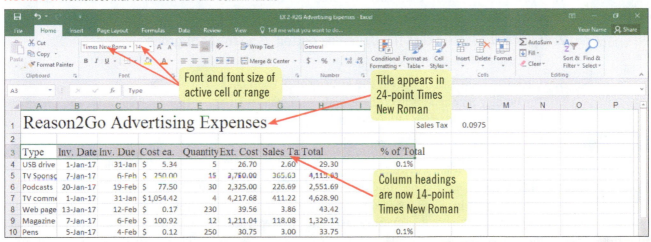

Inserting and adjusting online pictures and other images

You can illustrate your worksheets using online pictures and other images. Office.com makes many photos and animations available for your use. To add a picture to a worksheet, click the Online Pictures button in the Illustrations group on the Insert tab. The Insert Pictures window opens. Here you can search for online pictures (or Clip Art) from a variety of popular sources such as Facebook and Flickr, through the Bing search engine, or on OneDrive. To search, type one or more **keywords** (words related to your subject) in the appropriate Search text box, then press [Enter]. For example, pictures that relate to the keyword house in a search of Office.com appear in the Office.com window, as shown in **FIGURE 3-7**. When you double-click the image you want in the window, the image is inserted at the location of the active cell. To add images on your computer (or computers on your network) to a worksheet, click the Insert tab on the Ribbon, then click the Pictures button in the Illustrations group. Navigate to

the file you want, then click Insert. To resize an image, drag any corner sizing handle. To move an image, point inside the clip until the pointer changes to its, then drag it to a new location.

FIGURE 3-7: Results of Online Picture search

Change Font Styles and Alignment

Font styles are formats such as bold, italic, and underlining that you can apply to affect the way text and numbers look in a worksheet. You can also change the **alignment** of labels and values in cells to position them in relation to the cells' edges—such as left-aligned, right-aligned, or centered. You can apply font styles and alignment options using the Home tab, the Format Cells dialog box, or the Mini toolbar. See **TABLE 3-2** for a description of common font style and alignment buttons that are available on the Home tab and the Mini toolbar. Once you have formatted a cell the way you want it, you can "paint" or copy the cell's formats into other cells by using the Format Painter button in the Clipboard group on the Home tab. This is similar to using copy and paste, but instead of copying cell contents, it copies only the cell's formatting. **CASE** ▶ *You want to further enhance the worksheet's appearance by adding bold and underline formatting and centering some of the labels.*

STEPS

1. **Press [Ctrl][Home], then click the Bold button B in the Font group on the Home tab**
   The title in cell A1 appears in bold.

2. **Click cell A3, then click the Underline button U in the Font group**
   The column label is now underlined.

3. **Click the Italic button I in the Font group, then click B**
   The heading now appears in boldface, underlined, italic type. Notice that the Bold, Italic, and Underline buttons in the Font group are all selected.

4. **Click the Italic button I to deselect it**
   The italic font style is removed from cell A3, but the bold and underline font styles remain.

5. **Click the Format Painter button ✦ in the Clipboard group, then select the range B3:J3**
   The formatting in cell A3 is copied to the rest of the column labels. To paint the formats on more than one selection, double-click the Format Painter button to keep it activated until you turn it off. You can turn off the Format Painter by pressing [Esc] or by clicking ✦. You decide the title would look better if it were centered over the data columns.

6. **Select the range A1:H1, then click the Merge & Center button ▦ in the Alignment group**
   The Merge & Center button creates one cell out of the eight cells across the row, then centers the text in that newly created, merged cell. The title "Reason2Go Advertising Expenses" is centered across the eight columns you selected. To split a merged cell into its original components, select the merged cell, then click the Merge & Center button to deselect it. Occasionally, you may find that you want cell contents to wrap within a cell. You can do this by selecting the cells containing the text you want to wrap, then clicking the Wrap Text button ▦ in the Alignment group on the Home tab on the Ribbon.

7. **Select the range A3:J3, right-click, then click the Center button ≡ on the Mini toolbar**
   Compare your screen to **FIGURE 3-8**. Although they may be difficult to read, notice that all the headings are centered within their cells.

8. **Save your work**

FIGURE 3-8: Worksheet with font styles and alignment applied

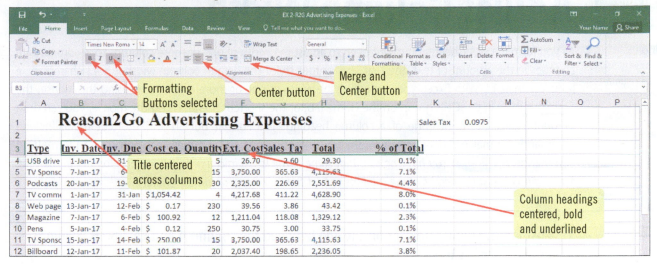

TABLE 3-2: Common font style and alignment buttons

button	description
B	Bolds text
I	Italicizes text
U	Underlines text
⬌	Centers text across columns, and combines two or more selected, adjacent cells into one cell
☰	Aligns text at the left edge of the cell
☰	Centers text horizontally within the cell
☰	Aligns text at the right edge of the cell
☰	Wraps long text into multiple lines

Rotating and indenting cell entries

In addition to applying fonts and font styles, you can rotate or indent data within a cell to further change its appearance. You can rotate text within a cell by altering its alignment. Click the Home tab, select the cells you want to modify, then click the launcher 🔲 in the Alignment group to open the Alignment tab of the Format Cells dialog box. Click a position in the Orientation box or type a number in the Degrees text box to rotate text from its default horizontal orientation, then click OK. You can indent cell contents using the Increase Indent button 🔲 in the Alignment group, which moves cell contents to the right one space, or the Decrease Indent button 🔲, which moves cell contents to the left one space.

Adjust Column Width

Learning
Outcomes
• Change a column
  width by dragging
• Resize a column
  with AutoFit
• Change the
  width of multiple
  columns

As you format a worksheet, you might need to adjust the width of one or more columns to accommodate changes in the amount of text, the font size, or font style. The default column width is 8.43 characters, a little less than 1". With Excel, you can adjust the width of one or more columns by using the mouse, the Format button in the Cells group on the Home tab, or the shortcut menu. Using the mouse, you can drag or double-click the right edge of a column heading. The Format button and shortcut menu include commands for making more precise width adjustments. **TABLE 3-3** describes common column formatting commands. **CASE** ▶ *You have noticed that some of the labels in columns A through J don't fit in the cells. You want to adjust the widths of the columns so that the labels appear in their entirety.*

STEPS

1. **Position the mouse pointer on the line between the column A and column B headings until it changes to ↔**

   See **FIGURE 3-9**. The **column heading** is the box at the top of each column containing a letter. Before you can adjust column width using the mouse, you need to position the pointer on the right edge of the column heading for the column you want to adjust. The cell entry "TV commercials" is the widest in the column.

   QUICK TIP

   If "######" appears after you adjust a column of values, the column is too narrow to display the values completely; increase the column width until the values appear.

2. **Click and drag the ↔ to the right until the column displays the "TV commercials" cell entries fully (approximately 15.29 characters, 1.23", or 112 pixels)**

   As you change the column width, a ScreenTip is displayed listing the column width. In Normal view, the ScreenTip lists the width in characters and pixels; in Page Layout view, the ScreenTip lists the width in inches and pixels.

3. **Position the pointer on the line between columns B and C until it changes to ↔, then double-click**

   Double-clicking the right edge of a column heading activates the **AutoFit** feature, which automatically resizes the column to accommodate the widest entry in the column. Column B automatically widens to fit the widest entry, which is the column label "Inv. Date".

4. **Use AutoFit to resize columns C, D, and J**

5. **Select the range E5:H5**

   You can change the width of multiple columns at once, by first selecting either the column headings or at least one cell in each column.

   QUICK TIP

   If an entire column rather than a column cell is selected, you can change the width of the column by right-clicking the column heading, then clicking Column Width on the short-cut menu.

6. **Click the Format button in the Cells group, then click Column Width**

   The Column Width dialog box opens. Column width measurement is based on the number of characters that will fit in the column when formatted in the Normal font and font size (in this case, 11-point Calibri).

7. **Drag the dialog box by its title bar if its placement obscures your view of the worksheet, type 11 in the Column width text box, then click OK**

   The widths of columns E, F, G, and H change to reflect the new setting. See **FIGURE 3-10**.

8. **Save your work**

TABLE 3-3: Common column formatting commands

command	description	available using
Column Width	Sets the width to a specific number of characters	Format button; shortcut menu
AutoFit Column Width	Fits to the widest entry in a column	Format button; mouse
Hide & Unhide	Hides or displays hidden column(s)	Format button; shortcut menu
Default Width	Resets column to worksheet's default column width	Format button

FIGURE 3-9: Preparing to change the column width

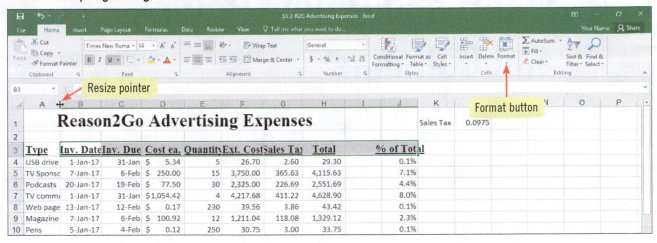

FIGURE 3-10: Worksheet with column widths adjusted

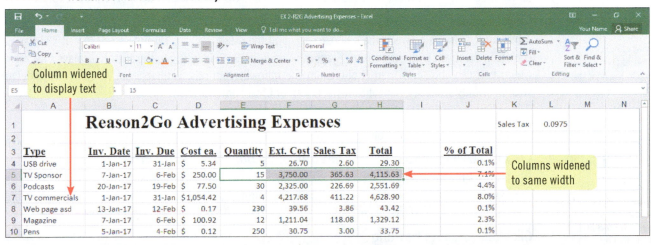

Changing row height

Changing row height is as easy as changing column width. Row height is calculated in points, the same units of measure used for fonts. The row height must exceed the size of the font you are using. Normally, you don't need to adjust row heights manually, because row heights adjust automatically to accommodate font size changes. If you format something in a row to be a larger point size, Excel adjusts the row to fit the largest point size in the row. However, you have just as many options for changing row height as you do column width. Using the mouse, you can place the ✛ pointer on the line dividing a row heading from the heading below, and then drag to the desired height; double-clicking the line AutoFits the row height where necessary. You can also select one or more rows, then use the Row Height command on the shortcut menu, or click the Format button on the Home tab and click the Row Height or AutoFit Row Height command.

Insert and Delete Rows and Columns

Learning Outcomes
• Use the Insert dialog box
• Use column and row heading buttons to insert and delete

As you modify a worksheet, you might find it necessary to insert or delete rows and columns to keep your worksheet current. For example, you might need to insert rows to accommodate new inventory products or remove a column of yearly totals that are no longer necessary. When you insert a new row, the row is inserted above the cell pointer and the contents of the worksheet shift down from the newly inserted row. When you insert a new column, the column is inserted to the left of the cell pointer and the contents of the worksheet shift to the right of the new column. To insert multiple rows, select the same number of row headings as you want to insert before using the Insert command. **CASE** *You want to improve the overall appearance of the worksheet by inserting a row between the last row of data and the totals. Also, you have learned that row 27 and column J need to be deleted from the worksheet.*

STEPS

1. **Right-click cell A32, then click Insert on the shortcut menu**

   The Insert dialog box opens. See **FIGURE 3-11**. You can choose to insert a column or a row; insert a single cell and shift the cells in the active column to the right; or insert a single cell and shift the cells in the active row down. An additional row between the last row of data and the totals will visually separate the totals.

2. **Click the Entire row option button, then click OK**

   A blank row appears between the Billboard data and the totals, and the formula result in cell E33 has not changed. The Insert Options button ▣ appears beside cell A33. Pointing to the button displays a list arrow, which you can click and then choose from the following options: Format Same As Above (the default setting, already selected), Format Same As Below, or Clear Formatting.

3. **Click the row 27 heading**

   All of row 27 is selected, as shown in **FIGURE 3-12**.

4. **Click the Delete button in the Cells group; *do not click the list arrow***

   Excel deletes row 27, and all rows below it shift up one row. You must use the Delete button or the Delete command on the shortcut menu to delete a row or column; pressing [Delete] on the keyboard removes only the *contents* of a selected row or column.

5. **Click the column J heading**

   The percentage information is calculated elsewhere and is no longer necessary in this worksheet.

6. **Click the Delete button in the Cells group**

   Excel deletes column J. The remaining columns to the right shift left one column.

7. **Use AutoFit to resize columns F and H, then save your work**

QUICK TIP
To insert a single row or column, right-click the row heading immediately below where you want the new row, or right-click the column heading to the right of where you want the new column, then click Insert on the shortcut menu.

QUICK TIP
If you inadvertently click the Delete list arrow instead of the button itself, click Delete Sheet Rows in the menu that opens.

QUICK TIP
After inserting or deleting rows or columns in a worksheet, be sure to proof formulas that contain relative cell references.

Hiding and unhiding columns and rows

When you don't want data in a column or row to be visible, but you don't want to delete it, you can hide the column or row. To hide a selected column, click the Format button in the Cells group on the Home tab, point to Hide & Unhide, then click Hide Columns. A hidden column is indicated by a dark green vertical line in its original position. This green line disappears when you click elsewhere in the worksheet. You can display a hidden column by selecting the columns on either side of the hidden column, clicking the Format button in the Cells group, pointing to Hide & Unhide, and then clicking Unhide Columns. (To hide or unhide one or more rows, substitute Hide Rows and Unhide Rows for the Hide Columns and Unhide Columns commands.)

FIGURE 3-11: Insert dialog box

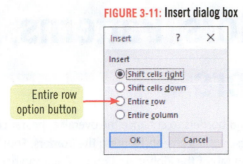

Entire row option button

FIGURE 3-12: Worksheet with row 27 selected

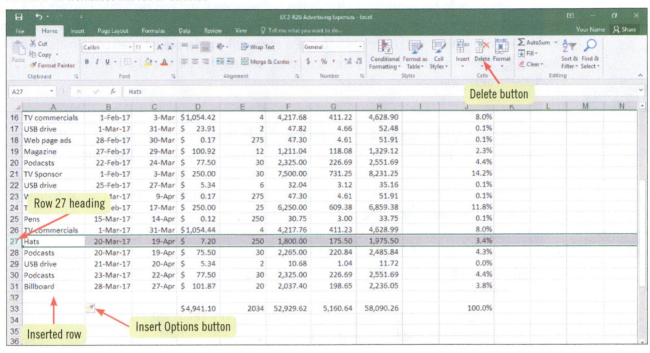

Adding and editing comments

Much of your work in Excel may be in collaboration with teammates with whom you share worksheets. You can share ideas with other worksheet users by adding comments within selected cells. To include a comment in a worksheet, click the cell where you want to place the comment, click the Review tab on the Ribbon, then click the New Comment button in the Comments group. You can type your comments in the resizable text box that opens containing the computer user's name. A small, red triangle appears in the upper-right corner of a cell containing a comment. If comments are not already displayed in a workbook, other users can point to the triangle to display the comment. To see all worksheet comments, as shown in **FIGURE 3-13**, click the Show All Comments button in the Comments group. To edit a comment, click the cell containing the comment, then click the Edit Comment button in the Comments

group. To delete a comment, click the cell containing the comment, then click the Delete button in the Comments group.

FIGURE 3-13: Comments displayed in a worksheet

21	TV Sponsor	1-Feb-16	2-Mar	Food Network
22	Newspaper	25-Feb-16	26-Mar	Village Reader
23	Web page ads	10-Mar-16	9-Apr	Advertising Concepts
24	TV Sponsor	15-Feb-16	16-Mar	Food Network
25	Pens	15-Mar-16	14-Apr	Mass Appeal, Inc.
26	TV commercials	1-Mar-16	31-Mar	Discovery Channel
27	Podcasts	20-Mar-16	19-Apr	iPodAds
28	Newspaper	1-Apr-16	1-May	University Voice
29	Podcasts	10-Apr-16	10-May	iPodAds
30	Billboard	28-Mar-16	27-Apr	Advertising Concepts

Harriet McDonald: I think this will turn out to be a very good decision.

Will Moss: Should we continue with this market, or expand to other types of publications?

Excel 2016

Apply Colors, Patterns, and Borders

You can use colors, patterns, and borders to enhance the overall appearance of a worksheet and make it easier to read. You can add these enhancements by using the Borders, Font Color, and Fill Color buttons in the Font group on the Home tab of the Ribbon and on the Mini toolbar, or by using the Fill tab and the Border tab in the Format Cells dialog box. You can open the Format Cells dialog box by clicking the dialog box launcher in the Font, Alignment, or Number group on the Home tab, or by right-clicking a selection, then clicking Format Cells on the shortcut menu. You can apply a color to the background of a cell or a range or to cell contents (such as letters and numbers), and you can apply a pattern to a cell or range. You can apply borders to all the cells in a worksheet or only to selected cells to call attention to selected information. To save time, you can also apply **cell styles**, predesigned combinations of formats. **CASE** *You want to add a pattern, a border, and color to the title of the worksheet to give the worksheet a more professional appearance.*

STEPS

1. **Select cell A1, click the Fill Color list arrow** ⬛ **in the Font group, then hover the pointer over the Turquoise, Accent 2 color (first row, sixth column from the left)**
   See **FIGURE 3-14**. Live Preview shows you how the color will look *before* you apply it. (Remember that cell A1 spans columns A through H because the Merge & Center command was applied.)

2. **Click the Turquoise, Accent 2 color**
   The color is applied to the background (or fill) of this cell. When you change fill or font color, the color on the Fill Color or Font Color button changes to the last color you selected.

3. **Right-click cell A1, then click Format Cells on the shortcut menu**
   The Format Cells dialog box opens.

4. **Click the Fill tab, click the Pattern Style list arrow, click the 6.25% Gray style (first row, sixth column from the left), then click OK**

5. **Click the Borders list arrow** ⬛ **in the Font group, then click Thick Bottom Border**
   Unlike underlining, which is a text-formatting tool, borders extend to the width of the cell, and can appear at the bottom of the cell, at the top, on either side, or on any combination of the four sides. It can be difficult to see a border when the cell is selected.

6. **Select the range A3:H3, click the Font Color list arrow** ⬛ **in the Font group, then click the Blue, Accent 1 color (first Theme Colors row, fifth column from the left) on the palette**
   The new color is applied to the labels in the selected range.

7. **Select the range J1:K1, click the Cell Styles button in the Styles group, click the Neutral cell style (first row, fourth column from the left) in the gallery, then AutoFit column J**
   The font and color change in the range, as shown in **FIGURE 3-15**.

8. **Save your work**

FIGURE 3-14: Live Preview of fill color

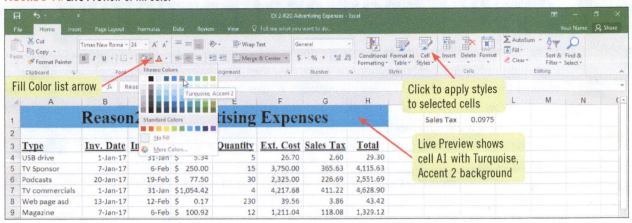

Fill Color list arrow

Click to apply styles to selected cells

Live Preview shows cell A1 with Turquoise, Accent 2 background

FIGURE 3-15: Worksheet with color, patterns, border, and style applied

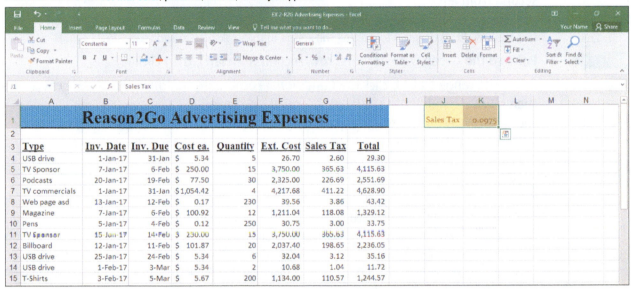

Working with themes and cell styles

Using themes and cell styles makes it easier to ensure that your worksheets are consistent. A **theme** is a predefined set of formats that gives your Excel worksheet a professional look. Formatting choices included in a theme are colors, fonts, and line and fill effects. To apply a theme, click the Themes button in the Themes group on the Page Layout tab to open the Themes gallery, as shown in **FIGURE 3-16**, then click a theme in the gallery. **Cell styles** are automatically updated if you change a theme. For example, if you apply the 20% - Accent1 cell style to cell A1 in a worksheet that has no theme applied, the fill color changes to light blue with no pattern, and the font changes to Calibri. If you change the theme of the worksheet to Ion Boardroom, cell A1's fill color changes to red and the font changes to Century Gothic, because these are the new theme's associated formats.

FIGURE 3-16: Themes gallery

Apply Conditional Formatting

Learning Outcomes
- Create conditional formatting in a range
- Change formatting and parameters in conditional formatting

So far, you've used formatting to change the appearance of different types of data, but you can also use formatting to highlight important aspects of the data itself. For example, you can apply formatting that changes the font color to red for any cells where the value is greater than $100 and to green where the value is below $50. This is called **conditional formatting** because Excel automatically applies different formats to data if the data meets conditions you specify. The formatting is updated if you change data in the worksheet. You can also copy conditional formats the same way you copy other formats. **CASE** ▶ *Mary is concerned about advertising costs exceeding the yearly budget. You decide to use conditional formatting to highlight certain trends and patterns in the data so that it's easy to spot the most expensive advertising.*

STEPS

QUICK TIP
You can also use the Quick Analysis tool to create data bars, but with fewer choices.

1. **Select the range H4:H30, click the Conditional Formatting button in the Styles group on the Home tab, point to Data Bars, then point to the Light Blue Data Bar (second row, second from left)**

   Data bars are colored horizontal bars that visually illustrate differences between values in a range of cells. Live Preview shows how this formatting will appear in the worksheet, as shown in **FIGURE 3-17**.

QUICK TIP
You can apply an Icon Set to a selected range by clicking the Conditional Formatting button in the Styles group, then pointing to Icon Sets; icons appear within the cells to illustrate differences in values.

2. **Point to the Green Data Bar (first row, second from left), then click it**

3. **Select the range F4:F30, click the Conditional Formatting button in the Styles group, then point to Highlight Cells Rules**

   The Highlight Cells Rules submenu displays choices for creating different formatting conditions. For example, you can create a rule for values that are greater than or less than a certain amount, or between two amounts.

4. **Click Between on the submenu**

   The Between dialog box opens, displaying input boxes you can use to define the condition and a default format (Light Red Fill with Dark Red Text) selected for cells that meet that condition. Depending on the condition you select in the Highlight Cells Rules submenu (such as "Greater Than" or "Less Than"), this dialog box displays different input boxes. You define the condition using the input boxes and then assign the formatting you want to use for cells that meet that condition. Values used in input boxes for a condition can be constants, formulas, cell references, or dates.

QUICK TIP
To define custom formatting for data that meets the condition, click Custom Format at the bottom of the with list, and then use the Format Cells dialog box to set the formatting to be applied.

5. **Type 2000 in the first text box, type 4000 in the second text box, click the with list arrow, click Light Red Fill, compare your settings to FIGURE 3-18, then click OK**

   All cells with values between 2000 and 4000 in column F appear with a light red fill.

6. **Click cell E7, type 3, then press [Enter]**

   When the value in cell E7 changes, the formatting also changes because the new value meets the condition you set. Compare your results to **FIGURE 3-19**.

7. **Press [Ctrl][Home] to select cell A1, then save your work**

FIGURE 3-17: Previewing data bars in a range

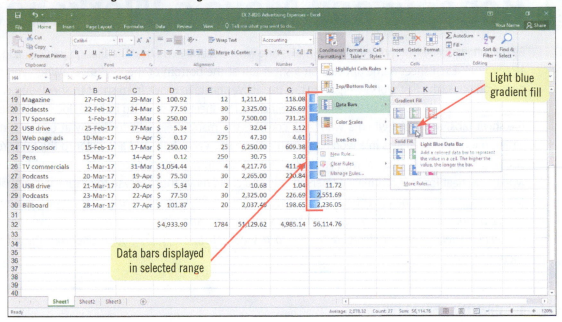

FIGURE 3-18: Between dialog box

FIGURE 3-19: Worksheet with conditional formatting

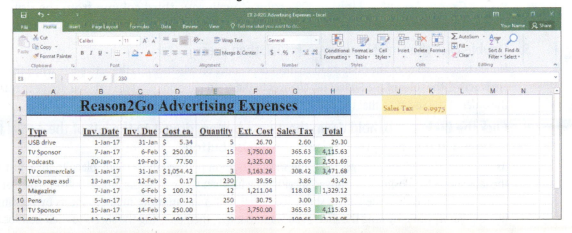

Managing conditional formatting rules

If you create a conditional formatting rule and then want to change a condition, you don't need to create a new rule; instead, you can modify the rule using the Rules Manager. Click the Conditional Formatting button in the Styles group, then click Manage Rules. The Conditional Formatting Rules Manager dialog box opens. Select the rule you want to edit, click Edit Rule, and then modify the settings in the Edit the Rule Description area in the Edit Formatting Rule dialog box. To change the formatting for a rule, click the Format Style button in the Edit the Rule Description area, select the formatting styles you want the text to have, then click OK three times to close the Format Cells dialog box, the Edit Formatting Rule dialog box, and the Conditional Formatting Rules Manager dialog box. The rule is modified, and the new conditional formatting is applied to the selected cells. To delete a rule, select the rule in the Conditional Formatting Rules Manager dialog box, then click the Delete Rule button.

Rename and Move a Worksheet

Learning Outcomes
- Rename a sheet
- Apply color to a sheet tab
- Reorder sheets in a workbook

By default, an Excel workbook initially contains one worksheet named Sheet1, although you can add sheets at any time. Each sheet name appears on a sheet tab at the bottom of the worksheet. When you open a new workbook, the first worksheet, Sheet1, is the active sheet. To move from sheet to sheet, you can click any sheet tab at the bottom of the worksheet window. The sheet tab scrolling buttons, located to the left of the sheet tabs, are useful when a workbook contains too many sheet tabs to display at once. To make it easier to identify the sheets in a workbook, you can rename each sheet and add color to the tabs. You can also organize them in a logical way. For instance, to better track performance goals, you could name each workbook sheet for an individual salesperson, and you could move the sheets so they appear in alphabetical order. **CASE** *In the current worksheet, Sheet1 contains information about actual advertising expenses. Sheet2 contains an advertising budget, and Sheet3 contains no data. You want to rename the two sheets in the workbook to reflect their contents, add color to a sheet tab to easily distinguish one from the other, and change their order.*

STEPS

1. **Click the Sheet2 tab**

   Sheet2 becomes active, appearing in front of the Sheet1 tab; this is the worksheet that contains the budgeted advertising expenses. See FIGURE 3-20.

2. **Click the Sheet1 tab**

   Sheet1, which contains the actual advertising expenses, becomes active again.

3. **Double-click the Sheet2 tab, type Budget, then press [Enter]**

   The new name for Sheet2 automatically replaces the default name on the tab. Worksheet names can have up to 31 characters, including spaces and punctuation.

4. **Right-click the Budget tab, point to Tab Color on the shortcut menu, then click the Bright Green, Accent 4, Lighter 40% color (fourth row, third column from the right) as shown in FIGURE 3-21**

5. **Double-click the Sheet1 tab, type Actual, then press [Enter]**

   Notice that the color of the Budget tab changes depending on whether it is the active tab; when the Actual tab is active, the color of the Budget tab changes to the green tab color you selected. You decide to rearrange the order of the sheets so that the Budget tab is to the left of the Actual tab.

6. **Click the Budget tab, hold down the mouse button, drag it to the left of the Actual tab, as shown in FIGURE 3-22, then release the mouse button**

   As you drag, the pointer changes to ▨, the sheet relocation pointer, and a small, black triangle just above the tabs shows the position the moved sheet will be in when you release the mouse button. The first sheet in the workbook is now the Budget sheet. See FIGURE 3-23. You can move multiple sheets by pressing and holding [Shift] while clicking the sheets you want to move, then dragging the sheets to their new location.

7. **Click the Actual sheet tab, click the Page Layout button 🔲 on the status bar to open Page Layout view, enter your name in the left header text box, then click anywhere in the worksheet to deselect the header**

8. **Click the Page Layout tab on the Ribbon, click the Orientation button in the Page Setup group, then click Landscape**

9. **Right-click the Sheet3 tab, click Delete on the shortcut menu, press [Ctrl][Home], then save your work**

FIGURE 3-20: Sheet tabs in workbook

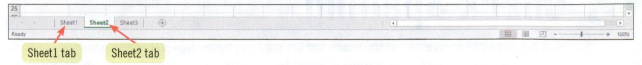

Sheet1 tab   Sheet2 tab

FIGURE 3-21: Tab Color palette

Sheet2 renamed

Bright Green, Accent 4, Lighter 40%

FIGURE 3-22: Moving the Budget sheet

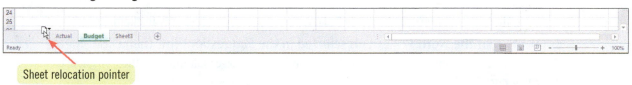

Sheet relocation pointer

FIGURE 3-23: Reordered sheets

Budget sheet comes before Actual sheet

Excel 2016

Copying, adding, and deleting worksheets

There are times when you may want to copy a worksheet. For example, a workbook might contain a sheet with Quarter 1 expenses, and you want to use that sheet as the basis for a sheet containing Quarter 2 expenses. To copy a sheet within the same workbook, press and hold [Ctrl], drag the sheet tab to the desired tab location, release the mouse button, then release [Ctrl]. A duplicate sheet appears with the same name as the copied sheet followed by "(2)" indicating that it is a copy. You can then rename the sheet to a more meaningful name. To copy a sheet to a different workbook, both the source and destination workbooks must be open. Select the sheet to copy or move, right-click the sheet tab, then click Move or Copy in the shortcut menu. Complete the information in the Move or Copy dialog box. Be sure to click the Create a copy check box if you are copying rather than moving the worksheet. Carefully check your calculation results whenever you move or copy a worksheet. You can add multiple worksheets to a workbook by clicking the Home tab on the Ribbon, pressing and holding [Shift], then clicking the number of existing worksheet tabs that correspond with the number of sheets you want to add, clicking the Insert list arrow in the Cells group on the Home tab, then clicking Insert Sheet. You can delete multiple worksheets from a workbook by clicking the Home tab, pressing and holding [Shift], clicking the sheet tabs of the worksheets you want to delete, clicking the Delete list arrow in the Cells group on the Home tab, then clicking Delete Sheet.

Check Spelling

Learning Outcomes
- Describe how spell checking works
- Change the spelling using a suggestion
- Replace a word using Find & Select

Excel includes a spell checker to help you ensure that the words in your worksheet are spelled correctly. The spell checker scans your worksheet, displays words it doesn't find in its built-in dictionary, and suggests replacements when they are available. To check all of the sheets in a multiple-sheet workbook, you need to display each sheet individually and run the spell checker for each one. Because the built-in dictionary cannot possibly include all the words that anyone needs, you can add words to the dictionary, such as your company name, an acronym, or an unusual technical term. Once you add a word or term, the spell checker no longer considers that word misspelled. Any words you've added to the dictionary using Word, Access, or PowerPoint are also available in Excel. **CASE** *Before you distribute this workbook to Mary, you check the spelling.*

STEPS

1. **Click the Review tab on the Ribbon, then click the Spelling button in the Proofing group**

   The Spelling: English (United States) dialog box opens, as shown in **FIGURE 3-24**, with "asd" selected as the first misspelled word in the worksheet, and with "ads" selected in the Suggestions list as a possible replacement. For any word, you have the option to Ignore this case of the flagged word, Ignore All cases of the flagged word, Change the word to the selected suggestion, Change All instances of the flagged word to the selected suggestion, or add the flagged word to the dictionary using Add to Dictionary.

2. **Click Change**

   Next, the spell checker finds the word "Podacsts" and suggests "Podcasts" as an alternative.

3. **Verify that the word Podcasts is selected in the Suggestions list, then click Change**

   When no more incorrect words are found, Excel displays a message indicating that the spell check is complete.

4. **Click OK**

5. **Click the Home tab, click Find & Select in the Editing group, then click Replace**

   The Find and Replace dialog box opens. You can use this dialog box to replace a word or phrase. It might be a misspelling of a proper name that the spell checker didn't recognize as misspelled, or it could simply be a term that you want to change throughout the worksheet. Mary has just told you that each instance of "Billboard" in the worksheet should be changed to "Sign."

6. **Type Billboard in the Find what text box, press [Tab], then type Sign in the Replace with text box**

   Compare your dialog box to **FIGURE 3-25**.

7. **Click Replace All, click OK to close the Microsoft Excel dialog box, then click Close to close the Find and Replace dialog box**

   Excel has made two replacements.

8. **Click the File tab, click Print on the navigation bar, click the No Scaling setting in the Settings section on the Print tab, then click Fit Sheet on One Page**

9. **Click the Return button ⊙ to return to your worksheet, save your work, submit it to your instructor as directed, close the workbook, then exit Excel**

   The completed worksheet is shown in **FIGURE 3-26**.

Emailing a workbook

You can send an entire workbook from within Excel using your installed email program, such as Microsoft Outlook. To send a workbook as an email message attachment, open the workbook, click the File tab, then click Share on the navigation bar. With the Email option selected in the Share section in Backstage view, click Send as Attachment in the right pane. An email message opens in your default email program with the workbook automatically attached; the filename appears in the Attached field. Complete the To and optional Cc fields, include a message if you wish, then click Send.

FIGURE 3-24: Spelling: English (United States) dialog box

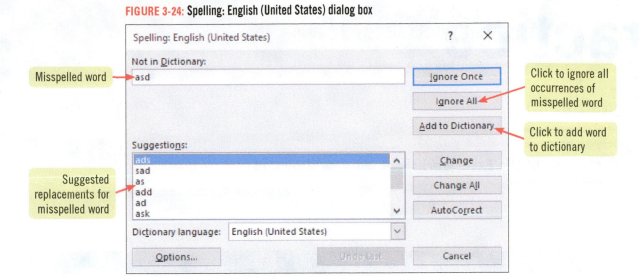

Misspelled word

Suggested replacements for misspelled word

Click to ignore all occurrences of misspelled word

Click to add word to dictionary

FIGURE 3-25: Find and Replace dialog box

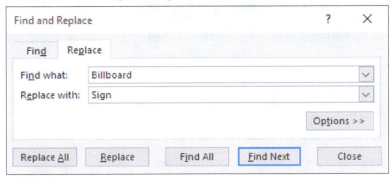

FIGURE 3-26: Completed worksheet

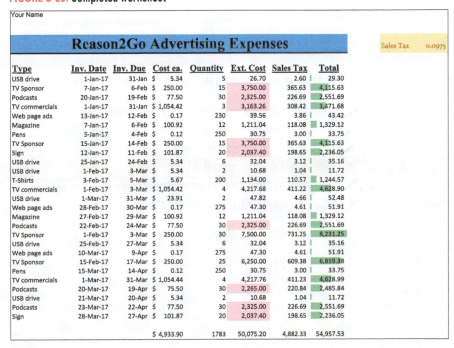

Excel 2016

Practice

Concepts Review

Label each element of the Excel worksheet window shown in FIGURE 3-27.

FIGURE 3-27

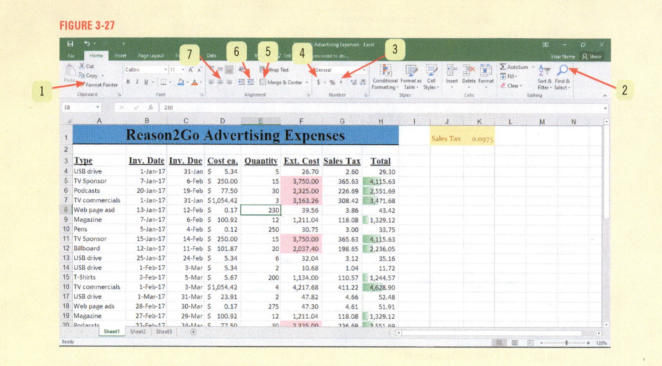

Match each command or button with the statement that best describes it.

8. Spelling button   a. Checks for apparent misspellings in a worksheet

9. $ b. Adds dollar signs and two decimal places to selected data

10.   c. Displays fill color options for a cell

11. [Ctrl][Home]   d. Moves cell pointer to cell A1

12.   e. Centers cell contents across multiple cells

13. Conditional formatting   f. Changes formatting of a cell that meets a certain rule

Select the best answer from the list of choices.

14. **Which of the following is an example of Accounting number format?**

  a. 5555

  b. $5,555.55

  c. 55.55%

  d. 5,555.55

15. **What is the name of the feature used to resize a column to accommodate its widest entry?**

  a. AutoFormat

  b. AutoFit

  c. AutoResize

  d. AutoRefit

16. **Which button copies multiple formats from selected cells to other cells?**

  a. ⟲

  b. 🔲

  c. A⁺

  d. 🖌

17. **Which button increases the number of decimal places in selected cells?**

  a. ⬅.00

  b. .00→

  c. ⮒

  d. ⬅

18. **Which button removes the italic font style from selected cells?**

  a. *I*

  b. B

  c. *I*

  d. U

19. **What feature is used to delete a conditional formatting rule?**

  a. Rules Reminder

  b. Conditional Formatting Rules Manager

  c. Condition Manager

  d. Format Manager

Skills Review

1. **Format values.**

  a. Start Excel, open the file EX 3-2.xlsx from the location where you store your Data Files, then save it as **EX 3-Health Insurance Premiums**.

  b. Use the Sum function to enter a formula in cell B10 that totals the number of employees.

  c. Create a formula in cell C5 that calculates the monthly insurance premium for the accounting department. (*Hint*: Make sure you use the correct type of cell reference in the formula. To calculate the department's monthly premium, multiply the number of employees by the monthly premium in cell B14.)

  d. Copy the formula in cell C5 to the range C6:C10.

  e. Format the range C5:C10 using Accounting number format.

  f. Change the format of the range C6:C9 to the Comma Style.

  g. Reduce the number of decimals in cell B14 to 0 using a button in the Number group on the Home tab.

  h. Save your work.

2. **Change font and font sizes.**

  a. Select the range of cells containing the column labels (in row 4).

  b. Change the font of the selection to Times New Roman.

  c. Increase the font size of the selection to 12 points.

  d. Increase the font size of the label in cell A1 to 14 points.

  e. Save your changes.

3. **Change font styles and alignment.**

  a. Apply the bold and italic font styles to the worksheet title in cell A1.

  b. Use the Merge & Center button to center the Health Insurance Premiums label over columns A–C.

  c. Apply the italic font style to the Health Insurance Premiums label.

  d. Add the bold font style to the labels in row 4.

  e. Use the Format Painter to copy the format in cell A4 to the range A5:A10.

  f. Apply the format in cell C10 to cell B14.

  g. Change the alignment of cell A10 to Align Right using a button in the Alignment group.

Skills Review (continued)

h. Select the range of cells containing the column labels, then center them.

i. Remove the italic font style from the Health Insurance Premiums label, then increase the font size to 14.

j. Move the Health Insurance Premiums label to cell A3, remove the Merge & Center format, then add the bold and underline font styles.

k. Save your changes.

4. **Adjust column width.**

   a. Resize column C to a width of 10.71 characters.

   b. Use the AutoFit feature to resize columns A and B.

   c. Clear the contents of cell A13 (do not delete the cell).

   d. Change the text in cell A14 to **Monthly Premium**, then change the width of the column to 25 characters.

   e. Save your changes.

5. **Insert and delete rows and columns.**

   a. Insert a new row between rows 5 and 6.

   b. Add a new department, **Donations**, in the newly inserted row. Enter **6** as the number of employees in the department.

   c. Copy the formula in cell C7 to C6.

   d. Add the following comment to cell A6: **New department**. Display the comment, then drag to move it out of the way, if necessary.

   e. Add a new column between the Department and Employees columns with the title **Family Coverage**, then resize the column using AutoFit.

   f. Delete the Legal row from the worksheet.

   g. Move the value in cell C14 to cell B14.

   h. Save your changes.

6. **Apply colors, patterns, and borders.**

   a. Add Outside Borders around the range A4:D10.

   b. Add a Bottom Double Border to cells C9 and D9 (above the calculated employee and premium totals).

   c. Apply the Aqua, Accent 5, Lighter 80% fill color to the labels in the Department column (do not include the Total label).

   d. Apply the Orange, Accent 6, Lighter 60% fill color to the range A4:D4.

   e. Change the color of the font in the range A4:D4 to Red, Accent 2, Darker 25%.

   f. Add a 12.5% Gray pattern style to cell A1.

   g. Format the range A14:B14 with a fill color of Dark Blue, Text 2, Lighter 40%, change the font color to White, Background 1, then apply the bold font style.

   h. Save your changes.

7. **Apply conditional formatting.**

   a. Select the range D5:D9, then create a conditional format that changes cell contents to green fill with dark green text if the value is between 150 and 275.

   b. Select the range C5:C9, then create a conditional format that changes cell contents to red text if the number of employees exceeds 10.

   c. Apply a purple gradient-filled data bar to the range C5:C9. (*Hint*: Click Purple Data Bar in the Gradient Fill section.)

   d. Use the Rules Manager to modify the conditional format in cells C5:C9 to display values greater than 10 in bold dark red text.

   e. Save your changes.

8. **Rename and move a worksheet.**

   a. Name the Sheet1 tab **Insurance Data**.

   b. Add a sheet to the workbook, then name the new sheet **Employee Data**.

   c. Change the Insurance Data tab color to Red, Accent 2, Lighter 40%.

Skills Review (continued)

    d. Change the Employee Data tab color to Aqua, Accent 5, Lighter 40%.

    e. Move the Employee Data sheet so it comes before (to the left of) the Insurance Data sheet.

    f. Make the Insurance Data sheet active, enter your name in cell A20, then save your work.

9. Check spelling.

    a. Move the cell pointer to cell A1.

    b. Use the Find & Select feature to replace the Accounting label with **Accounting/Legal**.

    c. Check the spelling in the worksheet using the spell checker, and correct any spelling errors if necessary.

    d. Save your changes, then compare your Insurance Data sheet to FIGURE 3-28.

    e. Preview the Insurance Data sheet in Backstage view, submit your work to your instructor as directed, then close the workbook and exit Excel.

FIGURE 3-28

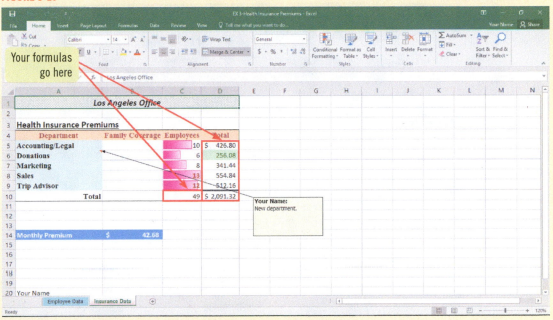

Independent Challenge 1

You run a freelance accounting business, and one of your newest clients is Fresh To You, a small local grocery store. Now that you've converted the store's accounting records to Excel, the manager would like you to work on an analysis of the inventory. Although more items will be added later, the worksheet has enough items for you to begin your modifications.

    a. Start Excel, open the file EX 3-3.xlsx from the location where you store your Data Files, then save it as **EX 3-Fresh To You Inventory**.

    b. Create a formula in cell E4 that calculates the value of the items in stock based on the price paid per item in cell B4. Format the cell in the Comma Style.

    c. In cell F4, calculate the sale value of the items in stock using an absolute reference to the markup value shown in cell H1.

    d. Copy the formulas created above into the range E5:F14; first convert any necessary cell references to absolute so that the formulas work correctly.

    e. Apply bold to the column labels, and italicize the inventory items in column A.

    f. Make sure that all columns are wide enough to display the data and labels.

    g. Format the values in the Sale Value column as Accounting number format with two decimal places.

    h. Format the values in the Price Paid column as Comma Style with two decimal places.

Independent Challenge 1 (continued)

i. Add a row under Cheddar Cheese for **Whole Wheat flour**, price paid **0.95**, sold by weight (**pound**), with **23** on hand. Copy the appropriate formulas to cells E7:F7.

j. Verify that all the data in the worksheet is visible and formulas are correct. Adjust any items as needed, and check the spelling of the entire worksheet.

k. Use conditional formatting to apply yellow fill with dark yellow text to items with a quantity of less than 25 on hand.

l. Use an icon set of your choosing in the range D4:D14 to illustrate the relative differences between values in the range.

m. Add an outside border around the data in the Item column (*do not* include the Item column label).

n. Delete the row containing the Resource Coffee - decaf entry.

o. Enter your name in an empty cell below the data, then save the file. Compare your worksheet to the sample in FIGURE 3-29.

p. Preview the worksheet in Backstage view, submit your work to your instructor as directed, close the workbook, then exit Excel.

FIGURE 3-29

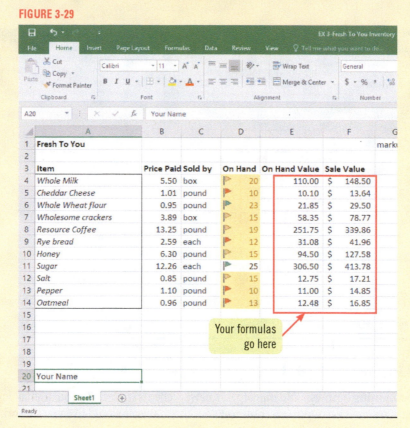

Independent Challenge 2

You volunteer several hours each week with the Assistance League of San Antonio, and you are in charge of maintaining the membership list. You're currently planning a mailing campaign to members in certain regions of the city. You also want to create renewal letters for members whose membership expires soon. You decide to format the list to enhance the appearance of the worksheet and make your upcoming tasks easier to plan.

a. Start Excel, open the file EX 3-4.xlsx from the location where you store your Data Files, then save it as **EX 3-Memphis Assistance League**.

b. Remove any blank columns.

c. Create a conditional format in the Zip Code column so that entries greater than 38249 appear in light red fill with dark red text.

d. Make all columns wide enough to fit their data and labels. (*Hint*: You can use any method to size the columns.)

e. Use formatting enhancements, such as fonts, font sizes, font styles, and fill colors, to make the worksheet more attractive.

Independent Challenge 2 (continued)

f. Center the column labels.

g. Use conditional formatting so that entries for Year of Membership Expiration that are between 2021 and 2023 appear in green fill with bold black text. (*Hint*: Create a custom format for cells that meet the condition.)

h. Adjust any items as necessary, then check the spelling.

i. Change the name of the Sheet1 tab to one that reflects the sheet's contents, then add a tab color of your choice.

j. Enter your name in an empty cell, then save your work.

k. Preview the worksheet, make any final changes you think necessary, then submit your work to your instructor as directed. Compare your work to the sample shown in FIGURE 3-30.

l. Close the workbook, then exit Excel.

FIGURE 3-30

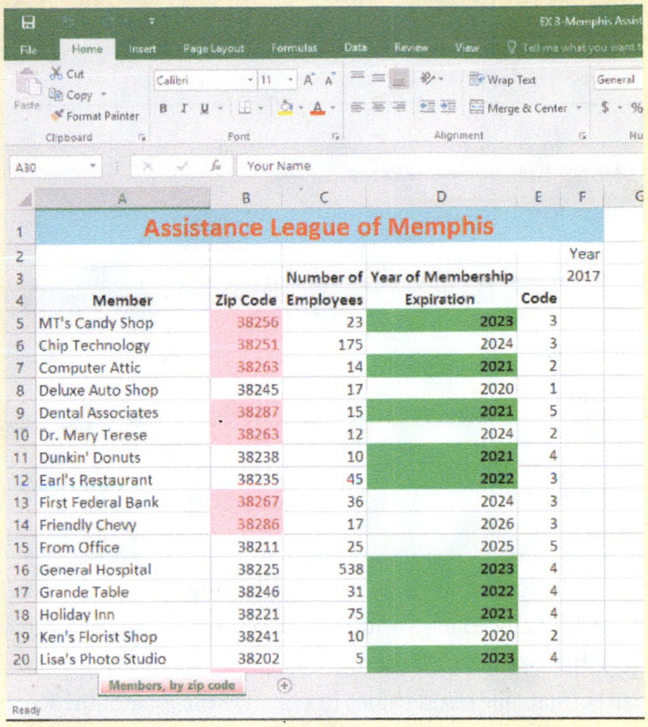

Independent Challenge 3

Advantage Calendars is a Dallas-based printer that prints and assembles calendars. As the finance manager for the company, one of your responsibilities is to analyze the monthly reports from the five district sales offices. Your boss, Joanne Bennington, has just asked you to prepare a quarterly sales report for an upcoming meeting. Because several top executives will be attending this meeting, Joanne reminds you that the report must look professional. In particular, she asks you to highlight the fact that the Northeastern district continues to outpace the other districts.

a. Plan a worksheet that shows the company's sales during the first quarter. Assume that all calendars are the same price. Make sure you include the following:
   - The number of calendars sold (units sold) and the associated revenues (total sales) for each of the five district sales offices. The five sales districts are Northeastern, Midwestern, Southeastern, Southern, and Western.
   - Calculations that show month-by-month totals for January, February, and March, and a 3-month cumulative total.
   - Calculations that show each district's share of sales (percent of Total Sales).
   - Labels that reflect the month-by-month data as well as the cumulative data.
   - Formatting enhancements such as data bars that emphasize the recent month's sales surge and the Northeastern district's sales leadership.

b. Ask yourself the following questions about the organization and formatting of the worksheet: What worksheet title and labels do you need, and where should they appear? How can you calculate the totals? What formulas can you copy to save time and keystrokes? Do any of these formulas need to use an absolute reference? How do you show dollar amounts? What information should be shown in bold? Do you need to use more than one font? Should you use more than one point size?

c. Start Excel, then save a new, blank workbook as **EX 3-Advantage Calendars** to the location where you store your Data Files.

Independent Challenge 3 (continued)

d. Build the worksheet with your own price and sales data. Enter the titles and labels first, then enter the numbers and formulas. You can use the information in **TABLE 3-4** to get started.

TABLE 3-4

Advantage Calendars											
1st Quarter Sales Report											
		January		February		March		Total			
Office	Price	Units Sold	Sales	Units Sold	Sales	Units Sold	Sales	Units Sold	Sales	Total % of Sales	
Northeastern											
Midwestern											
Southeastern											
Southern											
Western											

e. Add a row beneath the data containing the totals for each column.

f. Adjust the column widths as necessary.

g. Change the height of row 1 to 33 points.

h. Format labels and values to enhance the look of the worksheet, and change the font styles and alignment if necessary.

i. Resize columns and adjust the formatting as necessary.

j. Add data bars for the monthly Units Sold columns.

k. Add a column that calculates a 25% increase in total sales dollars. Use an absolute cell reference in this calculation. (*Hint:* Make sure that the current formatting is applied to the new information.)

l. Delete the contents of cells J4:K4 if necessary, then merge and center cell I4 over column I:K.

m. Add a bottom double border to cells I10:L10.

n. Enter your name in an empty cell.

o. Check the spelling in the workbook, change to a landscape orientation, save your work, then compare your work to **FIGURE 3-31**.

p. Preview the worksheet in Backstage view, then submit your work to your instructor as directed.

q. Close the workbook file, then exit Excel.

FIGURE 3-31

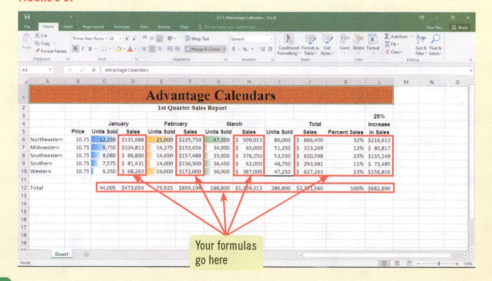

Formatting a Worksheet

Independent Challenge 4: Explore

This Independent Challenge requires an Internet connection.

Your corporate relocation company helps employees to settle quickly and easily into new cities around the world. Your latest client plans to send employees to seven different countries. All employees will receive the same weekly budget in American currency. You need to create a worksheet to help all the employees understand the currency conversion rates in the different countries so that they can plan their spending effectively.

a. Start Excel, then save a new, blank workbook as **EX 3-Foreign Currency Rates** to the location where you store your Data Files.

b. Add a title at the top of the worksheet.

c. Think of seven countries that each use a different currency, then enter column and row labels for your worksheet. (*Hint*: You may wish to include row labels for each country, plus column labels for the country, the $1 equivalent in native currency, the total amount of native currency employees will have in each country, and the name of each country's monetary unit.)

d. Decide how much money employees will bring to each country (for example, $1,000), and enter that in the worksheet.

e. Use your favorite search engine to find your own information sources on currency conversions for the countries you have listed.

f. Enter the cash equivalent to $1 in U.S. dollars for each country in your list.

g. Create an equation that calculates the amount of native currency employees will have in each country, using an absolute cell reference in the formula.

h. Format the entries in the column containing the native currency $1 equivalent as Number number format with three decimal places, and format the column containing the total native currency budget with two decimal places, using the correct currency number format for each country. (*Hint*: Use the Number tab in the Format cells dialog box; choose the appropriate currency number format from the Symbol list.)

i. Create a conditional format that changes the font style and color of the calculated amount in the $1,000 US column to light red fill with dark red text if the amount exceeds **1000** units of the local currency.

j. Merge and center the worksheet title over the column headings.

k. Add any formatting you want to the column headings, and resize the columns as necessary.

l. Add a background color to the title and change the font color if you choose.

m. Enter your name in the header of the worksheet.

n. Spell check the worksheet, save your changes, compare your work to FIGURE 3-32, then preview the worksheet, and submit your work to your instructor as directed.

o. Close the workbook and exit Excel.

FIGURE 3-32

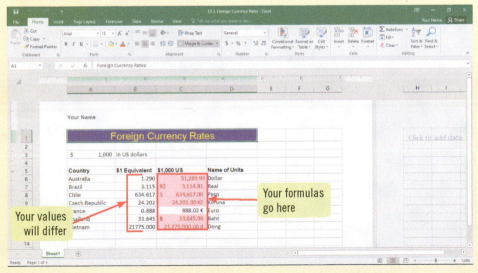

Visual Workshop

Open the file EX 3-5.xlsx from the location where you store your Data Files, then save it as **EX 3-London Employees**. Use the skills you learned in this module to format the worksheet so it looks like the one shown in FIGURE 3-33. Create a conditional format in the Level column so that entries greater than 3 appear in light red fill with dark red text. Create an additional conditional format in the Review Cycle column so that any value equal to 3 appears in black fill with white bold text. Replace the Accounting department label with **Legal**. (*Hint*: The only additional font used in this exercise is 18-point Times New Roman in row 1.) Enter your name in the upper-right part of the header, check the spelling in the worksheet, save your changes, then submit your work to your instructor as directed. (*Hint*: To match the figure exactly, remember to match the zoom level.)

FIGURE 3-33

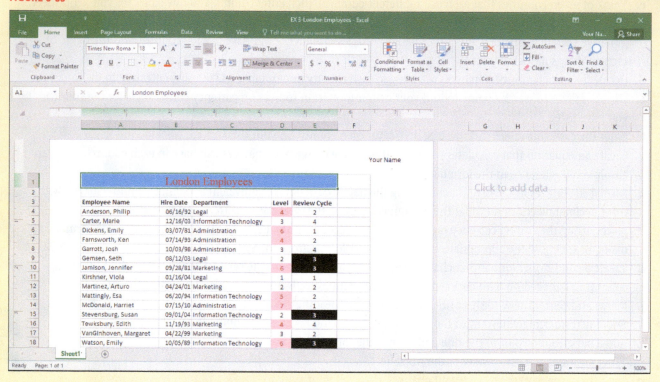

Working with Charts

CASE ▶ At the upcoming annual meeting, Yolanda Lee wants to discuss spending patterns at Reason2Go. She asks you to create a chart showing the trends in company expenses over the past four quarters.

Module Objectives

After completing this module, you will be able to:

- Plan a chart
- Create a chart
- Move and resize a chart
- Change the chart design
- Change the chart format
- Format a chart
- Annotate and draw on a chart
- Create a pie chart

Files You Will Need

EX 4-1.xlsx   EX 4-4.xlsx
EX 4-2.xlsx   EX 4-5.xlsx
EX 4-3.xlsx   EX 4-6.xlsx

Plan a Chart

Learning
Outcomes
• Prepare to create
  a chart
• Identify chart
  elements
• Explore common
  chart types

Before creating a chart, you need to plan the information you want your chart to show and how you want it to look. Planning ahead helps you decide what type of chart to create and how to organize the data. Understanding the parts of a chart makes it easier to format and change specific elements so that the chart best illustrates your data. **CASE** ▸ *In preparation for creating the chart for Yolanda's presentation, you identify your goals for the chart and plan its layout.*

DETAILS

Use the following guidelines to plan the chart:

- **Determine the purpose of the chart, and identify the data relationships you want to communicate graphically**

  You want to create a chart that shows quarterly tour expenses for each country where Reason2Go provides tours. This worksheet data is shown in **FIGURE 4-1**. You also want the chart to illustrate whether the quarterly expenses for each country increased or decreased from quarter to quarter.

QUICK TIP
The Quick Analysis tool recommends charts based on the selected data.

- **Determine the results you want to see, and decide which chart type is most appropriate**

  Different chart types display data in distinctive ways. For example, a pie chart compares parts to the whole, so it's useful for showing what proportion of a budget amount was spent on tours in one country relative to what was spent on tours in other countries. A line chart, in contrast, is best for showing trends over time. To choose the best chart type for your data, you should first decide how you want your data displayed and interpreted. **TABLE 4-1** describes several different types of charts you can create in Excel and their corresponding buttons on the Insert tab on the Ribbon. Because you want to compare R2G tour expenses in multiple countries over a period of four quarters, you decide to use a column chart.

- **Identify the worksheet data you want the chart to illustrate**

  Sometimes you use all the data in a worksheet to create a chart, while at other times you may need to select a range within the sheet. The worksheet from which you are creating your chart contains expense data for each of the past four quarters and the totals for the past year. You will need to use all the quarterly data except the quarterly totals.

- **Understand the elements of a chart**

  The chart shown in **FIGURE 4-2** contains basic elements of a chart. In the figure, R2G tour countries are on the horizontal axis (also called the **x-axis**) and expense dollar amounts are on the vertical axis (also called the **y-axis**). The horizontal axis is also called the **category axis** because it often contains the names of data groups, such as locations, months, or years. The vertical axis is also called the **value axis** because it often contains numerical values that help you interpret the size of chart elements. (3-D charts also contain a **z-axis**, for comparing data across both categories and values.) The area inside the horizontal and vertical axes is the **plot area**. The **tick marks**, on the vertical axis, and **gridlines** (extending across the plot area) create a scale of measure for each value. Each value in a cell you select for your chart is a **data point**. In any chart, a **data marker** visually represents each data point, which in this case is a column. A collection of related data points is a **data series**. In this chart, there are four data series (Quarter 1, Quarter 2, Quarter 3, and Quarter 4). Each is made up of column data markers of a different color, so a **legend** is included to make it easy to identify them.

FIGURE 4-1: Worksheet containing expense data

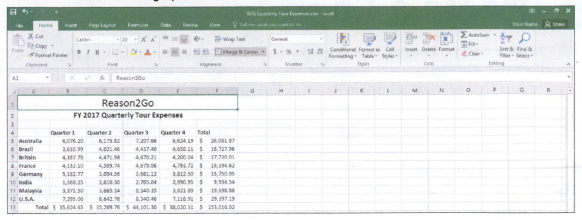

FIGURE 4-2: Chart elements

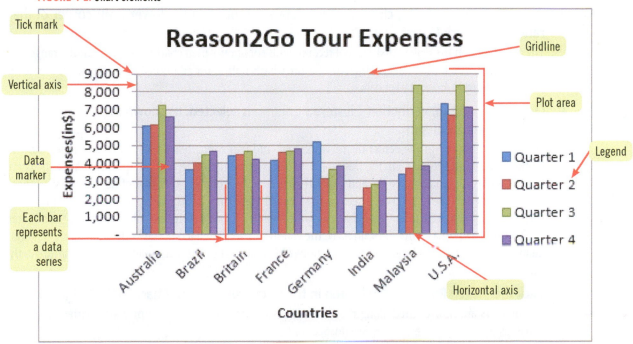

TABLE 4-1: Common chart types

type	button	description
Column		Compares data using columns; the Excel default; sometimes referred to as a bar chart in other spreadsheet programs
Line		Compares trends over even time intervals; looks similar to an area chart, but does not emphasize total
Pie		Compares sizes of pieces as part of a whole; used for a single series of numbers
Bar		Compares data using horizontal bars; sometimes referred to as a horizontal bar chart in other spreadsheet programs
Area		Shows how individual volume changes over time in relation to total volume
Scatter		Compares trends over uneven time or measurement intervals; used in scientific and engineering disciplines for trend spotting and extrapolation
Combo		Displays two or more types of data using different chart types; illustrates mixed or widely varying types of data

Create a Chart

Learning Outcomes
• Create a chart
• Switch a chart's columns/rows
• Add a chart title

To create a chart in Excel, you first select the range in a worksheet containing the data you want to chart. Once you've selected a range, you can use The Quick Analysis tool or the Insert tab on the Ribbon to create a chart based on the data in the range. **CASE** *Using the worksheet containing the quarterly expense data, you create a chart that shows how the expenses in each country varied across the quarters.*

STEPS

QUICK TIP
When charting data for a particular time period, make sure that all series are for the same time period.

1. **Start Excel, open the file EX 4-1.xlsx from the location where you store your Data Files, then save it as EX 4-R2G Quarterly Tour Expenses**
   You want the chart to include the quarterly tour expenses values, as well as quarter and country labels. You don't include the Total column and row because the figures in these cells would skew the chart.

2. **Select the range A4:E12, click the Quick Analysis tool 📊 in the lower-right corner of the range, then click Charts**
   The Charts tab on the Quick Analysis tool recommends commonly used chart types based on the range you have selected. The Charts tab also includes a More Charts button for additional chart types, such as stock charts for charting stock market data.

QUICK TIP
To base a chart on data in nonadjacent ranges, press and hold [Ctrl] while selecting each range, then use the Insert tab to create the chart.

3. **On the Charts tab, verify that Clustered Column is selected, as shown in FIGURE 4-3, then click Clustered Column**
   The chart is inserted in the center of the worksheet, and two contextual Chart Tools tabs appear on the Ribbon: Design and Format. On the Design tab, which is currently active, you can quickly change the chart type, chart layout, and chart style, and you can swap how the columns and rows of data in the worksheet are represented in the chart. When seen in the Normal view, three tools display to the right of the chart: these enable you to add, remove, or change chart elements ➕, set a style and color scheme 🖌, and filter the results shown in a chart 🔽. Currently, the countries are charted along the horizontal x-axis, with the quarterly expense dollar amounts charted along the y-axis. This lets you easily compare the quarterly expenses for each country.

4. **Click the Switch Row/Column button in the Data group on the Chart Tools Design tab**
   The quarters are now charted along the x-axis. The expense amounts per country are charted along the y-axis, as indicated by the updated legend. See **FIGURE 4-4**.

5. **Click the Undo button ↩ ▾ on the Quick Access Toolbar**
   The chart returns to its original design.

QUICK TIP
You can also triple-click to select the chart title text.

6. **Click the Chart Title placeholder to show the text box, click anywhere in the Chart Title text box, press [Ctrl][A] to select the text, type R2G Quarterly Tour Expenses, then click anywhere in the chart to deselect the title**
   Adding a title helps identify the chart. The border around the chart and the **sizing handles**, the small series of dots at the corners and sides of the chart's border, indicate that the chart is selected. See **FIGURE 4-5**. Your chart might be in a different location on the worksheet and may look slightly different; you will move and resize it in the next lesson. Any time a chart is selected, as it is now, a blue border surrounds the worksheet data range on which the chart is based, a purple border surrounds the cells containing the category axis labels, and a red border surrounds the cells containing the data series labels. This chart is known as an **embedded chart** because it is inserted directly in the current worksheet and doesn't exist in a separate file. Embedding a chart in the current sheet is the default selection when creating a chart, but you can also embed a chart on a different sheet in the workbook, or on a newly created chart sheet. A **chart sheet** is a sheet in a workbook that contains only a chart that is linked to the workbook data.

7. **Save your work**

FIGURE 4-3: Charts tab in Quick Analysis tool

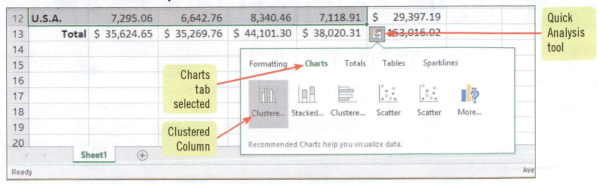

FIGURE 4-4: Clustered Column chart with different configuration of rows and columns

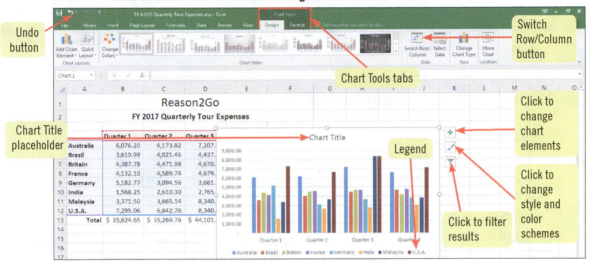

FIGURE 4-5: Chart with original configuration restored and title added

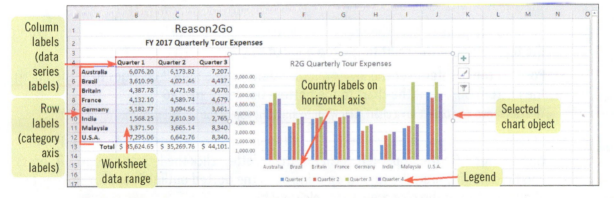

Creating sparklines

You can quickly create a miniature chart called a **sparkline** that serves as a visual indicator of data trends. You can create a sparkline by selecting a range of data, clicking the Quick Analysis tool, clicking the Sparklines tab, then clicking the type of sparkline you want. (The sparkline appears in the cell immediately adjacent to the selected range.) You can also select a range, click the Insert tab, then click the Line, Column, or Win/Loss button in the Sparklines group. In the Create Sparklines dialog box that opens, enter the cell in which you want the sparkline to appear,

then click OK. **FIGURE 4-6** shows a sparkline created in a cell. Any changes to data in the range are reflected in the sparkline. To delete a selected sparkline from a cell, click the Clear button in the Group group on the Sparkline Tools Design tab.

FIGURE 4-6: Sparklines in a cell

Move and Resize a Chart

A chart is an **object,** or an independent element on a worksheet, and is not located in a specific cell or range. You can select an object by clicking it; sizing handles around the object indicate it is selected. (When a chart is selected in Excel, the Name box, which normally tells you the address of the active cell, tells you the chart number.) You can move a selected chart anywhere on a worksheet without affecting formulas or data in the worksheet. Any data changed in the worksheet is automatically updated in the chart. You can even move a chart to a different sheet in the workbook, and it will still reflect the original data. You can resize a chart to improve its appearance by dragging its sizing handles. You can reposition chart objects (such as a title or legend) to predefined locations using commands using the Chart Elements button or the Add Chart Element button on the Chart Tools Design tab, or you can freely move any chart object by dragging it or by cutting and pasting it to a new location. When you point to a chart object, the name of the object appears as a ScreenTip. **CASE** ▶ *You want to resize the chart, position it below the worksheet data, and move the legend.*

STEPS

QUICK TIP
To delete a selected chart, press [Delete].

1. **Make sure the chart is still selected, then position the pointer over the chart**

   The pointer shape 🔓 indicates that you can move the chart. For a table of commonly used object pointers, refer to **TABLE 4-2.**

TROUBLE
Dragging a chart element instead of a blank area moves the element instead of the chart; if this happens, undo the action and try again.

2. **Position 🔓 on a blank area near the upper-left edge of the chart, press and hold the left mouse button, drag the chart until its upper-left corner is at the upper-left corner of cell A16, then release the mouse button**

   When you release the mouse button, the chart appears in the new location.

3. **Scroll down so you can see the whole chart, position the pointer on the right-middle sizing handle until it changes to ⇔, then drag the right border of the chart to the right edge of column G**

   The chart is widened. See **FIGURE 4-7.**

QUICK TIP
To resize a selected chart to an exact size, click the Chart Tools Format tab, then enter the desired height and width in the Size group.

4. **Position the pointer over the upper-middle sizing handle until it changes to ↕, then drag the top border of the chart to the top edge of row 15**

5. **Position the pointer over the lower-middle sizing handle until it changes to ↕, then drag the bottom border of the chart to the bottom border of row 26**

   You can move any object on a chart. You want to align the top of the legend with the top of the plot area.

QUICK TIP
You can move a legend to the right, top, left, or bottom of a chart by clicking Legend in the Add Chart Element button in the Chart Layouts group on the Chart Tools Design tab, then clicking a location option.

6. **Click the Quick Layout button in the Chart Layouts group of the Chart Tools Design tab, click Layout 1 (in the upper-left corner of the palette), click the legend to select it, press and hold [Shift], drag the legend up using 🔓 so the dotted outline is approximately 1/4" above the top of the plot area, then release [Shift]**

   When you click the legend, sizing handles appear around it and "Legend" appears as a ScreenTip when the pointer hovers over the object. As you drag, a dotted outline of the legend border appears. Pressing and holding the [Shift] key holds the horizontal position of the legend as you move it vertically. Although the sizing handles on objects within a chart look different from the sizing handles that surround a chart, they function the same way.

7. **Click cell A12, type United States, click the Enter button ✓ on the formula bar, use AutoFit to resize column A, then save your work**

   The axis label changes to reflect the updated cell contents, as shown in **FIGURE 4-8.** Changing any data in the worksheet modifies corresponding text or values in the chart. Because the chart is no longer selected, the Chart Tools tabs no longer appear on the Ribbon.

FIGURE 4-7: Moved and resized chart

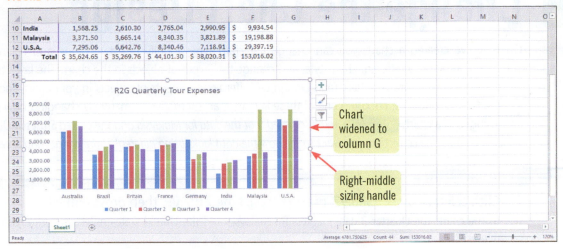

Chart widened to column G

Right-middle sizing handle

FIGURE 4-8: Worksheet with modified legend and label

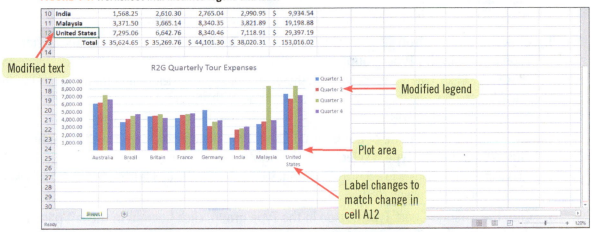

Modified text

Modified legend

Plot area

Label changes to match change in cell A12

TABLE 4-2: Common object pointers

name	pointer	use	name	pointer	use
Diagonal resizing	⤢ or ⤡	Change chart shape from corners	I-beam	I	Edit object text
Draw	+	Draw an object	Move	✛	Move object
Horizontal resizing	⇔	Change object width	Vertical resizing	↕	Change object height

Moving an embedded chart to a sheet

Suppose you have created an embedded chart that you decide would look better on a chart sheet or in a different worksheet. You can make this change without recreating the entire chart. To do so, first select the chart, click the Chart Tools Design tab, then click the Move Chart button in the Location group. The Move Chart dialog box opens. To move the chart to its own chart sheet, click the New sheet option button, type a name for the new sheet if desired, then click OK. If the chart is already on its own sheet or you want to move it to a different existing sheet, click the Object in option button, click the desired worksheet, then click OK.

Change the Chart Design

Learning Outcomes
- Change the chart design
- Change the chart type
- Apply a chart style

Once you've created a chart, you can change the chart type, modify the data range and column/row configuration, apply a different chart style, and change the layout of objects in the chart. The layouts in the Chart Layouts group on the Chart Tools Design tab offer arrangements of objects in your chart, such as its legend, title, or gridlines; choosing one of these layouts is an alternative to manually changing how objects are arranged in a chart. **CASE** ▶ *You discovered that the data for Malaysia and the United States in Quarter 3 is incorrect. After the correction, you want to see how the data looks using different chart layouts and types.*

STEPS

1. **Click cell D11, type 5568.92, press [Enter], type 7107.09, then press [Enter]**

   In the chart, the Quarter 3 data markers for Malaysia and the United States reflect the adjusted expense figures. See **FIGURE 4-9**.

2. **Select the chart by clicking a blank area within the chart border, click the Chart Tools Design tab on the Ribbon, click the Quick Layout button in the Chart Layouts group, then click Layout 3**

   The legend moves to the bottom of the chart. You prefer the original layout.

3. **Click the Undo button ↶ ▾ on the Quick Access Toolbar, then click the Change Chart Type button in the Type group**

   The Change Chart Type dialog box opens, as shown in **FIGURE 4-10**. The left pane of the dialog box lists the available categories, and the right pane shows the individual chart types. A pale gray border surrounds the currently selected chart type.

4. **Click Bar in the left pane of the Change Chart Type dialog box, confirm that the first Clustered Bar chart type is selected in the right pane, then click OK**

   The column chart changes to a clustered bar chart. See **FIGURE 4-11**. You decide to see how the data looks in a three-dimensional column chart.

5. **Click the Change Chart Type button in the Type group, click Column in the left pane of the Change Chart Type dialog box, click 3-D Clustered Column (fourth from the left in the top row) in the right pane, verify that the left-most 3-D chart is selected, then click OK**

   A three-dimensional column chart appears. You notice that the three-dimensional column format gives you a sense of volume, but it is more crowded than the two-dimensional column format.

6. **Click the Change Chart Type button in the Type group, click Clustered Column (first from the left in the top row) in the right pane of the Change Chart Type dialog box, then click OK**

7. **Click the Style 3 chart style in the Chart Styles group**

   The columns change to lighter shades of color. You prefer the previous chart style's color scheme.

8. **Click ↶ ▾ on the Quick Access Toolbar, then save your work**

Creating a combo chart

A **combo chart** presents two or more charts in one; a column chart with a line chart, for example. This type of chart is helpful when charting dissimilar but related data. For example, you can create a combo chart based on home price and home size data, showing home prices in a column chart and related home sizes in a line chart. Here a **secondary axis** (such as a vertical axis on the right side of the chart) would supply the scale for the home sizes.

To create a combo chart, select all the data you want to plot, click the Combo chart button 📊▾ in the Charts group in the Insert tab, click a suggested type or Create Custom Combo Chart, supply additional series information if necessary, then click OK. To change an existing chart to a combo chart, select the chart, click Change Chart Type in the Type group on the Chart Tools Design tab, then follow the same procedure.

FIGURE 4-9: Worksheet with modified data

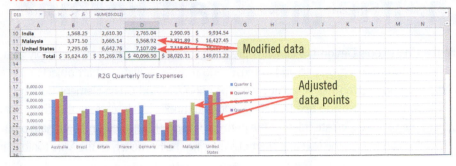

FIGURE 4-10: Change Chart Type dialog box

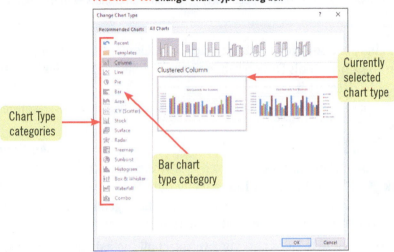

FIGURE 4-11: Column chart changed to bar chart

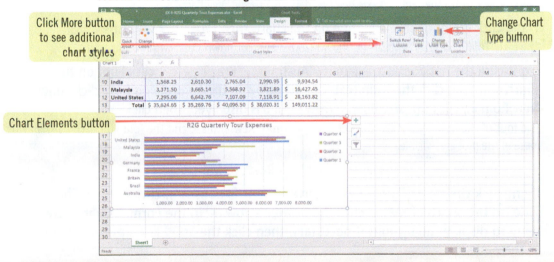

Working with a 3-D chart

Excel includes two kinds of 3-D chart types. In a true 3-D chart, a third axis, called the **z-axis**, lets you compare data points across both categories and values. The z-axis runs along the depth of the chart, so it appears to advance from the back of the chart. To create a true 3-D chart, look for chart types that begin with "3-D," such as 3-D Column. In a 3-D chart, data series can sometimes obscure other columns or bars in the same chart, but you can rotate the chart to obtain a better view. Right-click the chart, then click 3-D Rotation. The Format Chart Area pane opens with the 3-D Rotation category active. The 3-D Rotation options let you change the orientation and perspective of the chart area, plot area, walls, and floor. The 3-D Format category lets you apply three-dimensional effects to selected chart objects. (Not all 3-D Rotation and 3-D Format options are available on all charts.)

Change the Chart Format

Learning Outcomes
- Change the gridlines display
- Add axis titles
- Change the border color
- Add a shadow to an object

While the Chart Tools Design tab contains preconfigured chart layouts you can apply to a chart, the Chart Elements button makes it easy to add, remove, and modify individual chart objects such as a chart title or legend. Using options on this shortcut menu (or using the Add Chart Element button on the Chart Tools Design tab), you can also add text to a chart, add and modify labels, change the display of axes, modify the fill behind the plot area, create titles for the horizontal and vertical axes, and eliminate or change the look of gridlines. You can format the text in a chart object using the Home tab or the Mini toolbar, just as you would the text in a worksheet. **CASE** *You want to change the layout of the chart by creating titles for the horizontal and vertical axes. To improve the chart's appearance, you'll add a drop shadow to the chart title.*

STEPS

1. **With the chart still selected, click the Add Chart Element button in the Chart Layouts group on the Chart Tools Design tab, point to Gridlines, then click Primary Major Horizontal to deselect it**

   The gridlines that extend from the value axis tick marks across the chart's plot area are removed as shown in **FIGURE 4-12**.

2. **Click the Chart Elements button ⊞ in the upper-right corner *outside* the chart border, click the Gridlines arrow, click Primary Major Horizontal, click Primary Minor Horizontal, then click ⊞ to close the Chart Elements fly-out menu**

   Both major and minor gridlines now appear in the chart. **Major gridlines** represent the values at the value axis tick marks, and **minor gridlines** represent the values between the tick marks.

   > **QUICK TIP**
   > You can move any title to a new position by clicking one of its edges, then dragging it.

3. **Click ⊞, click the Axis Titles checkbox to select all the axis titles options, triple-click the vertical axis title on the chart, then type Expenses (in $)**

   Descriptive text on the category axis helps readers understand the chart.

   > **QUICK TIP**
   > You can also edit text in a chart or axis title by positioning the pointer over the selected title until it changes to I, clicking the title, then editing the text.

4. **Triple-click the horizontal axis title on the chart, then type Tour Countries**

   The text "Tour Countries" appears on the horizontal axis, as shown in **FIGURE 4-13**.

5. **Right-click the horizontal axis labels ("Australia", "Brazil", etc.), click Font on the shortcut menu, click the Latin text font list arrow in the Font dialog box, click Times New Roman, click the Size down arrow until 8 is displayed, then click OK**

   The font of the horizontal axis labels changes to Times New Roman, and the font size decreases, making more of the plot area visible.

   > **QUICK TIP**
   > You can also apply a border to a selected chart object by clicking the Shape Outline list arrow on the Chart Tools Format tab, and then selecting from the available options.

6. **Right-click the vertical axis labels, then click Reset to Match**

7. **Right-click the Chart Title ("R2G Quarterly Tour Expenses"), click Format Chart Title on the shortcut menu, click the Border arrow ▶ in the Format Chart Title pane to display the options if necessary, then click the Solid line option button in the pane**

   A solid border appears around the chart title with the default blue color.

   > **QUICK TIP**
   > You can also apply a shadow to a selected chart object by clicking the Shadow arrow, then clicking a shadow effect.

8. **Click the Effects button ⬠ in the Format Chart Title pane, click Shadow, click the Presets list arrow, click Offset Diagonal Bottom Right in the Outer group (first row, first from the left), click the Format Chart Title pane Close button ✕, then save your work**

   A blue border with a drop shadow surrounds the title. Compare your work to **FIGURE 4-14**.

FIGURE 4-12: Gridlines removed from chart

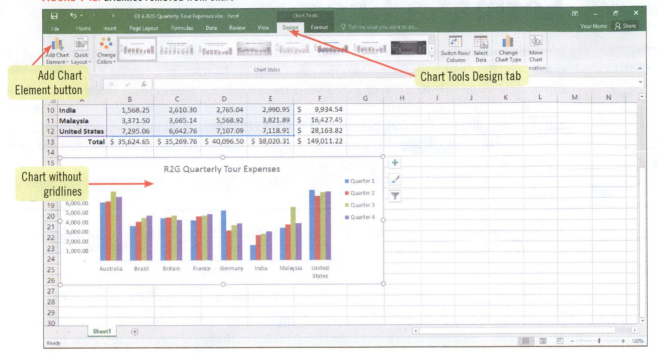

Add Chart Element button

Chart Tools Design tab

Chart without gridlines

FIGURE 4-13: Axis titles added to chart

Chart title

Vertical axis title

Vertical axis labels

Horizontal axis title

Horizontal axis labels

FIGURE 4-14: Enhanced chart

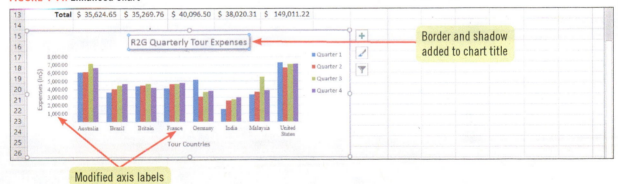

Border and shadow added to chart title

Modified axis labels

Adding data labels to a chart

There are times when your audience might benefit by seeing data labels on a chart. These labels appear next to the data markers in the chart and can indicate the series name, category name, and/or the value of one or more data points. Once your chart is selected, you can add this information to your chart by clicking the Chart Elements button in the upper-right corner outside the selected chart, clicking the Data Labels arrow, and then clicking a display option for the data labels. Once you have added the data labels, you can format them or delete individual data labels. To delete a data label, select it and then press [Delete].

Excel 2016

Format a Chart

Learning Outcomes
- Change the fill of a data series
- Use Live Preview to see a new data series color
- Apply a style to a data series

Formatting a chart can make it easier to read and understand. Many formatting enhancements can be made using the Chart Tools Format tab. You can change the fill color for a specific data series, or you can apply a shape style to a title or a data series using the Shape Styles group. Shape styles make it possible to apply multiple formats, such as an outline, fill color, and text color, all with a single click. You can also apply different fill colors, outlines, and effects to chart objects using arrows and buttons in the Shape Styles group. **CASE** *You want to use a different color for one data series in the chart and apply a shape style to another, to enhance the look of the chart.*

STEPS

QUICK TIP

You can change the chart type of a selected data series by clicking the Chart Tools Design tab on the Ribbon, clicking the Change Chart Type button in the Type group, selecting a chart type for that data series, then clicking OK.

1. **With the chart selected, click the Chart Tools Format tab on the Ribbon, then click any column in the Quarter 4 data series**

   Handles appear on each column in the Quarter 4 data series, indicating that the entire series is selected.

2. **Click the Shape Fill list arrow in the Shape Styles group on the Chart Tools Format tab**

3. **Click Orange, Accent 6 (first row, 10th from the left) as shown in FIGURE 4-15**

   All the columns for the series become orange, and the legend changes to match the new color. You can also change the color of selected objects by applying a shape style.

4. **Click any column in the Quarter 3 data series**

   Handles appear on each column in the Quarter 3 data series.

QUICK TIP

To apply a WordArt style to a text object (such as the chart title), select the object, then click a style in the WordArt Styles group on the Chart Tools Format tab.

5. **Click the More button ⊽ on the Shape Styles gallery, then *hover the pointer* over the Moderate Effect – Olive Green, Accent 3 shape style (fifth row, fourth from the left) in the gallery, as shown in FIGURE 4-16**

   Live Preview shows the data series in the chart with the shape style applied.

6. **Click the Subtle Effect – Olive Green, Accent 3 shape style**

   The style for the data series changes, as shown in FIGURE 4-17.

7. **Save your work**

Previewing a chart

To print or preview just a chart, select the chart (or make the chart sheet active), click the File tab, then click Print on the navigation bar. To reposition a chart by changing the page's margins, click the Show Margins button ▦ in the lower-right corner of the Print tab to display the margins in the preview. You can drag the margin lines to the exact settings you want; as the margins change, the size and placement of the chart on the page change too.

FIGURE 4-15: New shape fill applied to data series

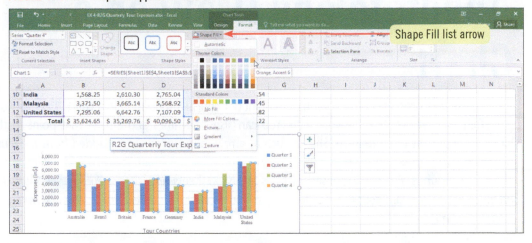

FIGURE 4-16: Live Preview of new style applied to data series

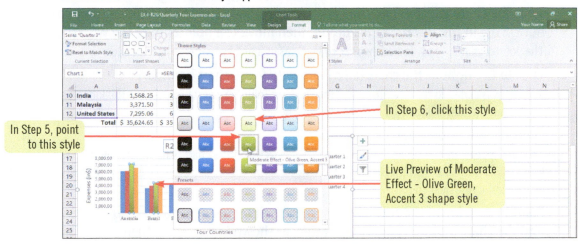

FIGURE 4-17: Style of data series changed

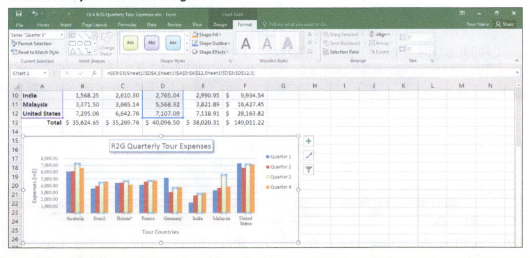

Changing alignment and angle in axis labels and titles

The buttons on the Chart Tools Design tab provide a few options for positioning axis labels and titles, but you can customize their position and rotation to exact specifications using the Format Axis pane or Format Axis Title pane. With a chart selected, right-click the axis text you want to modify, then click Format Axis or Format Axis Title on the shortcut menu. In the pane that opens, click the Size & Properties button, then select the appropriate option. You can also create a custom angle by clicking the Custom angle up and down arrows. When you have made the desired changes, close the pane.

Annotate and Draw on a Chart

You can use text annotations and graphics to point out critical information in a chart. **Text annotations** are labels that further describe your data. You can also draw lines and arrows that point to the exact locations you want to emphasize. Shapes such as arrows and boxes can be added from the Illustrations group on the Insert tab or from the Insert Shapes group on the Chart Tools Format tab on the Ribbon. The Insert group is also used to insert pictures into worksheets and charts. **CASE** *You want to call attention to the Germany tour expense decrease, so you decide to add a text annotation and an arrow to this information in the chart.*

STEPS

1. **With the chart selected and the Chart Tools Format tab active, click the Text Box button in the Insert Shapes group, then move the pointer over the worksheet**

   The pointer changes to ↓, indicating that you will insert a text box where you next click.

2. **Click to the right of the chart (anywhere *outside* the chart boundary)**

   A text box is added to the worksheet, and the Drawing Tools Format tab appears on the Ribbon so that you can format the new object. First you need to type the text.

3. **Type Great Improvement**

   The text appears in a selected text box on the worksheet, and the chart is no longer selected, as shown in **FIGURE 4-18**. Your text box may be in a different location; this is not important because you'll move the annotation in the next step.

4. **Point to an edge of the text box so that the pointer changes to ⸙, drag the text box into the chart to the left of the chart title, as shown in FIGURE 4-19, then release the mouse button**

   The text box is a text annotation for the chart. You also want to add a simple arrow shape in the chart.

5. **Click the chart to select it, click the Chart Tools Format tab, click the Arrow button in the Insert Shapes group, then move the pointer over the text box on the chart**

   The pointer changes to ✛, and the status bar displays "Click and drag to insert an AutoShape." When ✛ is over the text box, black handles appear around the text in the text box. A black handle can act as an anchor for the arrow.

6. **Position ✛ on the black handle to the right of the "t" in the word "improvement" (in the text box), press and hold the left mouse button, drag the line to the Quarter 2 column for the Germany category in the chart, then release the mouse button**

   An arrow points to the Quarter 2 expense for Germany, and the Drawing Tools Format tab displays options for working with the new arrow object. You can resize, format, or delete it just like any other object in a chart.

7. **Click the Shape Outline list arrow in the Shape Styles group, click the Automatic color, click the Shape Outline list arrow again, point to Weight, then click 1½ pt**

   Compare your finished chart to **FIGURE 4-20**.

8. **Save your work**

FIGURE 4-18: **Text box added**

Drawing Tools Format tab

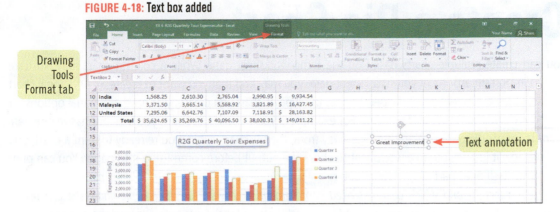

FIGURE 4-19: **Text annotation on the chart**

Text annotation

FIGURE 4-20: **Arrow shape added to chart**

Arrow drawn and formatted

Adding SmartArt graphics

In addition to charts, annotations, and drawn objects, you can create a variety of diagrams using SmartArt graphics. **SmartArt graphics** are available in List, Process, Cycle, Hierarchy, Relationship, Matrix, Pyramid, Picture, and Office.com categories. To insert SmartArt, click the Insert a SmartArt Graphic button in the Illustrations group on the Insert tab to open the Choose a SmartArt Graphic dialog box. Click a SmartArt category in the left pane, then click a layout for the graphic in the right pane. The right pane shows sample layouts for the selected SmartArt, as shown in **FIGURE 4-21**. The SmartArt graphic appears in the worksheet as an embedded object with sizing handles. Depending on the type of SmartArt graphic you selected, a text pane opens next to the graphic; you can enter text into the graphic using the text pane or by typing directly in the shapes in the diagram.

FIGURE 4-21: **Choose a SmartArt Graphic dialog box**

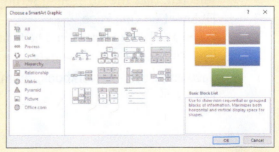

Create a Pie Chart

Learning
Outcomes
• Create a pie chart
• Explode a pie
  chart slice

You can create multiple charts based on the same worksheet data. While a column chart may illustrate certain important aspects of your worksheet data, you may find that you want to create an additional chart to emphasize a different point. Depending on the type of chart you create, you have additional options for calling attention to trends and patterns. For example, if you create a pie chart, you can emphasize one data point by **exploding**, or pulling that slice away from, the pie chart. When you're ready to print a chart, you can preview it just as you do a worksheet to check the output before committing it to paper. You can print a chart by itself or as part of the worksheet. **CASE** *At an upcoming meeting, Yolanda plans to discuss the total tour expenses and which countries need improvement. You want to create a pie chart she can use to illustrate total expenses. Finally, you want to fit the worksheet and the charts onto one worksheet page.*

STEPS

1. **Select the range A5:A12, press and hold [Ctrl], select the range F5:F12, click the Insert tab, click the Insert Pie or Doughnut Chart button in the Charts group, then click 3-D Pie in the chart gallery**

   The new chart appears in the center of the worksheet. You can move the chart and quickly format it using a chart layout.

2. **Drag the chart so its upper-left corner is at the upper-left corner of cell G1, click the Quick Layout button in the Chart Layouts group of the Chart Tools Design tab, then click Layout 2**

   The chart is repositioned on the page, and its layout changes so that a chart title is added, the percentages display on each slice, and the legend appears just below the chart title.

3. **Select the Chart Title text, then type R2G Total Expenses, by Country**

4. **Click the slice for the India data point, click it again so it is the only slice selected, right-click it, then click Format Data Point**

   The Format Data Point pane opens, as shown in **FIGURE 4-22**. You can use the Point Explosion slider to control the distance a pie slice moves away from the pie, or you can type a value in the Point Explosion text box.

5. **Double-click 0 in the Point Explosion text box, type 40, then click the Close button ⊠**

   Compare your chart to **FIGURE 4-23**. You decide to preview the chart and data before you print.

6. **Click cell A1, switch to Page Layout view, type your name in the left header text box, then click cell A1**

   You decide the chart and data would fit better on the page if they were printed in landscape orientation.

7. **Click the Page Layout tab, click the Orientation button in the Page Setup group, then click Landscape**

8. **Click the File tab, click Print on the navigation bar, verify that the correct printer is selected, click the No Scaling setting in the Settings section on the Print tab, then click Fit Sheet on One Page**

   The data and chart are positioned horizontally on a single page, as shown in **FIGURE 4-24**. The printer you have selected may affect the appearance of your preview screen.

9. **Save and close the workbook, submit your work to your instructor as directed, then exit Excel**

FIGURE 4-22: Format Data Point pane

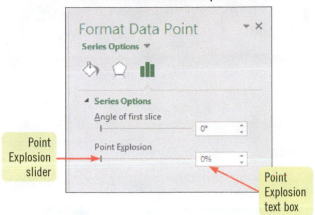

Point Explosion slider

Point Explosion text box

FIGURE 4-23: Exploded pie slice

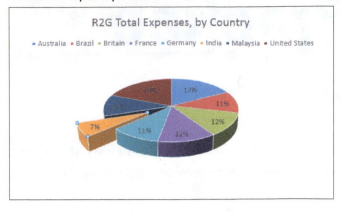

FIGURE 4-24: Preview of worksheet with charts in Backstage view

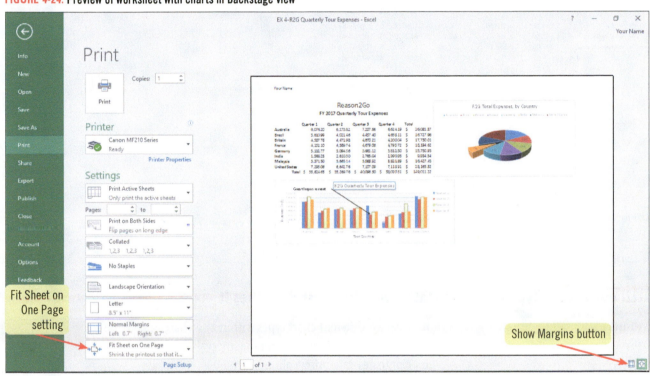

Fit Sheet on One Page setting

Show Margins button

Using the Insert Chart dialog box to discover new chart types

Excel 2016 includes five new chart types. You can explore these charts by clicking the Insert tab on the Ribbon, clicking Recommended Charts, then clicking the All Charts tab in the Insert Chart dialog box. Near the bottom of the list in the left panel are the new chart types: Treemap (which has nine variations), Sunburst, Histogram, Box & Whisker, and Waterfall. If cells are selected prior to opening the Insert Chart dialog box, you will see a sample of the chart type when you click each chart type; the sample will be magnified when you hover the mouse over the sample. The Treemap and Sunburst charts both offer visual comparisons of relative sizes. The Histogram looks like a column chart, but each column (or bin) represents a range of values. The Box & Whisker chart shows distribution details as well as the mean, quartiles, and outliers. The Waterfall chart shows results above and below an imaginary line.

Practice

Concepts Review

Label each element of the Excel chart shown in FIGURE 4-25.

FIGURE 4-25

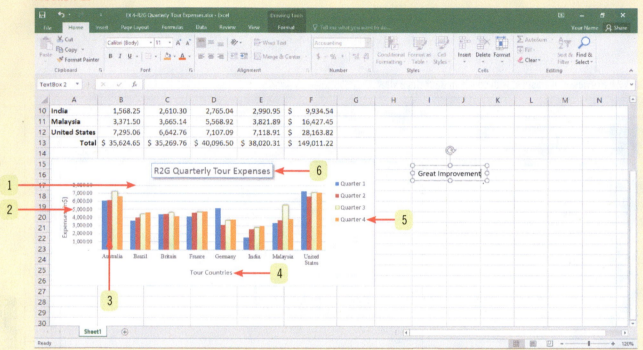

Match each chart type with the statement that best describes it.

7. Combo
8. Pie
9. Area
10. Column
11. Line

a. Displays different chart types within one chart
b. Compares trends over even time intervals
c. Compares data using columns
d. Compares data as parts of a whole
e. Shows how volume changes over time

Select the best answer from the list of choices.

12. **Which tab on the Ribbon do you use to create a chart?**
    a. Design
    b. Insert
    c. Page Layout
    d. Format

13. **A collection of related data points in a chart is called a:**
    a. Data series.
    b. Data tick.
    c. Cell address.
    d. Value title.

14. **The object in a chart that identifies the colors used for each data series is a(n):**
    a. Data marker.
    b. Data point.
    c. Organizer.
    d. Legend.

15. **How do you move an embedded chart to a chart sheet?**
    a. Click a button on the Chart Tools Design tab.
    b. Drag the chart to the sheet tab.
    c. Delete the chart, switch to a different sheet, then create a new chart.
    d. Use the Copy and Paste buttons on the Ribbon.

16. **Which is *not* an example of a SmartArt graphic?**
    a. Sparkline
    b. Basic Matrix
    c. Organization Chart
    d. Basic Pyramid

17. **Which tab appears only when a chart is selected?**
    a. Insert
    b. Chart Tools Format
    c. Review
    d. Page Layout

Skills Review

1. **Plan a chart.**
   a. Start Excel, open the Data File EX 4-2.xlsx from the location where you store your Data Files, then save it as **EX 4-Software Usage Polling Results**.
   b. Describe the type of chart you would use to plot this data.
   c. What chart type would you use to compare the number of Excel users in each type of business?

2. **Create a chart.**
   a. In the worksheet, select the range containing all the data and headings.
   b. Click the Quick Analysis tool.
   c. Create a Clustered Column chart, then add the chart title **Software Usage, by Business** above the chart.
   d. If necessary, click the Switch Row/Column button so the business type (Accounting, Advertising, etc.) appears as the x-axis.
   e. Save your work.

Skills Review (continued)

3. **Move and resize a chart.**
   a. Make sure the chart is still selected, and close any open panes if necessary.
   b. Move the chart beneath the worksheet data.
   c. Widen the chart so it extends to the right edge of column H.
   d. Use the Quick Layout button in the Chart Tools Design tab to move the legend to the right of the charted data. (*Hint*: Use Layout 1.)
   e. Resize the chart so its bottom edge is at the top of row 25.
   f. Save your work.

4. **Change the chart design.**
   a. Change the value in cell B3 to **8**. Observe the change in the chart.
   b. Select the chart.
   c. Use the Quick Layout button in the Chart Layouts group on the Chart Tools Design tab to apply the Layout 10 layout to the chart, then undo the change.
   d. Use the Change Chart Type button on the Chart Tools Design tab to change the chart to a Clustered Bar chart.
   e. Change the chart to a 3-D Clustered Column chart, then change it back to a Clustered Column chart.
   f. Save your work.

5. **Change the chart layout.**
   a. Use the Chart Elements button to turn off the primary major horizontal gridlines in the chart.
   b. Change the font used in the horizontal and vertical axis labels to Times New Roman.
   c. Turn on the primary major gridlines for both the horizontal and vertical axes.
   d. Change the chart title's font to Times New Roman if necessary, with a font size of 20.
   e. Insert **Business** as the primary horizontal axis title.
   f. Insert **Number of Users** as the primary vertical axis title.
   g. Change the font size of the horizontal and vertical axis titles to 10 and the font to Times New Roman, if necessary.
   h. Change "Personnel" in the worksheet column heading to **Human Resources**, then AutoFit column D, and any other columns as necessary.
   i. Change the font size of the legend to 14.
   j. Add a solid line border in the default color and a (preset) Offset Diagonal Bottom Right shadow to the chart title.
   k. Save your work.

6. **Format a chart.**
   a. Make sure the chart is selected, then select the Chart Tools Format tab, if necessary.
   b. Change the shape fill of the Excel data series to Dark Blue, Text 2.
   c. Change the shape style of the Excel data series to Subtle Effect – Orange, Accent 6.
   d. Save your work.

7. **Annotate and draw on a chart.**
   a. Make sure the chart is selected, then create the text annotation **Needs more users**.
   b. Position the text annotation so the word "Needs" is just below the word "Software" in the chart title.
   c. Select the chart, then use the Chart Tools Format tab to create a 1½ pt weight dark blue arrow that points from the bottom center of the text box to the Excel users in the Human Resources category.
   d. Deselect the chart.
   e. Save your work.

Skills Review (continued)

8. Create a pie chart.

   a. Select the range A1:F2, then create a 3-D Pie chart.

   b. Drag the 3-D pie chart beneath the existing chart.

   c. Change the chart title to **Excel Users**.

   d. Apply the Style 7 chart style to the chart, then apply Layout 6 using the Quick Layout button.

   e. Explode the Human Resources slice from the pie chart at **25%**.

   f. In Page Layout view, enter your name in the left section of the worksheet header.

   g. Preview the worksheet and charts in Backstage view, make sure all the contents fit on one page, then submit your work to your instructor as directed. When printed, the worksheet should look like **FIGURE 4-26**. (Note that certain elements such as the title may look slightly different when printed.)

   h. Save your work, close the workbook, then exit Excel.

FIGURE 4-26

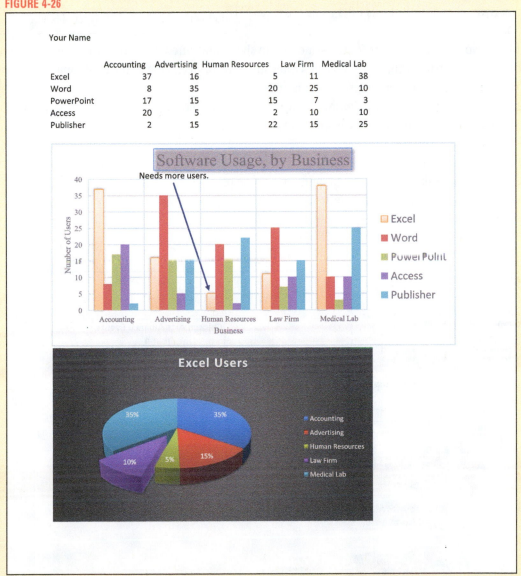

Independent Challenge 1

You are the operations manager for the Chicago Arts Alliance. Each year the group revisits the number and types of activities they support to better manage their budgets. For this year's budget, you need to create charts to document the number of events in previous years.

a. Start Excel, open the file EX 4-3.xlsx from the location where you store your Data Files, then save it as **EX 4-Chicago Arts Alliance**.

b. Take some time to plan your charts. Which type of chart or charts might best illustrate the information you need to display? What kind of chart enhancements do you want to use? Will a 3-D effect make your chart easier to understand?

c. Create a Clustered Column chart for the data.

d. Change at least one of the colors used in a data series.

e. Make the appropriate modifications to the chart to make it visually attractive and easier to read and understand. Include a legend to the right of the chart, and add chart titles and horizontal and vertical axis titles using the text shown in **TABLE 4-3**.

TABLE 4-3

title	text
Chart title	Chicago Arts Alliance Events
Vertical axis title	Number of Events
Horizontal axis title	Types of Events

f. Create at least two additional charts for the same data to show how different chart types display the same data. Reposition each new chart so that all charts are visible in the worksheet. One of the additional charts should be a pie chart for an appropriate data set; the other is up to you.

g. Modify each new chart as necessary to improve its appearance and effectiveness. A sample worksheet containing three charts based on the worksheet data is shown in **FIGURE 4-27**.

h. Enter your name in the worksheet header.

i. Save your work. Before printing, preview the worksheet in Backstage view, then adjust any settings as necessary so that all the worksheet data and charts will print on a single page.

j. Submit your work to your instructor as directed.

k. Close the workbook, then exit Excel.

FIGURE 4-27

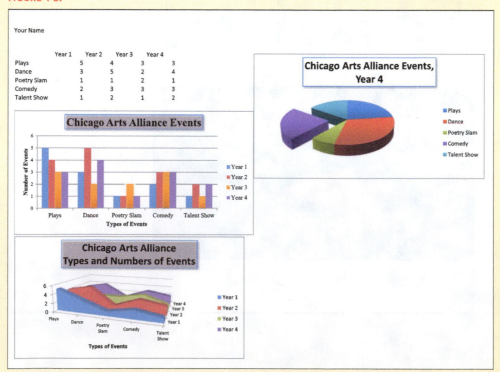

Independent Challenge 2

You work at Canine Companions, a locally owned dog obedience school. One of your responsibilities at the school is to manage the company's sales and expenses using Excel. As part of your efforts, you want to help the staff better understand and manage the school's largest sources of both expenses and sales. To do this, you've decided to create charts using current operating expenses including rent, utilities, and payroll. The manager will use these charts at the next monthly meeting.

a. Start Excel, open EX 4-4.xlsx from the location where you store your Data Files, then save it as **EX 4-Canine Companions Expense Analysis**.

b. Decide which data in the worksheet should be charted. What chart types are best suited for the information you need to show? What kinds of chart enhancements are necessary?

c. Create a 3-D Clustered Column chart in the worksheet showing the expense data for all four quarters. (*Hint*: The expense categories should appear on the x-axis. Do not include the totals.)

d. Change the vertical axis labels (Expenses data) so that no decimals are displayed. (*Hint*: Use the Number category in the Format Axis pane.)

e. Using the sales data, create two charts on this worksheet that compare the sales amounts. (*Hint*: Move each chart to a new location on the worksheet, then deselect it before creating the next one.)

f. In one chart of the sales data, add data labels, then add chart titles as you see fit.

g. Make any necessary formatting changes to make the charts look more attractive, then enter your name in a worksheet cell.

h. Save your work.

i. Preview each chart in Backstage view, and adjust any items as needed. Fit the worksheet to a single page, then submit your work to your instructor as directed. A sample of a printed worksheet is shown in FIGURE 4-28.

j. Close the workbook, then exit Excel.

FIGURE 4-28

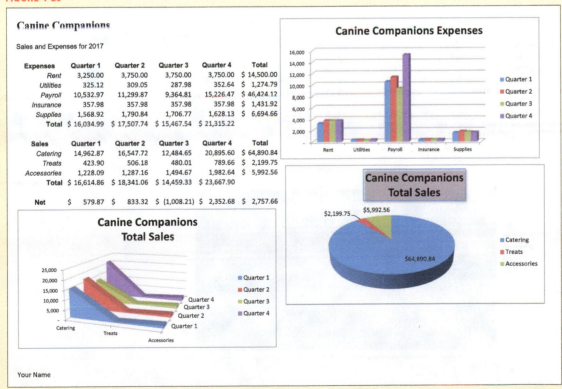

Independent Challenge 3

You are working as an account representative at a clothing store called Zanzibar. You have been examining the advertising expenses incurred recently. The CEO wants to examine expenses designed to increase sales and has asked you to prepare charts that can be used in this evaluation. In particular, you want to see how dollar amounts compare among the different expenses, and you also want to see how expenses compare with each other proportional to the total budget.

a. Start Excel, open the Data File EX 4-5.xlsx from the location where you store your Data Files, then save it as **EX 4-Zanzibar Advertising Expenses**.

b. Identify three types of charts that seem best suited to illustrate the data in the range A16:B24. What kinds of chart enhancements are necessary?

c. Create at least two different types of charts that show the distribution of advertising expenses. (*Hint*: Move each chart to a new location on the same worksheet.) One of the charts should be a 3-D pie chart.

d. In at least one of the charts, add annotated text and arrows highlighting important data, such as the largest expense.

e. Change the color of at least one data series in at least one of the charts.

f. Add chart titles and category and value axis titles where appropriate. Format the titles with a font of your choice. Apply a shadow to the chart title in at least one chart.

g. Add your name to a section of the header, then save your work.

h. Explode a slice from the 3-D pie chart.

i. Add a data label to the exploded pie slice.

j. Preview the worksheet in Backstage view. Adjust any items as needed. Be sure the charts are all visible on one page. Compare your work to the sample in FIGURE 4-29.

k. Submit your work to your instructor as directed, close the workbook, then exit Excel.

FIGURE 4-29

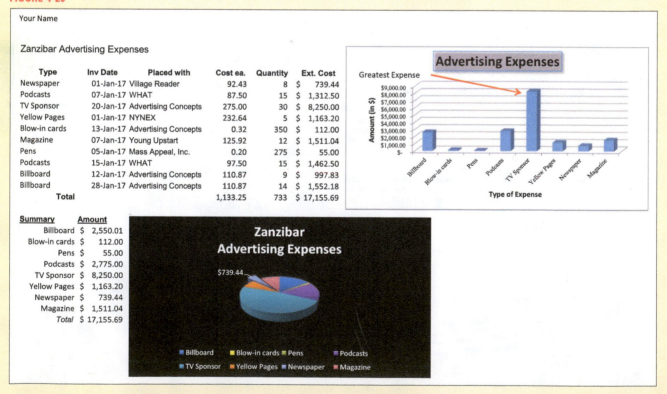

Independent Challenge 4: Explore

This Independent Challenge requires an Internet connection.

All the years of hard work and saving money have paid off, and you have decided to purchase a home. You know where you'd like to live, and you decide to use the web to find out more about houses that are currently available. A worksheet would be a great place to compare the features and prices of potential homes.

a. Start Excel, then save a new, blank workbook as **EX 4-My New House** to the location where you save your Data Files.

b. Decide on where you would like to live, and use your favorite search engine to find information sources on homes for sale in that area. (*Hint*: Try using realtor.com or other realtor-sponsored sites.)

c. Determine a price range and features within the home. Find data for at least five homes that meet your location and price requirements, and enter them in the worksheet. See **TABLE 4-4** for a suggested data layout.

TABLE 4-4

suggested data layout					
Location					
Price range					
	House 1	House 2	House 3	House 4	House 5
Asking price					
Bedrooms					
Bathrooms					
Year built					
Size (in sq. ft.)					

d. Format the data so it looks attractive and professional.

e. Create any type of column chart using only the House and Asking Price data. Place it on the same worksheet as the data. Include a descriptive title.

f. Change the colors in the chart using the chart style of your choice.

g. Enter your name in a section of the header.

h. Create an additional chart: a combo chart that plots the asking price on one axis and the size of the home on the other axis. (*Hint*: Use the Tell me what you want to do text box above the Ribbon to get more guidance on creating a Combo Chart.)

i. Save the workbook. Preview the worksheet in Backstage view and make adjustments if necessary to fit all of the information on one page. See **FIGURE 4-30** for an example of what your worksheet might look like.

j. Submit your work to your instructor as directed.

k. Close the workbook, then exit Excel.

FIGURE 4-30

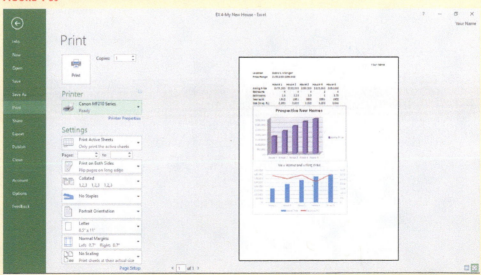

Visual Workshop

Open the Data File EX 4-6.xlsx from the location where you store your Data Files, then save it as **EX 4-Estimated Cost Center Expenses**. Format the worksheet data so it looks like **FIGURE 4-31**, then create and modify two charts to match the ones shown in the figure. You will need to make formatting, layout, and design changes once you create the charts. (*Hint*: The shadow used in the 3-D pie chart title is made using the Outer Offset Diagonal Top Right shadow.) Enter your name in the left text box of the header, then save and preview the worksheet. Submit your work to your instructor as directed, then close the workbook and exit Excel.

FIGURE 4-31

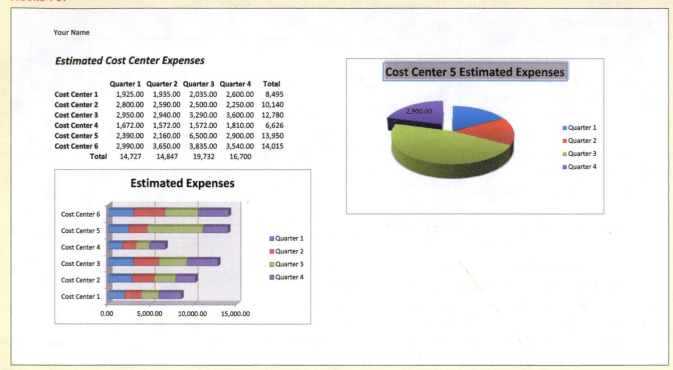

Analyzing Data Using Formulas

CASE ▶ Mary Watson, Reason2Go's vice president of sales and marketing, uses Excel formulas and functions to analyze sales data for the U.S. region and to consolidate sales data from branch offices. Because management is considering adding a new regional branch, Mary asks you to estimate the loan costs for a new office facility and to compare sales in the existing U.S. offices.

Module Objectives

After completing this module, you will be able to:

- Format data using text functions
- Sum a data range based on conditions
- Consolidate data using a formula
- Check formulas for errors
- Construct formulas using named ranges
- Build a logical formula with the IF function
- Build a logical formula with the AND function
- Calculate payments with the PMT function

Files You Will Need

EX 5-1.xlsx	EX 5-5.xlsx
EX 5-2.xlsx	EX 5-6.xlsx
EX 5-3.xlsx	EX 5-7.xlsx
EX 5-4.xlsx	

Format Data Using Text Functions

Learning Outcomes
- Separate text data using Flash Fill
- Format text data using the PROPER function
- Format text data using the CONCATENATE function

Often, you need to import data into Excel from an outside source, such as another program or the Internet. Sometimes you need to reformat this data to make it understandable and attractive. Instead of handling these formatting tasks manually in each cell, you can use Excel text functions to perform them automatically for an entire range. The Flash Fill feature can be used to break data fields in one column into separate columns. The text function PROPER capitalizes the first letter in a string of text as well as any text following a space. You can use the CONCATENATE function to join two or more strings into one text string. **CASE** ▶ *Mary has received the U.S. sales representatives' data from the Human Resources Department, and has imported it into Excel. She asks you to use text formulas to format the data into a more useful layout.*

STEPS

1. **Start Excel, open EX 5-1.xlsx from the location where you store your Data Files, then save it as EX 5-Sales**

2. **On the Sales Reps sheet, click cell B4, type troy silva, press [Tab], type new york, press [Tab], type 5, then click the Enter button ✓ on the formula bar**
   You are manually separating the data in cell A4 into the adjacent cells, as shown in **FIGURE 5-1**. You will let Excel follow your pattern for the rows below using Flash Fill. **Flash Fill** uses worksheet data you have entered as an example to predict what should be entered into similar column cells.

3. **With cell D4 selected, click the Data tab, then click the Flash Fill button in the Data Tools group**
   The years of service number is copied from cell D4 into the range D5:D15. You will use Flash Fill to fill in the names and cities.

4. **Click cell B4, click the Flash Fill button in the Data Tools group, click cell C4, then click the Flash Fill button again**
   The column A data is separated into columns B, C and D. You want to format the letters in the names and cities to the correct cases.

QUICK TIP
You can move the Function Arguments dialog box if it overlaps a cell or range that you need to click. You can also click the Collapse Dialog box button 📧, select the cell or range, then click the Expand Dialog box button 📧 to return to the Function Arguments dialog box.

5. **Click cell E4, click the Formulas tab, click the Text button in the Function Library group, click PROPER, with the insertion point in the Text text box click cell B4, then click OK**
   The name is copied from cell B4 to cell E4 with the correct uppercase letters for proper names. The name is formatted in green, taking on the column's previously applied formatting.

6. **Drag the fill handle to copy the formula in cell E4 to cell F4, then copy the formulas in cells E4:F4 into the range E5:F15**
   You want to format the years data to be more descriptive.

QUICK TIP
Excel automatically inserts quotation marks to enclose the space and the Years text.

7. **Click cell G4, click the Text button in the Function Library group, click CONCATENATE, with the insertion point in the Text1 text box click cell D4, press [Tab], with the insertion point in the Text2 text box press [Spacebar], type Years, then click OK**

8. **Copy the formula in cell G4 into the range G5:G15, click cell A1, compare your work to FIGURE 5-2, click the Insert tab, click the Header & Footer button in the Text group, click the Go to Footer button in the Navigation group, enter your name in the center text box, click on the worksheet, scroll up and click cell A1, then click the Normal button ▦ in the Workbook Views group on the View tab**

9. **Save your file, then preview the worksheet**

FIGURE 5-1: Worksheet with data separated into columns

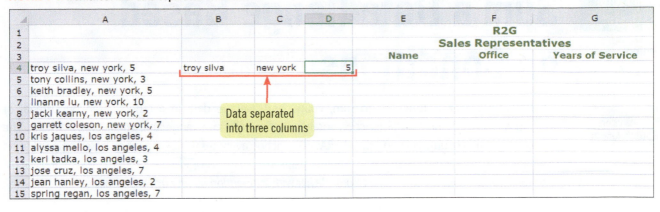

FIGURE 5-2: Worksheet with data formatted in columns

	A	B	C	D	E	F	G
1						R2G	
2						Sales Representatives	
3					Name	Office	Years of Service
4	troy silva, new york, 5	troy silva	new york	5	Troy Silva	New York	5 Years
5	tony collins, new york, 3	tony collins	new york	3	Tony Collins	New York	3 Years
6	keith bradley, new york, 5	keith bradley	new york	5	Keith Bradley	New York	5 Years
7	linanne lu, new york, 10	linanne lu	new york	10	Linanne Lu	New York	10 Years
8	jacki kearny, new york, 2	jacki kearny	new york	2	Jacki Kearny	New York	2 Years
9	garrett coleson, new york, 7	garrett coleson	new york	7	Garrett Coleson	New York	7 Years
10	kris jaques, los angeles, 4	kris jaques	los angeles	4	Kris Jaques	Los Angeles	4 Years
11	alyssa mello, los angeles, 4	alyssa mello	los angeles	4	Alyssa Mello	Los Angeles	4 Years
12	keri tadka, los angeles, 3	keri tadka	los angeles	3	Keri Tadka	Los Angeles	3 Years
13	jose cruz, los angeles, 7	jose cruz	los angeles	7	Jose Cruz	Los Angeles	7 Years
14	jean hanley, los angeles, 2	jean hanley	los angeles	2	Jean Hanley	Los Angeles	2 Years
15	spring regan, los angeles, 7	spring regan	los angeles	7	Spring Regan	Los Angeles	7 Years
16							

Working with text in other ways

Other useful text functions include UPPER, LOWER, and SUBSTITUTE. The UPPER function converts text to all uppercase letters, the LOWER function converts text to all lowercase letters, and SUBSTITUTE replaces text in a text string. For example, if cell A1 contains the text string "Today is Wednesday", then =LOWER(A1) would produce "today is wednesday"; =UPPER(A1) would produce "TODAY IS WEDNESDAY"; and =SUBSTITUTE(A1, "Wednesday", "Tuesday") would result in "Today is Tuesday". You can also use functions to display one or more characters at certain locations within a string. Use the RIGHT function to find the last characters with the syntax =RIGHT(string, # characters), the LEFT function to find the first characters with the syntax =LEFT(string, # characters), or the MID function to display the middle characters with the syntax =MID(string, starting character, # characters). You can separate text data stored in one column into multiple columns by clicking the Data tab, clicking the Text to Columns button in the Data Tools group, and specifying the delimiter for your data. A **delimiter** is a separator, such as a space, comma, or semicolon, that should separate your data. Excel then separates your data into columns at the delimiter.

Sum a Data Range Based on Conditions

Learning Outcomes
- Count data using the COUNTIF function
- Total data using the SUMIF function
- Summarize data using the AVERAGEIF function

You can also use Excel functions to sum, count, and average data in a range based on criteria, or conditions, you set. The SUMIF function totals only the cells in a range that meet given criteria. The COUNTIF function counts cells and the AVERAGEIF function averages values in a range based on a specified condition. The format for the SUMIF function appears in **FIGURE 5-3**. **CASE** *Mary asks you to analyze the New York branch's January sales data to provide her with information about each experience.*

STEPS

1. **Click the NY sheet tab, click cell G7, click the Formulas tab, click the More Functions button in the Function Library group, point to Statistical, scroll down the list of functions if necessary, then click COUNTIF**

   You want to count the number of times Wildlife Care appears in the Experience Category column. The formula you use will say, in effect, "Examine the range I specify, then count the number of cells in that range that contain "Wildlife Care."" You will specify absolute addresses for the range so you can copy the formula later on in the worksheet when the same range will be used.

2. **With the insertion point in the Range text box select the range A6:A25, press [F4], press [Tab], with the insertion point in the Criteria text box, click cell F7, then click OK**

   Your formula, as shown in the formula bar in **FIGURE 5-4**, asks Excel to search the range A6:A25, and where it finds the value shown in cell F7 (that is, when it finds the value "Wildlife Care"), to add one to the total count. The number of Wildlife Care experiences, 4, appears in cell G7. You want to calculate the total sales revenue for the Wildlife Care experiences.

QUICK TIP

You can also sum, count, and average ranges with multiple criteria using the functions SUMIFS, COUNTIFS, and AVERAGEIFS.

3. **Click cell H7, click the Math & Trig button in the Function Library group, scroll down the list of functions, then click SUMIF**

   The Function Arguments dialog box opens. You want to enter two ranges and a criterion; the first range is the one where you want Excel to search for the criteria entered. The second range contains the corresponding cells that Excel will total when it finds the criterion you specify in the first range.

4. **With the insertion point in the Range text box, select the range A6:A25, press [F4], press [Tab], with the insertion point in the Criteria text box click cell F7, press [Tab], with the insertion point in the Sum_range text box select the range B6:B25, press [F4], then click OK**

   Your formula asks Excel to search the range A6:A25, and where it finds Wildlife Care to add the corresponding amounts from column B. The revenue for the Wildlife Care experiences, $4,603, appears in cell H7. You want to calculate the average price paid for the Wildlife Care experiences.

5. **Click cell I7, click the More Functions button in the Function Library group, point to Statistical, then click AVERAGEIF**

6. **With the insertion point in the Range text box select the range A6:A25, press [F4], press [Tab], with the insertion point in the Criteria text box click cell F7, press [Tab], with the insertion point in the Average_range text box select the range B6:B25, press [F4], then click OK**

   The average price paid for the Wildlife Care experiences, $1,151, appears in cell I7.

TROUBLE

Follow the same steps that you used to add a footer to the Sales Reps worksheet in the previous lesson.

7. **Select the range G7:I7, then drag the fill handle to fill the range G8:I10**

   Compare your results with those in **FIGURE 5-5**.

8. **Add your name to the center of the footer, save the workbook, then preview the sheet**

FIGURE 5-3: Format of SUMIF function

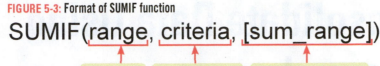

SUMIF(range, criteria, [sum_range])

| The range the function searches | The condition that must be satisfied in the range | The range where the cells that meet the condition will be totaled |

FIGURE 5-4: COUNTIF function in the formula bar

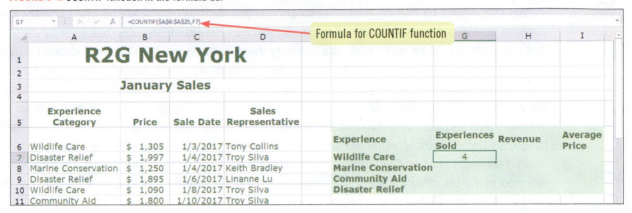

FIGURE 5-5: Worksheet with conditional statistics

Experience	Experiences Sold	Revenue	Average Price
Wildlife Care	4	$ 4,603	$1,151
Marine Conservation	5	$ 5,613	$1,123
Community Aid	5	$ 9,016	$1,803
Disaster Relief	6	$ 11,864	$1,977

Entering date and time functions

Microsoft Excel stores dates as sequential serial numbers and uses them in calculations. January 1, 1900 is assigned serial number 1 and numbers are represented as the number of days following that date. You can see the serial number of a date by using the DATE function. For example, to see the serial number of January, 1, 2017 you would enter =DATE(2017,1,1). The result would be in date format, but if you formatted the cell as Number, it would display the serial number 42736 for this date. Because Excel uses serial numbers, you can perform calculations that include dates and times using the Excel date and time functions. To enter a date or time function, click the Formulas tab on the Ribbon, click the Date & Time button in the Function Library group, then click the Date or Time function you want. All of the date and time functions will be displayed as dates and times unless you change the formatting to Number. See **TABLE 5-1** for some of the available Date and Time functions in Excel.

TABLE 5-1: Date and Time functions

function	calculates	example
TODAY	The current date	=TODAY()
NOW	The current date and time	=NOW()
DATE	Displays a date you enter	=DATE(2017,1,2)
TIME	A serial number from hours, minutes, and seconds	=TIME(5,12,20)
YEAR	A year portion of a date	=YEAR(1/20/2017)
HOUR	The hour portion of a time	=HOUR("15:30:30")
MINUTE	The minute portion of a time	=MINUTE("15:30:30")

Excel 2016

Learning Outcomes
- Consolidate data on multiple sheets using AutoSum
- Consolidate data on multiple sheets using 3-D references

Consolidate Data Using a Formula

When you want to summarize similar data that exists in different sheets or workbooks, you can **consolidate**, or combine and display, the data in one sheet. For example, you might have entered departmental sales figures on four different store sheets that you want to consolidate on one summary sheet, showing total departmental sales for all stores. Or, you may have quarterly sales data on separate sheets that you want to total for yearly sales on a summary sheet. The best way to consolidate data is to use cell references to the various sheets on a consolidation, or summary, sheet. Because they reference other sheets that are usually behind the summary sheet, such references effectively create another dimension in the workbook and are called **3-D references**, as shown in FIGURE 5-6. You can reference, or **link** to, data in other sheets and in other workbooks. Linking to a worksheet or workbook is better than retyping calculated results from another worksheet or workbook because the data values that the calculated totals depend on might change. If you reference the cells, any changes to the original values are automatically reflected in the consolidation sheet. **CASE** *Mary asks you to prepare a January sales summary sheet comparing the total U.S. revenue for the experiences sold in the month.*

STEPS

1. **Click the US Summary Jan sheet tab**

   Because the US Summary Jan sheet (which is the consolidation sheet) will contain references to the data in the other sheets, the cell pointer must reside there when you begin entering the reference.

2. **Click cell B7, click the Formulas tab, click the AutoSum button in the Function Library group, click the NY sheet tab, press and hold [Shift], click the LA sheet tab, scroll up if necessary and click cell G7, then click the Enter button ☑ on the formula bar**

   The US Summary Jan sheet becomes active, and the formula bar reads =SUM(NY:LA!G7), as shown in FIGURE 5-7. "NY:LA" references the NY and LA sheets. The exclamation point (!) is an **external reference indicator**, meaning that the cells referenced are outside the active sheet; G7 is the actual cell reference you want to total in the external sheets. The result, 7, appears in cell B7 of the US Summary Jan sheet; it is the sum of the number of Wildlife Care experiences sold and referenced in cell G7 of the NY and LA sheets. Because the Revenue data is in the column to the right of the Experiences Sold column on the NY and LA sheets, you can copy the experiences sold summary formula, with its relative addresses, into the cell that holds the revenue summary information.

3. **Drag the fill handle to copy the formula in cell B7 to cell C7, click the Auto Fill Options list arrow 🔡, then click the Fill Without Formatting option button**

   The result, $8,004, appears in cell C7 of the US Summary Jan sheet, showing the sum of the Wildlife Care experience revenue referenced in cell H7 of the NY and LA sheets.

4. **In the US Summary Jan sheet, with the range B7:C7 selected, drag the fill handle to fill the range B8:C10**

   You can test a consolidation reference by changing one cell value on which the formula is based and seeing if the formula result changes.

5. **Click the LA sheet tab, edit cell A6 to read Wildlife Care, then click the US Summary Jan sheet tab**

   The number of Wildlife Care experiences sold is automatically updated to 8, and the revenue is increased to $9,883, as shown in FIGURE 5-8.

6. **Save the workbook, then preview the worksheet**

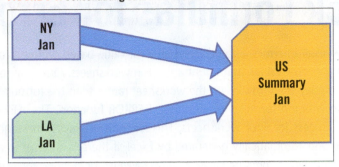

FIGURE 5-6: Consolidating data from two worksheets

FIGURE 5-7: Worksheet showing total Wildlife Care experiences sold

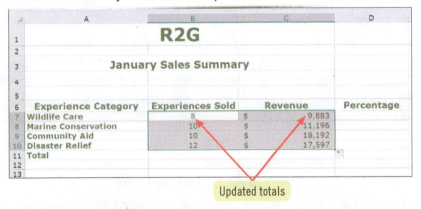

FIGURE 5-8: US Summary Jan worksheet with updated totals

Linking data between workbooks

Just as you can link data between cells in a worksheet and between sheets in a workbook, you can link workbooks so that changes made in referenced cells in one workbook are reflected in the consolidation sheet in the other workbook. To link a single cell between workbooks, open both workbooks, select the cell to receive the linked data, type the equal sign (=), select the cell in the other workbook containing the data to be linked, then press [Enter]. Excel automatically inserts the name of the referenced workbook in the cell reference. For example, if the linked data is contained in cell C7 of the Sales worksheet in the Product workbook, the cell entry reads =[Product.xlsx]Sales!$C$7. To perform calculations, enter formulas on the consolidation sheet using cells in the supporting sheets.

Check Formulas for Errors

Learning Outcomes
- Check for formula errors using IFERROR
- Display worksheet formulas

When formulas result in errors, Excel displays an error value based on the error type. See **TABLE 5-2** for an explanation of the error values that might appear in worksheets. One way to check worksheet formulas for errors is to display the formulas on the worksheet rather than the formula results. You can also check for errors when entering formulas by using the IFERROR function. The IFERROR function simplifies the error-checking process for your worksheets. This function displays a message or value that you specify, rather than the one automatically generated by Excel, if there is an error in a formula. **CASE** *Mary asks you to use formulas to compare the experiences revenues for January. You will use the IFERROR function to help catch formula errors.*

STEPS

1. **On the US Summary Jan sheet, click cell B11, click the Formulas tab, click the AutoSum button in the Function Library group, then click the Enter button ✓ on the formula bar**
   The number of experiences sold, 40, appears in cell B11.

2. **Drag the fill handle to copy the formula in cell B11 into cell C11, click the Auto Fill options list arrow ⊞ ▾, then click the Fill Without Formatting option button**
   The experience revenue total of $56,868 appears in cell C11. You decide to enter a formula to calculate the percentage of revenue the Wildlife Care experience represents by dividing the individual experience revenue figures by the total revenue figure. To help with error checking, you decide to enter the formula using the IFERROR function.

3. **Click cell D7, click the Logical button in the Function Library group, click IFERROR, with the insertion point in the Value text box click cell C7, type /, click cell C11, press [Tab], in the Value_if_error text box type ERROR, then click OK**
   The Wildlife Care experience revenue percentage of 17.38% appears in cell D7. You want to be sure that your error message will be displayed properly, so you decide to test it by intentionally creating an error. You copy and paste the formula—which has a relative address in the denominator, where an absolute address should be used.

4. **Drag the fill handle to copy the formula in cell D7 into the range D8:D10**
   The ERROR value appears in cells D8:D10, as shown in **FIGURE 5-9**. The errors are a result of the relative address for C11 in the denominator of the copied formula. Changing the relative address of C11 in the copied formula to an absolute address of $C$11 will correct the errors.

5. **Double-click cell D7, select C11 in the formula, press [F4], then click ✓ on the formula bar**
   The formula now contains an absolute reference to cell C11.

6. **Copy the corrected formula in cell D7 into the range D8:D10**
   The experience revenue percentages now appear in all four cells, without error messages, as shown in **FIGURE 5-10**. You want to check all of your worksheet formulas by displaying them on the worksheet.

7. **Click the Show Formulas button in the Formula Auditing group**
   The formulas appear in columns B, C, and D. You want to display the formula results again. The Show Formulas button works as a toggle, turning the feature on and off with each click.

8. **Click the Show Formulas button in the Formula Auditing group**
   The formula results appear on the worksheet.

9. **Add your name to the center section of the footer, save the workbook, preview the worksheet, close the workbook, then submit the workbook to your instructor**

FIGURE 5-9: Worksheet with error codes

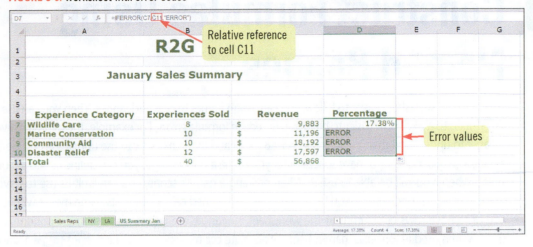

Relative reference to cell C11

Error values

FIGURE 5-10: Worksheet with experience percentages

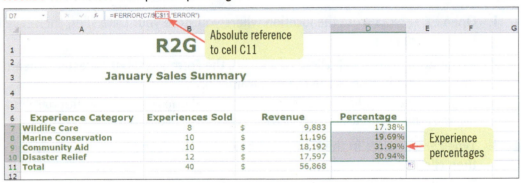

Absolute reference to cell C11

Experience percentages

TABLE 5-2: Understanding error values

error value	cause of error	error value	cause of error
#DIV/0!	A number is divided by 0	#NAME?	Formula contains text error
#NA	A value in a formula is not available	#NULL!	Invalid intersection of areas
#NUM!	Invalid use of a number in a formula	#REF!	Invalid cell reference
#VALUE!	Wrong type of formula argument or operand	#####	Column is not wide enough to display data

Correcting circular references

A cell with a circular reference contains a formula that refers to its own cell location. If you accidentally enter a formula with a circular reference, a warning box opens, alerting you to the problem. Click Help to open a Help window explaining how to find the circular reference. In simple formulas, a circular reference is easy to spot. To correct it, edit the formula to remove any reference to the cell where the formula is located.

If the circular reference is intentional, you can avoid this error by enabling the iteration feature. Excel then recalculates

the formula for the number of times you specify. To enable iterative calculations, click the File tab on the Ribbon, click Options, click Formulas to view the options for calculations, click the Enable iterative calculation check box in the Calculation options group, enter the maximum number of iterations in the Maximum Iterations text box, enter the maximum amount of change between recalculation results in the Maximum Change text box, then click OK.

Construct Formulas Using Named Ranges

To make your worksheet easier to follow, you can assign names to cells and ranges. Then you can use the names in formulas to make them easier to build and to reduce formula errors. For example, the formula "revenue-cost" is easier to understand than the formula "A5-A8". Cell and range names can use uppercase or lowercase letters as well as digits, but cannot have spaces. After you name a cell or range, you can define its **scope**, or the worksheets where you will be able to use it. When defining a name's scope, you can limit its use to a worksheet or make it available to the entire workbook. If you move a named cell or range, its name moves with it, and if you add or remove rows or columns to the worksheet the ranges are adjusted to their new position in the worksheet. When used in formulas, names become absolute cell references by default. **CASE** *Mary asks you to calculate the number of days before each experience departs. You will use range names to construct the formula.*

STEPS

1. Open **EX 5-2.xlsx** from the location where you store your Data Files, then save it as **EX 5-Experiences**

2. In the April Sales sheet, click cell **B4**, click the **Formulas tab** if necessary, then click the **Define Name button** in the Defined Names group

   The New Name dialog box opens, as shown in **FIGURE 5-11**. You can give a cell that contains a date a name that will make it easier to build formulas that perform date calculations.

3. Type **current_date** in the Name text box, click the **Scope list arrow**, click **April Sales**, then click **OK**

   The name assigned to cell B4, current_date, appears in the Name Box. Because its scope is the April Sales worksheet, the range name current_date will appear on the name list only on that worksheet.

4. Select the range **B7:B13**, click the **Define Name button** in the Defined Names group, enter **experience_date** in the Name text box, click the **Scope list arrow**, click **April Sales**, then click **OK**

   Now you can use the named cell and named range in a formula. The formula =experience_date–current_date is easier to understand than =B7-$B$4.

5. Click cell **C7**, type **=**, click the **Use in Formula button** in the Defined Names group, click **experience_date**, type **–**, click the **Use in Formula button**, click **current_date**, then click the **Enter button** ✓ on the formula bar

   The number of days before the elephant conservation experience departs, 6, appears in cell C7. You can use the same formula to calculate the number of days before the other experiences depart.

6. Drag the **fill handle** to copy the formula in cell C7 into the range **C8:C13**, then compare your formula results with those in **FIGURE 5-12**

7. Save the workbook

Consolidating data using named ranges

You can consolidate data using named cells and ranges. For example, you might have entered team sales figures using the names team1, team2, and team3 on different sheets that you want to consolidate on one summary sheet. As you enter the summary formula you can click the Formulas tab, click the Use in Formula button in the Defined Names group, and select the cell or range name.

FIGURE 5-11: New Name dialog box

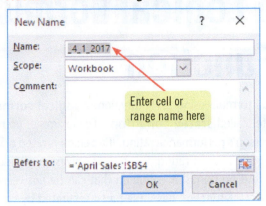

FIGURE 5-12: Worksheet with days before departure

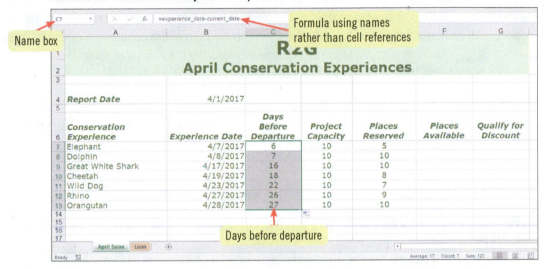

Managing workbook names

You can use the Name Manager to create, delete, and edit names in a workbook. Click the Name Manager button in the Defined Names group on the Formulas tab to open the Name Manager dialog box, shown in FIGURE 5-13. Click the New button to create a new named cell or range, click Delete to remove a highlighted name, and click Filter to see options for displaying specific criteria for displaying names. Clicking Edit opens the Edit Name dialog box where you can change a highlighted cell name, edit or add comments, and change the cell or cells that the name refers to on the worksheet.

FIGURE 5-13: Name Manager dialog box

Excel 2016

Learning Outcomes
- Build a logical formula using the IF function
- Apply comparison operators in a logical test

Build a Logical Formula with the IF Function

You can build a logical formula using an IF function. A **logical formula** makes calculations based on criteria that you create, called **stated conditions**. For example, you can build a formula to calculate bonuses based on a person's performance rating. If a person is rated a 5 (the stated condition) on a scale of 1 to 5, with 5 being the highest rating, he or she receives an additional 10% of his or her salary as a bonus; otherwise, there is no bonus. A condition that can be answered with a true or false response is called a **logical test**. The IF function has three parts, separated by commas: a condition or logical test, an action to take if the logical test or condition is true, and an action to take if the logical test or condition is false. Another way of expressing this is: IF(test_cond,do_this,else_this). Translated into an Excel IF function, the formula to calculate bonuses might look like this: IF(Rating=5,Salary*0.10,0). In other words, if the rating equals 5, multiply the salary by 0.10 (the decimal equivalent of 10%), then place the result in the selected cell; if the rating does not equal 5, place a 0 in the cell. When entering the logical test portion of an IF statement, you typically use some combination of the comparison operators listed in **TABLE 5-3**. **CASE** *Mary asks you to use an IF function to calculate the number of places available for each experience in April, and to display "None" if no places are available.*

STEPS

1. **Click cell F7, on the Formulas tab click the Logical button in the Function Library group, then click IF**

   The Function Arguments dialog box opens. You want the function to do the following: If the project capacity is greater than the number of places reserved, calculate the number of places that are available (capacity minus number reserved), and place the result in cell F7; otherwise, place the text "None" in the cell.

2. **With the insertion point in the Logical_test text box, click cell D7, type >, click cell E7, then press [Tab]**

   The symbol (>) represents "greater than." So far, the formula reads "If the project capacity is greater than the number of reserved places,". The next part of the function tells Excel the action to take if the capacity exceeds the reserved number of places.

3. **With the insertion point in the Value_if_true text box, click cell D7, type –, click cell E7, then press [Tab]**

   This part of the formula tells the program what you want it to do if the logical test is true. Continuing the translation of the formula, this part means "Subtract the number of reserved places from the project capacity." The last part of the formula tells Excel the action to take if the logical test is false (that is, if the project capacity does not exceed the number of reserved places).

QUICK TIP
You can nest IF functions to test several conditions in a formula. A nested IF function contains IF functions inside other IF functions to test these multiple conditions. The second IF statement is actually the value_if_false argument of the first IF statement.

4. **Type None in the Value_if_false text box, then click OK**

   The function is complete, and the result, 5 (the number of available places), appears in cell F7, as shown in **FIGURE 5-14**.

5. **Drag the fill handle to copy the formula in cell F7 into the range F8:F13**

   Compare your results with **FIGURE 5-15**.

6. **Save the workbook**

FIGURE 5-14: Worksheet with IF function

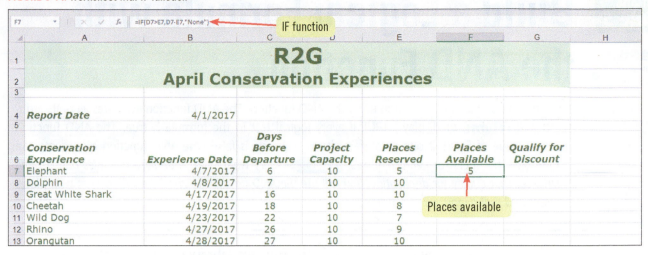

FIGURE 5-15: Worksheet showing places available

April Conservation Experiences

Conservation Experience	Experience Date	Days Before Departure	Project Capacity	Places Reserved	Places Available	Qualify for Discount
Report Date	4/1/2017					
Elephant	4/7/2017	6	10	5	5	
Dolphin	4/8/2017	7	10	10	None	
Great White Shark	4/17/2017	16	10	10	None	
Cheetah	4/19/2017	18	10	8	2	
Wild Dog	4/23/2017	22	10	7	3	
Rhino	4/27/2017	26	10	9	1	
Orangutan	4/28/2017	27	10	10	None	

Places available

April Sales   Loan

Ready   Average: 3   Count: 7   Sum: 11   120%

TABLE 5-3: Comparison operators

operator	meaning	operator	meaning
<	Less than	<=	Less than or equal to
>	Greater than	>=	Greater than or equal to
=	Equal to	<>	Not equal to

Build a Logical Formula with the AND Function

You can also build a logical function using the AND function. The AND function evaluates all of its arguments and **returns**, or displays, TRUE if every logical test in the formula is true. The AND function returns a value of FALSE if one or more of its logical tests is false. The AND function arguments can include text, numbers, or cell references. **CASE** *Mary wants you to analyze the sales data to find experiences that qualify for discounting. You will use the AND function to check for experiences with places available and that depart within 21 days.*

STEPS

TROUBLE
If you get a formula error, check to be sure that you typed the quotation marks around None.

1. **Click cell G7, click the Logical button in the Function Library group, then click AND**
   The Function Arguments dialog box opens. You want the function to evaluate the discount qualification as follows: There must be places available, and the experience must depart within 21 days.

2. **With the insertion point in the Logical1 text box, click cell F7, type < >, type "None", then press [Tab]**
   The symbol (<>) represents "not equal to." So far, the formula reads "If the number of places available is not equal to None"—in other words, if it is an integer. The next logical test checks the number of days before the experience departs.

QUICK TIP
Functions can be placed inside of an IF function. For example, the formula in cell G7 could be replaced by the formula =IF(AND(F7<> "None", C7<21), "TRUE", "FALSE")

3. **With the insertion point in the Logical2 text box, click cell C7, type <21, then click OK**
   The function is complete, and the result, TRUE, appears in cell G7, as shown in **FIGURE 5-16**.

4. **Drag the fill handle to copy the formula in cell G7 into the range G8:G13**
   Compare your results with **FIGURE 5-17**.

QUICK TIP
You can fit your worksheet on one page to print by clicking the Page Layout tab, clicking the Width list arrow in the Scale to Fit group, then clicking 1 page.

5. **Add your name to the center of the footer, save the workbook, then preview the worksheet**

Using the OR and NOT logical functions

The OR logical function has the same syntax as the AND function, but rather than returning TRUE if every argument is true, the OR function will return TRUE if any of its arguments are true. It will only return FALSE if all of its arguments are false. The NOT logical function reverses the value of its argument. For example NOT(TRUE) reverses its argument of TRUE and returns FALSE. This can be used in a worksheet to ensure that a cell is not equal to a particular value. See **TABLE 5-4** for examples of the AND, OR, and NOT functions.

TABLE 5-4: Examples of AND, OR, and NOT functions with cell values A1=10 and B1=20

function	formula	result
AND	=AND(A1>5,B1>25)	FALSE
OR	=OR(A1>5,B1>25)	TRUE
NOT	=NOT(A1=0)	TRUE

FIGURE 5-16: Worksheet with AND function

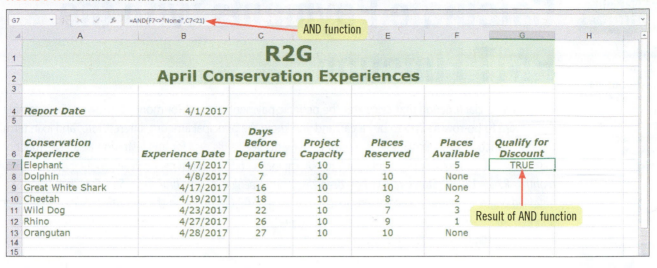

FIGURE 5-17: Worksheet with discount status evaluated

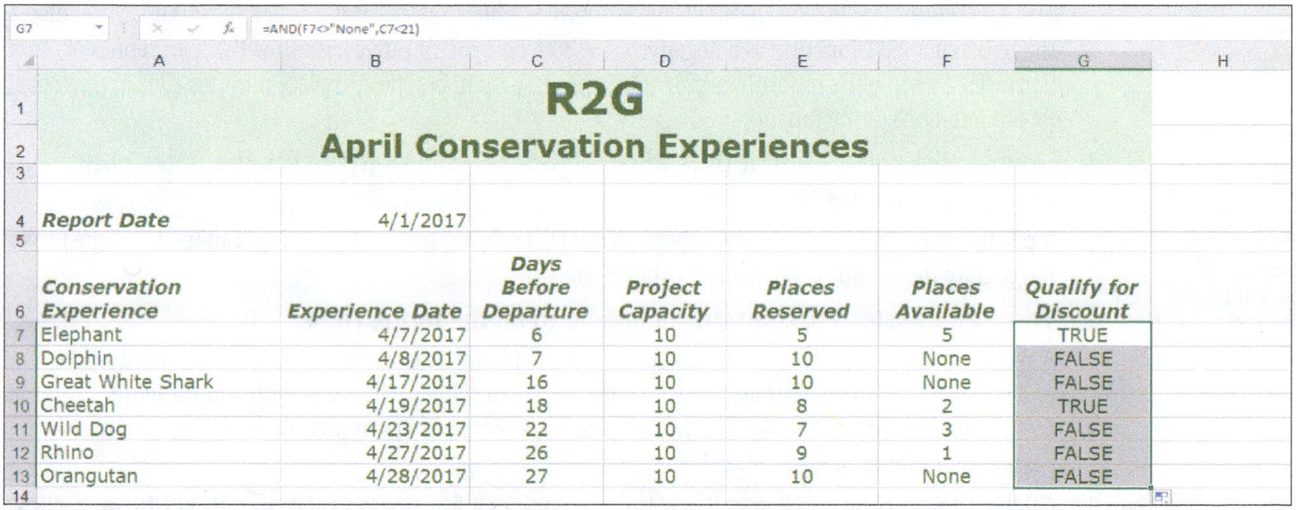

Conservation Experience	Experience Date	Days Before Departure	Project Capacity	Places Reserved	Places Available	Qualify for Discount
Report Date	4/1/2017					
Elephant	4/7/2017	6	10	5	5	TRUE
Dolphin	4/8/2017	7	10	10	None	FALSE
Great White Shark	4/17/2017	16	10	10	None	FALSE
Cheetah	4/19/2017	18	10	8	2	TRUE
Wild Dog	4/23/2017	22	10	7	3	FALSE
Rhino	4/27/2017	26	10	9	1	FALSE
Orangutan	4/28/2017	27	10	10	None	FALSE

Excel 2016

Calculate Payments with the PMT Function

Learning Outcomes
- Calculate monthly payments using the PMT function
- Edit the PMT function to display payments as a positive value

PMT is a financial function that calculates the periodic payment amount for money borrowed. For example, if you want to borrow money to buy a car, and you know the principal amount, interest rate, and loan term, the PMT function can calculate your monthly payment. See FIGURE 5-18 for an illustration of a PMT function that calculates the monthly payment for a $20,000 car loan at 6.5% interest over 5 years. **CASE** *For several months, R2G's United States region has been discussing opening a new branch in San Francisco. Mary has obtained quotes from three different lenders on borrowing $500,000 to begin the expansion. She obtained loan quotes from a commercial bank, a venture capitalist, and an investment banker. She wants you to summarize the information using the Excel PMT function.*

STEPS

1. **Click the Loan sheet tab, click cell F5, click the Formulas tab, click the Financial button in the Function Library group, scroll down the list of functions, then click PMT**

2. **With the insertion point in the Rate text box, click cell D5 on the worksheet, type /12, then press [Tab]**

   You must divide the annual interest by 12 because you are calculating monthly, not annual, payments. You need to be consistent about the units you use for rate and nper. If you express nper as the number of monthly payments, then you must express the interest rate as a monthly rate.

QUICK TIP

The Fv and Type arguments are optional: Fv is the future value, or the total amount you want to obtain after all payments. If you omit it, Excel assumes you want to pay off the loan completely, so the default Fv is 0. Type indicates when the payments are made; 0 is the end of the period, and 1 is the beginning of the period. The default is the end of the period.

3. **With the insertion point in the Nper text box click cell E5, click the Pv text box, click cell B5, then click OK**

   The payment of ($5,242.39) in cell F5 appears in red, indicating that it is a negative amount. Excel displays the result of a PMT function as a negative value to reflect the negative cash flow the loan represents to the borrower. To show the monthly payment as a positive number, you can place a minus sign in front of the Pv cell reference in the function.

4. **Double-click cell F5, edit it to read =PMT(D5/12,E5,-B5), then click the Enter button ☑ on the formula bar**

   A positive value of $5,242.39 now appears in cell F5, as shown in FIGURE 5-19. You can use the same formula to generate the monthly payments for the other loans.

5. **With cell F5 selected, drag the fill handle to fill the range F6:F7**

   A monthly payment of $9,424.17 for the venture capitalist loan appears in cell F6. A monthly payment of $14,996.68 for the investment banker loan appears in cell F7. The loans with shorter terms have much higher monthly payments. But you will not know the entire financial picture until you calculate the total payments and total interest for each lender.

QUICK TIP

You can use the keyboard shortcut of [Ctrl][Enter] rather than clicking the Enter button. This enters the formula and leaves the cell selected.

6. **Click cell G5, type =, click cell E5, type *, click cell F5, press [Tab], in cell H5 type =, click cell G5, type –, click cell B5, then click ☑**

7. **Copy the formulas in cells G5:H5 into the range G6:H7, then click cell A1**

   You can experiment with different interest rates, loan amounts, or terms for any one of the lenders; the PMT function generates a new set of values automatically.

8. **Add your name to the center section of the footer, save the workbook, preview the worksheet, submit the workbook to your instructor, close the workbook, then exit Excel**

   Your worksheet appears as shown in FIGURE 5-20.

FIGURE 5-18: Example of PMT function for car loan

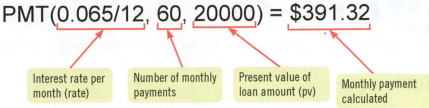

PMT(0.065/12, 60, 20000) = $391.32

Interest rate per month (rate)

Number of monthly payments

Present value of loan amount (pv)

Monthly payment calculated

FIGURE 5-19: PMT function calculating monthly loan payment

F5		✕ ✓ fx	=PMT(D5/12,E5,-B5)				

R2G
Expansion Loan Summary

Lender	Loan Amount	Term (Years)	Interest Rate	Term (Months)	Monthly Payment	Total Payments	Total Interest
Commercial Bank	$ 500,000	10	4.75%	120	$5,242.39		
Venture Capitalist	$ 500,000	5	4.95%	60			
Investment Banker	$ 500,000	3	5.05%	36			

Minus sign before present value displays payment as a positive amount

FIGURE 5-20: Completed worksheet

R2G
Expansion Loan Summary

Lender	Loan Amount	Term (Years)	Interest Rate	Term (Months)	Monthly Payment	Total Payments	Total Interest
Commercial Bank	$ 500,000	10	4.75%	120	$5,242.39	$629,086.46	$ 129,086.46
Venture Capitalist	$ 500,000	5	4.95%	60	$9,424.17	$565,450.05	$ 65,450.05
Investment Banker	$ 500,000	3	5.05%	36	$14,996.68	$539,880.32	$ 39,880.32

Calculating future value with the FV function

You can use the FV (Future Value) function to determine the amount of money a given monthly investment will amount to, at a given interest rate, after a given number of payment periods. The syntax is similar to that of the PMT function: FV(rate,nper,pmt,pv,type). The rate is the interest paid by the financial institution, the nper is the number of periods, and the pmt is the amount that you deposit. For example, suppose you want to invest $1,000 every month for the next 12 months into an account that pays 2% a year, and you want to know how much you will have at the end of 12 months (that is, its future value). You enter the function FV(.02/12,12,-1000), and Excel returns the value $12,110.61 as the future value of your investment. As with the PMT function, the units for the rate and nper must be consistent.

Practice

Concepts Review

FIGURE 5-21

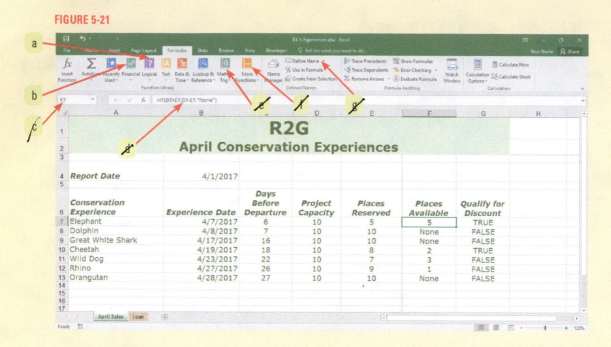

1. Which element do you click to name a cell or range and define its scope?
2. Which element do you click to add a statistical function to a worksheet?
3. Which element points to a logical formula?
4. Which element points to the area where the name of a selected cell or range appears?
5. Which element do you click to add a SUMIF function to a worksheet?
6. Which element do you click to insert a PMT function into a worksheet?
7. Which element do you click to add an IF function to a worksheet?

Match each term with the statement that best describes it.

8. FV	a. Function used to change the first letter of a string to uppercase
9. PV	b. Function used to determine the future amount of an investment
10. SUMIF	c. Part of the PMT function that represents the loan amount
11. PROPER	d. Part of the IF function that the conditions are stated in
12. test_cond	e. Function used to conditionally total cells

Select the best answer from the list of choices.

13. To express conditions such as less than or equal to, you can use a:
    a. Text formula.
    b. Comparison operator.
    c. PMT function.
    d. Statistical function.

14. When you enter the rate and nper arguments in a PMT function, you must:
    a. Be consistent in the units used.
    b. Multiply both units by 12.
    c. Divide both values by 12.
    d. Always use annual units.

15. **Which of the following is an external reference indicator in a formula?**

a. &
c. !
b. :
d. =

16. **Which of the following statements is false?**

a. When used in formulas, names become relative cell references by default.

b. Names cannot contain spaces.

c. Named ranges make formulas easier to build.

d. If you move a named cell or range, its name moves with it.

17. **Which function joins text strings into one text string?**

a. Proper
c. Combine
b. Join
d. Concatenate

18. **When using text in logical tests, the text must be enclosed in:**

a. " "
c. !
b. ( )
d. < >

Skills Review

1. **Format data using text functions.**

a. Start Excel, open EX 5-3.xlsx from the location where you store your Data Files, then save it as **EX 5-North Systems**.

b. On the Managers worksheet, select cell B4 and use the Flash Fill button on the Data tab to enter the names into column B.

c. In cell D2, use a text function to convert the first letter of the department in cell C2 to uppercase, then copy the formula in cell D2 into the range D3:D9.

d. In cell E2, use a text function to convert all letters of the department in cell C2 to uppercase, then copy the formula in cell E2 into the range E3:E9. Widen column E to fit the uppercase entries.

e. In cell F2, use a text function to convert all letters of the department in cell C2 to lowercase, then copy the formula in cell F2 into the range F3:F9.

f. In cell G2, use a text function to substitute "IT" for "operations" if that text exists in cell F2. (*Hint*: In the Function Arguments dialog box, Text is F2, Old_text is "operations", and New_text is "IT".) Copy the formula in cell G2 into the range G3:G9 to change any cells containing "operations" to "IT."

g. Save your work, then enter your name in the worksheet footer. Switch back to Normal view, then compare your screen to **FIGURE 5-22**.

h. Display the formulas in the worksheet.

i. Redisplay the formula results.

FIGURE 5-22

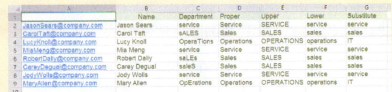

2. **Sum a data range based on conditions.**

a. Make the Service sheet active.

b. In cell B20, use the COUNTIF function to count the number of employees with a rating of 5.

c. In cell B21, use the AVERAGEIF function to average the salaries of those with a rating of 5.

d. In cell B22, enter the SUMIF function that totals the salaries of employees with a rating of 5.

e. Format cells B21 and B22 with the Number format using commas and no decimals. Save your work, then compare your formula results to **FIGURE 5-23**.

FIGURE 5-23

18	**Department Statistics**	
19	**Top Rating**	
20	**Number**	4
21	**Average Salary**	58,110
22	**Total Salary**	232,440
23		

Skills Review (continued)

3. **Consolidate data using a formula.**

   a. Make the Summary sheet active.

   b. In cell B4, use the AutoSum function to total cell F15 on the Service and Accounting sheets.

   c. Format cell B4 with the Accounting Number format with two decimal places.

   d. Enter your name in the worksheet footer, then save your work. Return to Normal view, then compare your screen to **FIGURE 5-24**.

   e. Display the formula in the worksheet, then redisplay the formula results in the worksheet.

4. **Check formulas for errors.**

   a. Make the Service sheet active.

   b. In cell I6, use the IFERROR function to display "ERROR" in the event that the formula F6/F15 results in a formula error. (*Note*: This formula will generate an intentional error after the next step, which you will correct in a moment.)

   c. Copy the formula in cell I6 into the range I7:I14.

   d. Correct the formula in cell I6 by making the denominator, F15, an absolute address.

   e. Copy the new formula in cell I6 into the range I7:I14, then save your work.

5. **Construct formulas using named ranges.**

   a. On the Service sheet, name the range C6:C14 **review_date**, and limit the scope of the name to the Service worksheet.

   b. In cell E6, enter the formula **=review_date+183**, using the Use in Formula button to enter the cell name.

   c. Copy the formula in cell E6 into the range E7:E14.

   d. Use the Name Manager to add a comment of **Date of last review** to the review_date name. (*Hint*: In the Name Manager dialog box, click the review_date name, then click Edit to enter the comment.) Widen the worksheet columns to display all of the data as necessary, then save your work.

6. **Build a logical formula with the IF function.**

   a. In cell G6, use the Function Arguments dialog box to enter the formula **=IF(D6=5,F6*0.05,0)**.

   b. Copy the formula in cell G6 into the range G7:G14.

   c. In cell G15, use AutoSum to total the range G6:G14.

   d. Save your work.

7. **Build a logical formula with the AND function.**

   a. In cell H6, use the Function Arguments dialog box to enter the formula **=AND(G6>0,B6>6)**.

   b. Copy the formula in cell H6 into the range H7:H14.

   c. Enter your name in the footers of the Service and Accounting sheets, save your work, then return to Normal view and compare your Service worksheet to **FIGURE 5-25**.

FIGURE 5-24

	A	B
1	Salary Summary	
2		
3		Salary
4	TOTAL	$ 852,035.00
5		

FIGURE 5-25

	A	B	C	D	E	F	G	H	I
1					Service Department				
2					Bonus Pay				
3									
4									
5	Last Name	Professional Development Hours	Review Date	Rating	Next Review	Salary	Bonus	Pay Bonus	Percentage of Total
6	Boady	5	1/7/2017	5	7/9/2017	$ 59,740.00	$2,987.00	FALSE	13.73%
7	Cane	9	4/1/2017	4	10/1/2017	$ 66,800.00	$0.00	FALSE	15.35%
8	Dugal	1	6/1/2017	4	12/1/2017	$ 33,400.00	$0.00	FALSE	7.67%
9	Hennely	7	4/1/2017	5	10/1/2017	$ 45,500.00	$2,275.00	TRUE	10.45%
10	Krones	10	3/1/2017	4	8/31/2017	$ 37,500.00	$0.00	FALSE	8.62%
11	Malone	4	5/15/2017	3	11/14/2017	$ 36,500.00	$0.00	FALSE	8.39%
12	Mercy	4	6/1/2017	5	12/1/2017	$ 57,500.00	$2,875.00	FALSE	13.21%
13	Stone	6	8/1/2017	3	1/31/2018	$ 28,600.00	$0.00	FALSE	6.57%
14	Storey	8	7/23/2017	5	1/22/2018	$ 69,700.00	$3,485.00	TRUE	16.01%
15	Totals					$ 435,240.00	$11,622.00		

Skills Review (continued)

8. Calculate payments with the PMT function.

FIGURE 5-26

a. Make the Loan sheet active.

b. In cell B9, determine the monthly payment using the loan information shown: Use the Function Arguments dialog box to enter the formula **=PMT(B5/12,B6,-B4)**.

c. In cell B10, enter a formula that multiplies the number of payments by the monthly payment.

d. In cell B11, enter the formula that subtracts the loan amount from the total payment amount, then compare your screen to **FIGURE 5-26**.

e. Enter your name in the worksheet footer, save the workbook, then submit your workbook to your instructor.

f. Close the workbook, then exit Excel.

	A	B	C	D	E	F
1	Service Department					
2	Equipment Loan Quote					
3						
4	Loan Amount	$ 125,000.00				
5	Interest Rate	4.75%				
6	Term In Months	48				
7						
8						
9	Monthly Payment:	$2,864.53				
10	Total Payments: $	137,497.31				
11	Total Interest: $	12,497.31				
12						
13						

Independent Challenge 1

As the accounting manager of Ace Floors, a carpet and flooring company, you are reviewing the accounts payable information for your advertising accounts and prioritizing the overdue invoices for your collections service. You will analyze the invoices and use logical functions to emphasize priority accounts.

a. Start Excel, open EX 5-4.xlsx from the location where you store your Data Files, then save it as **EX 5-Ace**.

b. Name the range B7:B13 **invoice_date**, and give the name a scope of the accounts payable worksheet.

c. Name the cell B4 **current_date**, and give the name a scope of the accounts payable worksheet.

d. Enter a formula using the named range invoice_date in cell E7 that calculates the invoice due date by adding 30 to the invoice date.

e. Copy the formula in cell E7 to the range E8:E13.

f. In cell F7, enter a formula using the named range invoice_date and the named cell current_date that calculates the invoice age by subtracting the invoice date from the current date.

g. Copy the formula in cell F7 to the range F8:F13.

h. In cell G7, enter an IF function that calculates the number of days an invoice is overdue, assuming that an invoice must be paid in 30 days. (*Hint*: The Logical_test should check to see if the age of the invoice is greater than 30, the Value_if_true should calculate the current date minus the invoice due date, and the Value_if_false should be 0.) Copy the IF function into the range G8:G13.

i. In cell H7, enter an AND function to prioritize the overdue invoices that are more than $1,000 for collection services. (*Hint*: The Logical1 condition should check to see if the number of days overdue is more than 0, and the Logical2 condition should check if the amount is more than 1,000.) Copy the AND function into the range H8:H13.

j. Use the Name Manager to name the range H7:H13 **Priority** and give the name a scope of the accounts payable worksheet. (*Hint*: In the Name Manager dialog box, click New to enter the range name.)

k. Enter your name in the worksheet footer, save the workbook, preview the worksheet, then submit the workbook to your instructor.

l. Close the workbook, then exit Excel.

Excel 2016

Independent Challenge 2

You are an auditor with a certified public accounting firm. Boston Paper, an online seller of office products, has contacted you to audit its first-quarter sales records. The management is considering expanding and needs its sales records audited to prepare the business plan. Specifically, they want to show what percent of annual sales each category represents. You will use a formula on a summary worksheet to summarize the sales for January, February, and March and to calculate the overall first-quarter percentage of the sales categories.

a. Start Excel, open EX 5-5.xlsx from the location where you store your Data Files, then save it as **EX 5-Paper**.

b. In cell B10 of the Jan, Feb, and Mar sheets, enter the formulas to calculate the sales totals for the month.

c. For each month, in cell C5, create a formula calculating the percent of sales for the Equipment sales category. Use a function to display "INCORRECT" if there is a mistake in the formula. Verify that the percent appears with two decimal places. Copy this formula as necessary to complete the % of sales for all sales categories on all sheets. If any cells display "INCORRECT", fix the formulas in those cells.

d. In column B of the Summary sheet, use formulas to total the sales categories for the Jan, Feb, and Mar worksheets.

e. Enter the formula to calculate the first quarter sales total in cell B10 using the sales totals on the Jan, Feb, and Mar worksheets.

f. Calculate the percent of each sales category on the Summary sheet. Use a function to display "MISCALCULATION" if there is a mistake in the formula. Copy this formula as necessary. If any cells display "MISCALCULATION", fix the formulas in those cells.

g. Enter your name in the Summary worksheet footer, save the workbook, preview the worksheet, then submit it to your instructor.

FIGURE 5-27

	A	B	C	D	E
1	equipment	paper	stationery	ink	toner
2	EQUIPMENT	PAPER	STATIONERY	INK	TONER
3					

h. On the Products sheet, separate the product list in cell A1 into separate columns of text data. (*Hint*: With cell A1 as the active cell, use the Text to Columns button in the Data Tools group of the Data tab. The products are delimited with commas.) Use the second row to display the products in uppercase, as shown in **FIGURE 5-27**. Widen the columns as necessary.

i. Enter your name in the Products worksheet footer, save the workbook, preview the worksheet, then submit the workbook to your instructor.

Independent Challenge 3

As the owner of GWW, an advertising firm, you are planning to expand your business. Because you will have to purchase additional equipment and hire a new part-time accounts manager, you decide to take out a $100,000 loan to finance your expansion expenses. You check three loan sources: the Small Business Administration (SBA), your local bank, and a consortium of investors. The SBA will lend you the money at 4.5% interest, but you have to pay it off in 4 years. The local bank offers you the loan at 5.75% interest over 5 years. The consortium offers you a 8.25% loan, and they require you to pay it back in 2 years. To analyze all three loan options, you decide to build a loan summary worksheet. Using the loan terms provided, build a worksheet summarizing your options.

a. Start Excel, open a new workbook, save it as **EX 5-Options**, then rename Sheet1 **Loan Summary**.

b. Using **FIGURE 5-28** as a guide, enter labels and worksheet data for the three loan sources in columns A through D. Use the formatting of your choice.

FIGURE 5-28

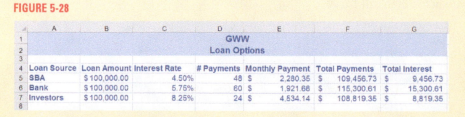

	A	B	C	D	E	F	G
1				GWW			
2				Loan Options			
3							
4	Loan Source	Loan Amount	Interest Rate	# Payments	Monthly Payment	Total Payments	Total Interest
5	SBA	$100,000.00	4.50%	48	$ 2,280.35	$ 109,456.73	$ 9,456.73
6	Bank	$100,000.00	5.75%	60	$ 1,921.68	$ 115,300.61	$ 15,300.61
7	Investors	$100,000.00	8.25%	24	$ 4,534.14	$ 108,819.35	$ 8,819.35
8							

Analyzing Data Using Formulas

Independent Challenge 3 (continued)

c. Enter the monthly payment formula for your first loan source (making sure to show the payment as a positive amount), copy the formula as appropriate, then name the range containing the monthly payment formulas **Monthly_Payment** with a scope of the workbook.

d. Name the cell range containing the number of payments **Number_Payments** with the scope of the workbook.

e. Enter the formula for total payments for your first loan source using the named ranges Monthly_Payment and Number_Payments, then copy the formula as necessary.

f. Name the cell range containing the formulas for Total payments **Total_Payments**. Name the cell range containing the loan amounts **Loan_Amount**. Each name should have the workbook as its scope.

g. Enter the formula for total interest for your first loan source using the named ranges Total_Payments and Loan_Amount, then copy the formula as necessary.

h. Format the worksheet using appropriate formatting, then enter your name in the worksheet footer.

i. Save the workbook, preview the worksheet and change it to landscape orientation on a single page, then submit the workbook to your instructor.

j. Close the workbook, then exit Excel.

Independent Challenge 4: Explore

As the physical therapist at NE Rehab, you are using a weekly worksheet to log and analyze the training for each of your patients. As part of this therapy, you record daily walking, biking, swimming, and weight training data and analyze it on a weekly basis.

a. Start Excel, open EX 5-6.xlsx from the location where you store your Data Files, then save it as **EX 5-Activity**.

b. Use SUMIF functions in cells G5:G8 to calculate the total minutes spent on each corresponding activity in cells F5:F8.

c. Use AVERAGEIF functions in cells H5:H8 to calculate the average number of minutes spent on each corresponding activity in cells F5:F8.

d. Use COUNTIF functions in cells I5:I8 to calculate the number of times each activity in cells F5:F8 was performed. (*Hint*: The Range of cells to count is $B$4:$B$15.)

e. Use the SUMIFS function in cell G9 to calculate the total number of minutes spent walking outdoors.

f. Use the AVERAGEIFS function in cell H9 to calculate the average number of minutes spent walking outdoors.

g. Use the COUNTIFS function in cell I9 to calculate the number of days spent walking outdoors. Compare your worksheet to **FIGURE 5-29** and adjust your cell formatting as needed to match the figure.

h. Enter your name in the worksheet footer, save the workbook, preview the worksheet, then submit it to your instructor.

i. Close the workbook, then exit Excel.

FIGURE 5-29

	A	B	C	D	E	F	G	H	I
1					NE Rehab				
2	Client Name:	Karl Logan							
3	Date	Activity	Minutes	Location			Week of January 2nd		
4						Activity	Total Minutes	Average Minutes	Number of Workouts
5	1/2/2017	Walk	40	Gym		Walk	172	43.00	4
6	1/2/2017	Swim	30	Aquatics Center		Swim	125	41.67	3
7	1/3/2017	Walk	50	Outdoors		Bike	80	26.67	3
8	1/3/2017	Bike	25	Outdoors		Weights	60	30.00	2
9	1/4/2017	Walk	42	Outdoors		Walk Outdoors	92	46	2
10	1/4/2017	Weights	30	Gym					
11	1/5/2017	Swim	50	Aquatics Center					
12	1/6/2017	Weights	30	Gym					
13	1/6/2017	Bike	30	Outdoors					
14	1/7/2017	Walk	40	Gym					
15	1/7/2017	Swim	45	Aquatics Center					
16	1/8/2017	Bike	25	Gym					

Analyzing Data Using Formulas

Visual Workshop

Open EX 5-7.xlsx from the location where you store your Data Files, then save it as **EX 5-Bonus**. Create the worksheet shown in FIGURE 5-30 using the data in columns B, C, and D along with the following criteria:

- The employee is eligible for a bonus if:
    - The employee has sales that exceed the sales quota.

      AND
    - The employee has a performance rating of seven or higher.
- If the employee is eligible for a bonus, the bonus amount is calculated as three percent of the sales amount. Otherwise the bonus amount is 0. (*Hint:* Use an AND formula to determine if a person is eligible for a bonus, and use an IF formula to check eligibility and to enter the bonus amount.) Enter your name in the worksheet footer, save the workbook, preview the worksheet, then submit the worksheet to your instructor.

FIGURE 5-30

	A	B	C	D	E	F	G
1	Fitness Unlimited						
2	Bonus Pay Summary						
3	Last Name	Quota	Sales	Performance Rating	Eligible	Bonus Amount	
4	Andrews	$145,000	$157,557	7	TRUE	$4,727	
5	Lee	$78,587	$91,588	3	FALSE	$0	
6	Atkinson	$113,984	$125,474	9	TRUE	$3,764	
7	Halley	$135,977	$187,255	5	FALSE	$0	
8	Pratt	$187,900	$151,228	8	FALSE	$0	
9	Balla	$128,744	$152,774	5	FALSE	$0	
10	Cruz	$129,855	$160,224	7	TRUE	$4,807	
11	Yanck	$94,000	$87,224	3	FALSE	$0	
12	Green	$79,500	$86,700	9	TRUE	$2,601	
13							

Managing Workbook Data

CASE ▶ Mary Watson, the vice president of sales and marketing at Reason2Go, asks for your help in analyzing yearly sales data from the U.S. branches. When the analysis is complete, she will distribute the workbook for branch managers to review.

Module Objectives

After completing this module, you will be able to:

- View and arrange worksheets
- Protect worksheets and workbooks
- Save custom views of a worksheet
- Add a worksheet background

- Prepare a workbook for distribution
- Insert hyperlinks
- Save a workbook for distribution
- Group worksheets

Files You Will Need

EX 6-1.xlsx	EX 6-8.jpg
EX 6-2.xlsx	EX 6-Classifications.xlsx
EX 6-3.jpg	EX 6-Equipment.xlsx
EX 6-4.xlsx	EX 6-Expenses.xlsx
EX 6-5.xlsx	EX 6-Information.xlsx
EX 6-6.xlsx	EX 6-LA Sales.xlsx
EX 6-7.xlsx	EX 6-Logo.jpg

View and Arrange Worksheets

Learning Outcomes
- Compare worksheet data by arranging worksheets
- View and hide instances of a workbook

As you work with workbooks made up of multiple worksheets, you might need to compare data in the various sheets. To do this, you can view each worksheet in its own workbook window, called an **instance**, and display the windows in an arrangement that makes it easy to compare data. When you work with worksheets in separate windows, you are working with different views of the same workbook; the data itself remains in one file. **CASE** *Mary asks you to compare the monthly store sales totals for the Los Angeles and New York branches. Because the sales totals are on different worksheets, you want to arrange the worksheets side by side in separate windows.*

STEPS

1. **Start Excel, open EX 6-1.xlsx from the location where you store your Data Files, then save it as EX 6-Store Sales**

2. **With the Los Angeles sheet active, click the View tab, then click the New Window button in the Window group**

   There are now two instances of the Store Sales workbook open. You can see them when you place the mouse pointer over the Excel icon on the task bar: EX 6-Store Sales.xlsx:1 and EX 6-Store Sales.xlsx:2. The EX 6-Store Sales.xlsx:2 window appears in front, indicating that it's the active instance.

3. **Click the New York sheet tab, click the View tab, click the Switch Windows button in the Window group, then click EX 6-Store Sales.xlsx:1**

   The EX 6-Store Sales.xlsx:1 instance moves to the front. The Los Angeles sheet is active in the EX 6-Store Sales.xlsx:1 workbook, and the New York sheet is active in the EX 6-Store Sales.xlsx:2 workbook.

4. **Click the Arrange All button in the Window group**

   The Arrange Windows dialog box, shown in **FIGURE 6-1**, lets you choose how to display the instances. You want to view the workbooks next to each other.

5. **Click the Vertical option button to select it, then click OK**

   The windows are arranged next to each other, as shown in **FIGURE 6-2**. The second instance of the workbook opens at a zoom of 100%, not the 120% zoom of the workbook. You can activate a workbook by clicking one of its cells. You can also view only one of the workbooks by hiding the one you do not wish to see.

6. **Scroll horizontally to view the data in the EX 6-Store Sales.xlsx:1 workbook, click anywhere in the EX 6-Store Sales.xlsx:2 workbook, scroll horizontally to view the data in it, then click the Hide Window button in the Window group**

   When you hide the second instance, only the EX 6-Store Sales.xlsx:1 workbook is visible.

7. **In the EX 6-Store Sales.xlsx:1 window, click the Unhide Window button in the Window group; click EX 6-Store Sales.xlsx:2 if necessary in the Unhide dialog box, then click OK**

   The EX 6-Store Sales.xlsx:2 instance appears.

8. **Click the Close Window button ⊠ in the title bar to close the EX 6-Store Sales.xlsx:2 instance, then maximize the Los Angeles worksheet in the EX 6-Store Sales.xlsx workbook**

   Closing the EX 6-Store Sales.xlsx:2 instance leaves only the first instance open. Its name in the title bar returns to EX 6-Store Sales.xlsx. When closing an instance of a workbook, it is important to use the close button and not the Close command on the File menu, which closes the workbook.

Managing Workbook Data

FIGURE 6-1: Arrange Windows dialog box

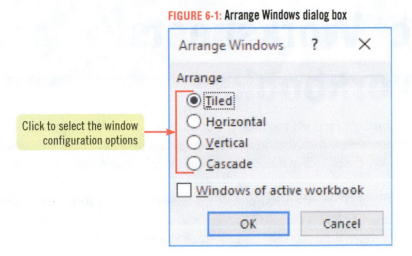

Click to select the window configuration options

FIGURE 6-2: Windows instances displayed vertically

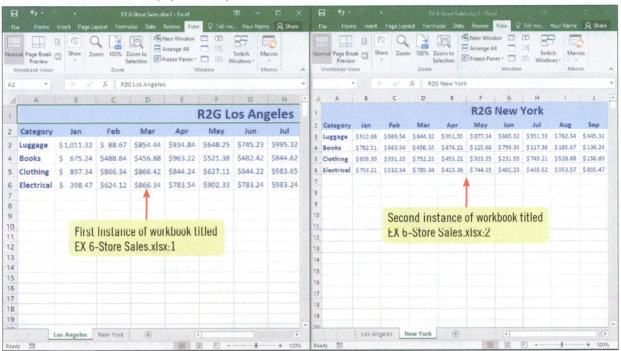

First instance of workbook titled EX 6-Store Sales.xlsx:1

Second instance of workbook titled EX 6-Store Sales.xlsx:2

Splitting the worksheet into multiple panes

Excel lets you split the worksheet area into vertical and/or horizontal panes, so that you can click inside any one pane and scroll to locate information in that pane while the other panes remain in place, as shown in **FIGURE 6-3**. To split a worksheet area into multiple panes, click a cell below and to the right of where you want the split to appear, click the View tab, then click the Split button in the Window group. You can also split a worksheet into only two panes by selecting the row or column below or to the right of where you want the split to appear, clicking the View tab, then clicking Split in the Window group. To remove a split, click the View tab, then click Split in the Window group.

FIGURE 6-3: Worksheet split into four panes

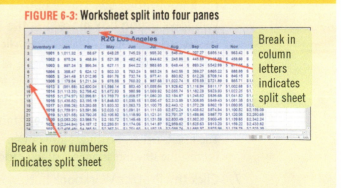

Break in column letters indicates split sheet

Break in row numbers indicates split sheet

Excel 2016

Protect Worksheets and Workbooks

To protect sensitive information, Excel lets you **lock** one or more cells so that other people can view the values and formulas in those cells, but not change it. Excel locks all cells by default, but this locking does not take effect until you activate the protection feature. A common worksheet protection strategy is to unlock cells in which data will be changed, sometimes called the **data entry area**, and to lock cells in which the data should not be changed. Then, when you protect the worksheet, the unlocked areas can still be changed. **CASE** ▸ *Because the Los Angeles sales figures for January through March have been finalized, Mary asks you to protect that worksheet area. That way, users cannot change the figures for those months.*

STEPS

1. **On the Los Angeles sheet, select the range E3:M6, click the Home tab, click the Format button in the Cells group, click Format Cells, then in the Format Cells dialog box click the Protection tab**

   The Locked check box in the Protection tab is already checked, as shown in **FIGURE 6-4**. All the cells in a new workbook start out locked. The protection feature is inactive by default.

2. **Click the Locked check box to deselect it, click OK, click the Review tab, then click the Protect Sheet button in the Changes group**

   The Protect Sheet dialog box opens, as shown in **FIGURE 6-5**. The default options protect the worksheet while allowing users to select locked or unlocked cells only. You choose not to use a password.

3. **Verify that Protect worksheet and contents of locked cells is checked, that the password text box is blank, and that Select locked cells and Select unlocked cells are checked, then click OK**

   You are ready to test the new worksheet protection.

4. **Click cell B3, type 1 to confirm that locked cells cannot be changed, click OK, click cell F3, type 1, notice that Excel lets you begin the entry, press [Esc] to cancel the entry, then save your work**

   When you try to change a locked cell on a protected worksheet, a dialog box, shown in **FIGURE 6-6**, reminds you of the protected cell's status and provides instructions to unprotect the worksheet. These cells are in **Read-only format**, which means they can be viewed in the worksheet but not changed. Because you unlocked the cells in columns E through M before you protected the worksheet, these cells are not in read-only format and you can change these cells. You want to add more protection by protecting the workbook from changes to the workbook's structure, but decide not to require a password.

5. **Click the Protect Workbook button in the Changes group, in the Protect Structure and Windows dialog box make sure the Structure check box is selected, verify that the password text box is blank, then click OK**

   The Protect Workbook button is a toggle, which means it's like an on/off switch. When it is highlighted, the workbook is protected. Clicking it again removes the highlighting indicating the protection is removed from the workbook. You are ready to test the new workbook protection.

6. **Right-click the Los Angeles sheet tab**

   The Insert, Delete, Rename, Move or Copy, Tab Color, Hide, and Unhide menu options are not available because the structure is protected. You decide to remove the workbook and worksheet protections.

7. **Click the Protect Workbook button in the Changes group to turn off the protection, click the Unprotect Sheet button, then save your changes**

Managing Workbook Data

FIGURE 6-4: Protection tab in Format Cells dialog box

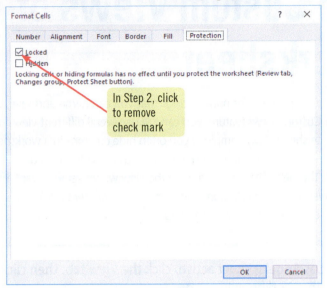

FIGURE 6-5: Protect Sheet dialog box

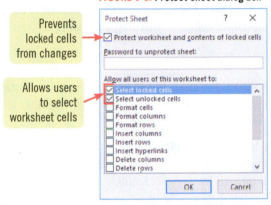

FIGURE 6-6: Reminder of protected worksheet status

Freezing rows and columns

As the rows and columns of a worksheet fill up with data, you might want to Freeze panes to hold headers in place so you can see them as you scroll through the worksheet. Freezing panes is similar to splitting panes except that the panes do not move, so you can keep column or row labels in view as you scroll. **Panes** are the columns and rows that **freeze**, or remain in place, while you scroll through your worksheet. To freeze panes, click the first cell in the area you want to scroll, click the View tab, click the Freeze Panes button in the Window group, then click Freeze Panes. Excel freezes the columns to the left and the rows above the selected cell, as shown in **FIGURE 6-7**. You can also select Freeze Top Row or Freeze First Column to freeze the top row or left worksheet column. To unfreeze panes, click the View tab, click Freeze panes, then click Unfreeze Panes.

FIGURE 6-7: Worksheet with top row and left column frozen

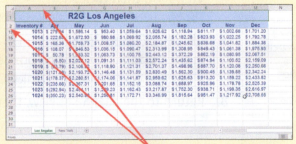

Break in column letters and row numbers indicates first column and first two rows are frozen

Managing Workbook Data

Save Custom Views of a Worksheet

Learning Outcomes
- Create different views of worksheet data using custom views
- Display different views of worksheet data using custom views

A **view** is a set of display and/or print settings that you can name and save, then access at a later time. By using the Excel Custom Views feature, you can create several different views of a worksheet without having to create separate sheets. For example, if you often hide columns in a worksheet, you can create two views, one that displays all of the columns and another with the columns hidden. You set the worksheet display first, then name the view. Then you can open the view whenever you want. **CASE** ▶ *Because Mary wants to generate a sales report from the final sales data for January through March, she asks you to create a custom view that shows only the first-quarter sales data.*

STEPS

1. **With the Los Angeles sheet active, click the** View tab, **then click the** Custom Views button **in the Workbook Views group**

   The Custom Views dialog box opens. Any previously defined views for the active worksheet appear in the Views box. No views are defined for the Los Angeles worksheet. You decide to add a named view for the current view, which shows all the worksheet columns. That way, you can easily return to it from any other views you create.

   QUICK TIP
   To delete views from the active worksheet, select the view in the Custom Views dialog box, then click Delete.

2. **Click** Add

   The Add View dialog box opens, as shown in **FIGURE 6-8**. Here, you enter a name for the view and decide whether to include print settings and/or hidden rows, columns, and filter settings. You want to include these options, which are already selected.

3. **In the Name box, type** Year Sales, **then click** OK

   You have created a view called Year Sales that shows all the worksheet columns. You want to set up another view that will hide the April through December columns.

4. **Select columns** E through M, **right-click the selected area, then click** Hide **on the shortcut menu**

   You are ready to create a custom view of the January through March sales data.

5. **Click cell** A1, **click the** Custom Views button **in the Workbook Views group, click** Add, **in the Name box type** First Quarter, **then click** OK

   You are ready to test the two custom views.

   TROUBLE
   If you receive the message "Some view settings could not be applied", turn off worksheet protection by clicking the Unprotect Sheet button in the Changes group of the Review tab.

6. **Click the** Custom Views button **in the Workbook Views group, click** Year Sales **in the Views list, then click** Show

   The Year Sales custom view displays all of the months' sales data.

7. **Click the** Custom Views button **in the Workbook Views group, then with** First Quarter **in the Custom Views dialog box selected, click** Show

   Only the January through March sales figures appear on the screen, as shown in **FIGURE 6-9**.

8. **Return to the** Year Sales view, **then save your work**

FIGURE 6-8: Add View dialog box

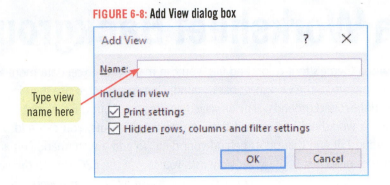

Type view name here

FIGURE 6-9: First Quarter view

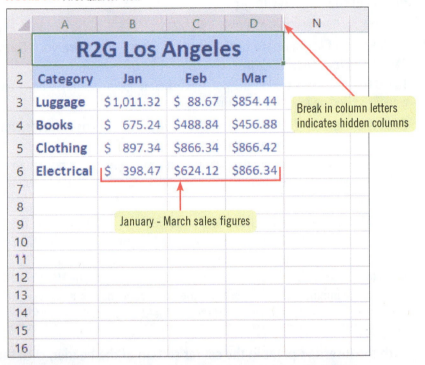

Break in column letters indicates hidden columns

January - March sales figures

Using Page Break Preview

The vertical and horizontal dashed lines in the Normal view of worksheets represent page breaks. Excel automatically inserts a page break when your worksheet data doesn't fit on one page. These page breaks are **dynamic**, which means they adjust automatically when you insert or delete rows and columns and when you change column widths or row heights. Everything to the left of the first vertical dashed line and above the first horizontal dashed line is printed on the first page. You can manually add or remove page breaks by clicking the Page Layout tab, clicking the Breaks button in the Page Setup group, then clicking the appropriate command. You can also view and change page breaks manually by clicking the View tab, then clicking the Page Break Preview button in the Workbook Views group, or by clicking the Page Break Preview button on the status bar. You can drag the blue page break lines to the desired location. Some cells may temporarily display ##### while you are in Page Break Preview. If you drag a page break to the right to include more data on a page, Excel shrinks the type to fit the data on that page. To exit Page Break Preview, click the Normal button in the Workbook Views group.

Add a Worksheet Background

In addition to using a theme's font colors and fills, you can make your Excel data more attractive on the screen by adding a picture to the worksheet background. Companies often use their logo as a worksheet background. A worksheet background will be displayed on the screen but will not print with the worksheet. If you want to add a worksheet background that appears on printouts, you can add a **watermark**, a translucent background design that prints behind your data. To add a watermark, you add the image to the worksheet header or footer. **CASE** ▸ *Mary asks you to add the R2G logo to the background of the Los Angeles worksheet. You want to explore the difference between adding it as a worksheet background and adding it as a watermark.*

STEPS

1. **With the Los Angeles sheet active, click the Page Layout tab, then click the Background button in the Page Setup group**

   The Insert Pictures dialog box opens.

2. **Click From a file, navigate to the location where you store your Data Files, click EX 6-Logo.jpg, then click Insert**

   The R2G logo appears behind the worksheet data. It appears multiple times on your screen because the graphic is **tiled**, or repeated, to fill the background.

3. **Click the File tab, click Print, view the preview of the Los Angeles worksheet, then click the Back button ⊙ to return to the worksheet**

   Because the logo is a background image, it will not print with the worksheet, so it is not visible in the Print preview. You want the logo to print with the worksheet, so you decide to remove the background and add the logo to the worksheet header.

4. **On the Page Layout tab, click the Delete Background button in the Page Setup group, click the Insert tab, then click the Header & Footer button in the Text group**

   The Header & Footer Tools Design tab appears, as shown in **FIGURE 6-10**. You can use the buttons in this group to add preformatted headers and footers to a worksheet. The Header & Footer Elements buttons let you add page numbers, the date, the time, the file location, names, and pictures to the header or footer. The Navigation group buttons move the insertion point from the header to the footer and back. You want to add a picture to the header.

5. **With the insertion point in the center section of the header, click the Picture button in the Header & Footer Elements group, click Browse, navigate to where you store your Data Files, click EX 6-Logo.jpg, then click Insert**

   A code representing a picture, "&[Picture]", appears in the center of the header.

6. **Click cell A1, click the Page Layout tab, click the Width list arrow in the Scale to Fit group, click 1 page, click the Height list arrow in the Scale to Fit group, click 1 page, then preview the worksheet**

   Your worksheet should look like **FIGURE 6-11**, with all the data fitting on one page.

7. **Return to the worksheet, switch to Normal view, click the Home tab, then save the workbook**

FIGURE 6-10: Header & Footer Tools Design tab

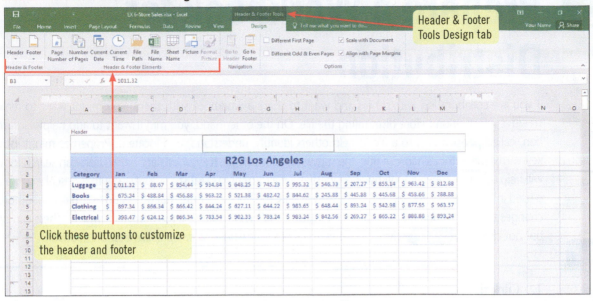

FIGURE 6-11: Preview of Los Angeles worksheet with logo in the background

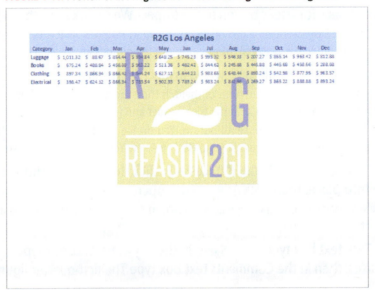

Working with screenshots in Excel

You can paste an image of an open file, called a **screenshot**, into an Excel workbook or another Office document. The pasted screenshot is an image that you can move, copy, or edit. To do so, click the Insert tab, click the Take a Screenshot button in the Illustrations group to see a gallery of other available open windows, then click one of the windows in the gallery. This pastes a screenshot of the window you clicked into the current Excel document. You can also click the Screen Clipping button in the gallery to select and paste an area from an open window. Once you have created a screenshot and positioned it in your worksheet, you can modify it using tools on the Picture Tools Format tab. You can change the overall visual style of the image by clicking the More button in the Picture Styles group, then clicking a style. In the Picture Styles group you can also use the Picture Effects button to apply a visual effect to the image, the Picture Border button to enhance the border surrounding the image, and the Picture Layout button to convert the image to a SmartArt Graphic. The Picture Tools tab also has other tools to correct images. For example, you can sharpen and soften an image and make corrections for brightness and contrast by clicking the Corrections button in the Adjust group. Clicking a choice in the Sharpen/Soften section allows you to change the visual acuity of the image and choosing an option in the Brightness/Contrast section adjusts the lightness of an image.

Prepare a Workbook for Distribution

If you are collaborating with others and want to share a workbook with them, you might want to remove sensitive information before distributing the file. On the other hand, you might want to add helpful information, called **properties**, to a file to help others identify, understand, and locate it. Properties might include keywords, the author's name, a title, the status, and comments. **Keywords** are terms users can search for that will help them locate your workbook. Properties are a form of **metadata**, information that describes data and is used in Microsoft Windows document searches. In addition, to ensure that others do not make unauthorized changes to your workbook, you can mark a file as final. This makes it a read-only file, which others can open but not change. **CASE** *Mary wants you to protect the workbook and prepare it for distribution.*

STEPS

1. **Click the File tab**

   Backstage view opens, and displays the Info place. It shows you information about your file. It also includes tools you can use to check for security issues.

   > **TROUBLE**
   > If asked to save your file, click Yes.

2. **Click the Check for Issues button in the Inspect Workbook area, then click Inspect Document**

   The Document Inspector dialog box opens, as shown in **FIGURE 6-12**. It lists items from which you can have Excel evaluate hidden or personal information. All the options are selected by default.

3. **Click Inspect, then scroll to view the inspection results**

   Areas with data have a red "**!**" in front of them. If there are hidden names they will be flagged. Headers and footers is flagged. You want to keep the file's header and footer. If personal information is flagged, you can remove it by clicking the Remove All button. You decide to add keywords to help the sales managers find the worksheet. The search words "Los Angeles" or "New York" would be good keywords for this workbook.

   > **QUICK TIP**
   > You can view and edit a file's summary information by clicking the File tab and reviewing the information on the right side of the info place. You can also edit some of the information in this area.

4. **Click Close, click the File tab if necessary, click the Properties list arrow on the right side of the Info place, then click Advanced Properties**

   The file's properties dialog box opens, as shown in **FIGURE 6-13**. You decide to add a title, keywords, and comments.

5. **In the Title text box type Store Sales, in the Keywords text box type Los Angeles New York store sales, then in the Comments text box type The first-quarter figures are final., then click OK**

   You are ready to mark the workbook as final.

6. **Click the Protect Workbook button in the Info place, click Mark as Final, click OK, then click OK again**

   "[Read-Only]" appears in the title bar indicating the workbook is saved as a read-only file. A yellow bar also appears below the tabs indicating the workbook is marked as final. The yellow bar also has an Edit Anyway button.

7. **Click the Home tab, click cell B3, type 1 to confirm that the cell cannot be changed, click the Edit Anyway button above the formula bar, then save the workbook**

   Marking a workbook as final is not a strong form of workbook protection because a workbook recipient can remove this Final status. By clicking Edit Anyway, you remove the read-only status, which makes the workbook editable again.

FIGURE 6-12: Document Inspector Properties dialog box

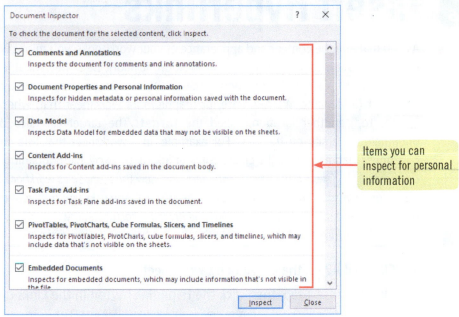

Items you can inspect for personal information

FIGURE 6-13: Document Properties panel

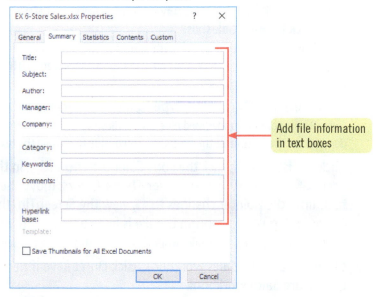

Add file information in text boxes

Sharing a workbook using OneDrive

Once you set up a Windows Live account you can save your Excel files to the cloud using OneDrive. This allows you to access your Excel files from any computer and share Excel files with others. When saving an Excel file to the cloud, click the File tab, click Save As, then click OneDrive, which is the default location. After you save an Excel file to your OneDrive, you can share it by

clicking the File tab, clicking Share, clicking Share with People, entering the email addresses of the people you wish to invite to share the file in the Invite people text box, and then clicking Share. An email with a link to the Excel file on your OneDrive will be sent to the addresses you entered. The recipients can view or edit the file using the Excel web app.

Insert Hyperlinks

As you manage the content and appearance of your workbooks, you might want the workbook user to view information that exists in another location. It might be nonessential information or data that is too detailed to place in the workbook itself. In these cases, you can create a hyperlink. A **hyperlink** is an object (a filename, word, phrase, or graphic) in a worksheet that, when you click it, displays, or "jumps to," another location, called the **target**. The target can also be a worksheet, another document, or a site on the web. For example, in a worksheet that lists customer invoices, at each customer's name, you might create a hyperlink to an Excel file containing payment terms for each customer. **CASE** *Mary wants managers who view the Store Sales workbook to be able to view the item totals for each sales category in the Los Angeles sheet. She asks you to create a hyperlink at the Category heading so that users can click it to view the items for each category.*

STEPS

1. **Click cell A2 on the Los Angeles worksheet**

2. **Click the Insert tab, then click the Hyperlink button in the Links group**

   The Insert Hyperlink dialog box opens, as shown in **FIGURE 6-14**. The icons under "Link to" on the left side of the dialog box let you select the type of location to where you want the link to jump: an existing file or webpage, a place in the same document, a new document, or an e-mail address. Because you want the link to display an already existing document, the selected first icon, Existing File or webpage, is correct, so you won't have to change it.

3. **Click the Look in list arrow, navigate to where you store your Data Files if necessary, then click EX 6-LA Sales.xlsx**

   The filename you selected and its path appear in the Address text box. This is the document users will see when they click the hyperlink. You can also specify the ScreenTip that users see when they hold the pointer over the hyperlink.

4. **Click the ScreenTip button, type Items in each category, click OK, then click OK again**

   Cell A2 now contains underlined blue text, indicating that it is a hyperlink. The default color of a hyperlink depends on the worksheet theme colors. You decide to change the text color of the hyperlink.

5. **Click the Home tab, click the Font Color list arrow** ![A] **in the Font group, click the Green, Accent 6, Darker 50% color under Theme Colors, move the pointer over the Category text, until the pointer changes to 🖑, view the ScreenTip, then click once; if a dialog box opens asking you to confirm the file is from a trustworthy source, click OK**

   After you click, the EX 6-LA Sales workbook opens, displaying the Sales sheet, as shown in **FIGURE 6-15**.

6. **Close the EX 6-LA Sales workbook, click Don't Save if necessary, then save the EX 6-Store Sales workbook**

Working with Headers and Footers

You may want to add a different header or footer to the first page of your worksheet. You can do this by clicking the Insert tab on the Ribbon, clicking the Header & Footer button in the Text group, then clicking the Different First Page check box in the Options group of the Header & Footer Tools Design tab to select it. You can also have different headers or footers on odd and even pages of your worksheet by clicking the Different Odd & Even Pages check box to select it. In the Options group of the Header & Footer Tools Design tab, you can also adjust the header and footer size relative to the rest of the document by using the Scale with Document check box. You can use the Align with Page Margins check box to place the header or footer at the margins of the worksheet. You can also add the name of the worksheet by clicking the Sheet Name button in the Header and Footer Elements group of the Header & Footer Tools Design tab.

Managing Workbook Data

FIGURE 6-14: Insert Hyperlink dialog box

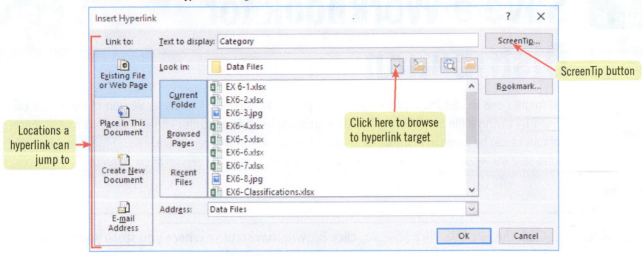

FIGURE 6-15: Target document

	A	B	C	D
1	R2G LA			
2	Store Sales			
3	Item	Total Sales	Category	
4	Maps	$ 1,500.36	Books	
5	Language Aids	$ 4,234.31	Books	
6	Guide Books	$ 3,625.14	Books	
7	Computer Case	$ 1,855.65	Luggage	
8	Backpack	$ 1,836.91	Luggage	
9	Chargers	$ 1,099.15	Electrical	
10	Travel Socks	$ 1,108.16	Clothing	
11	Men's Sandals	$ 1,103.14	Clothing	
12	Women's Sandals	$ 1,954.19	Clothing	
13	Hats	$ 975.44	Clothing	
14	Men's T-Shirts	$ 3,111.76	Clothing	
15	Women's T-Shirts	$ 1,108.41	Clothing	
16	Converter	$ 2,578.31	Electrical	
17				

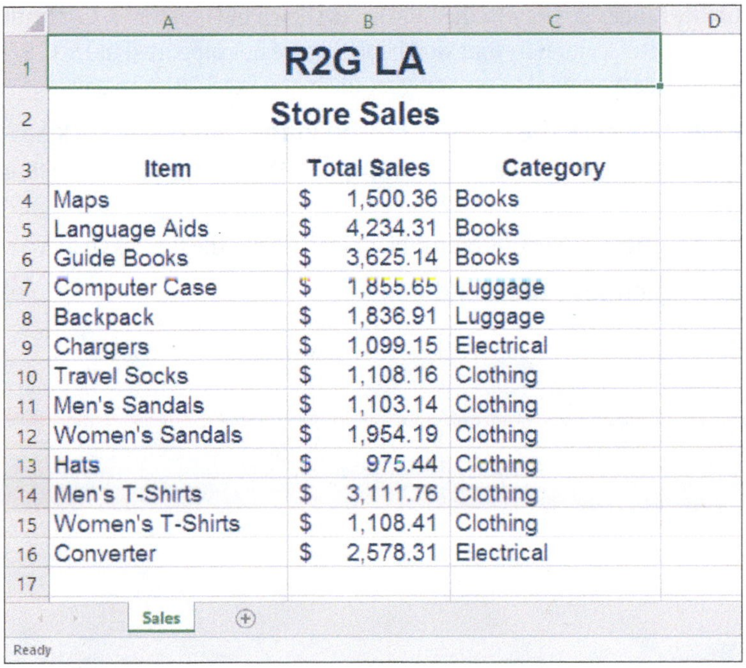

Using research tools

You can access resources online and locally on your computer using the Insights task pane. The research results are based on selected data on your Excel worksheet. To open the Insights task pane, click the Review tab, then click the Smart Lookup button in the Insights group. The Insights pane shows results for your selected data in the Explore and Define areas. The Explore area displays Wikipedia information, images, maps, and web searches. The Define pane displays definitions and pronunciation help.

Save a Workbook for Distribution

Learning Outcomes
- Save a workbook in earlier formats of Excel
- Convert an Excel 97-2003 workbook to the 2016 format

You might need to distribute your Excel files to people working with an earlier version of Excel. You can do this by saving a file as an Excel 97-2003 workbook. In addition to this earlier workbook format, Excel workbooks can be saved in many other different formats as summarized in **TABLE 6-1**. **CASE** *Mary asks you to save the workbook in a format that managers running an earlier version of Excel can use.*

STEPS

QUICK TIP
You can also export an Excel file into another format by clicking the File tab, clicking Export, clicking Change File Type, then clicking a file type.

1. **Click the File tab, click Save As, click Browse, navigate to where you store your Data Files, click the Save as type list arrow in the Save As dialog box, click Excel 97-2003 Workbook (*.xls), then click Save**

   The Compatibility Checker dialog box opens as shown in **FIGURE 6-16**. It alerts you to the features that will be lost or converted by saving in the earlier format. Some Excel 2016 features are not available in earlier versions of Excel.

2. **Click Continue, close the workbook, then reopen the EX 6-Store Sales.xls workbook**

   "[Compatibility Mode]" appears in the title bar, as shown in **FIGURE 6-17**. Compatibility mode prevents you from including Excel features in your workbook that are not supported in Excel 97-2003 workbooks. To exit compatibility mode, you need to convert your file to the Excel 2016 format.

3. **Click the File tab, click the Convert button in the Info place, click Save, click Yes if you are asked if you want to replace the existing file, then click Yes to close and reopen the workbook**

   The title bar no longer displays "[Compatibility Mode]" and the file has changed to .xlsx format.

4. **Click cell A1, then save the workbook**

Saving a workbook in other formats

Excel data can be shared by **publishing**, the data on a network or on the web so that others can access it using a web browser. To publish an Excel document to an **intranet** (a company's internal website) or the web, you can save it in an HTML format. **HTML (Hypertext Markup Language)** is the coding format used for all web documents. You can also save your Excel file as a **single-file web page** that integrates all of the worksheets and graphical elements from the workbook into a single file. This file format is called MHTML, also known as MHT.

If you want to ensure that your workbook is displayed the same way on different computer platforms and screen settings, you can publish it in PDF format by clicking File, clicking Export, then clicking the Create PDF/XPS button. You can also save a workbook as a pdf file using the Save As dialog box and selecting PDF (*.pdf) in the Save as type list.

FIGURE 6-16: Compatibility Checker dialog box

FIGURE 6-17: Workbook in compatibility mode

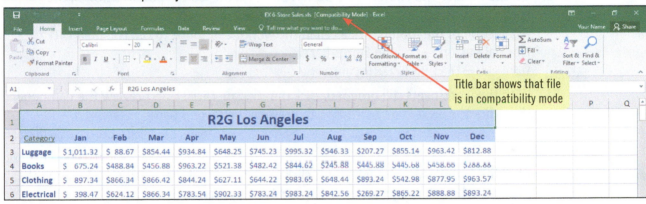

TABLE 6-1: Workbook formats

type of file	file extension(s)	used for
Macro-enabled workbook	.xlsm	Files that contain macros
Excel 97 – 2003 workbook	.xls	Working with people using older versions of Excel
Single file webpage	.mht, .mhtml	Websites with multiple pages and graphics
webpage	.htm, .html	Simple single-page websites
Excel template	.xltx	Excel files that will be reused with small changes
Excel macro-enabled template	.xltm	Excel files that will be used again and contain macros
PDF (Portable document format)	.pdf	Files with formatting that needs to be preserved
XML paper specification	.xps	Files with formatting that needs to be preserved and files that need to be shared
OpenDocument spreadsheet	.ods	Files created with OpenOffice

Group Worksheets

Learning Outcomes
• Group worksheets
• Edit grouped worksheets
• Add custom margins to worksheets

You can group worksheets to work on them as a collection. When you enter data into one grouped worksheet, that data is also automatically entered into all of the worksheets in the group. This is useful for data that is common to every sheet of a workbook, such as headers and footers, or for column headings that will apply to all monthly worksheets in a yearly summary. Grouping worksheets can also be used to print multiple worksheets at one time. **CASE** Mary asks you to add the text "R2G" to the footer of both the Los Angeles and New York worksheets. You will also add half-inch margins to the top of both worksheets.

STEPS

1. **With the Los Angeles sheet active, press and hold [Shift], click the New York sheet, then release [Shift]**

   Both sheet tabs are selected, and the title bar now contains "[Group]", indicating that the worksheets are grouped together. Now any changes you make to the Los Angeles sheet will also be made to the New York sheet.

2. **Click the Insert tab, then click the Header & Footer button in the Text group**

3. **On the Header and Footer Tools Design tab, click the Go to Footer button in the Navigation group, type R2G in the center section of the footer, type your name in the left section of the footer, click a cell in the worksheet, move to cell A1, then click the Normal button ▦ on the Status Bar**

   You decide to check the footers in Print Preview.

4. **With the worksheets still grouped, click the File tab, click Print, preview the first page, then click the Next Page button ▶ to preview the second page**

   Because the worksheets are grouped, both worksheets are ready to print and both pages contain the footer with "R2G" and your name. The worksheets would look better with a smaller top margin.

5. **Click the Normal Margins list arrow, click Custom Margins, in the Top text box on the Margins tab of the Page Setup dialog box type .5, then click OK**

   You decide to ungroup the worksheets.

6. **Return to the worksheet, right-click the Los Angeles worksheet sheet tab, then click Ungroup Sheets**

7. **Save and close the workbook, exit Excel, then submit the workbook to your instructor**

   The completed worksheets are shown in **FIGURES 6-18** and **6-19**.

FIGURE 6-18: Los Angeles worksheet

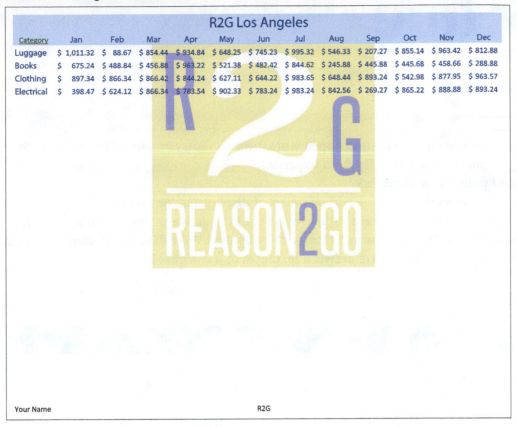

R2G Los Angeles

Category	Jan	Feb	Mar	Apr	May	Jun	Jul	Aug	Sep	Oct	Nov	Dec
Luggage	$ 1,011.32	$ 88.67	$ 854.44	$ 934.84	$ 648.25	$ 745.23	$ 995.32	$ 546.33	$ 207.27	$ 855.14	$ 963.42	$ 812.88
Books	$ 675.24	$ 488.84	$ 456.88	$ 963.22	$ 521.38	$ 482.42	$ 844.62	$ 245.88	$ 445.88	$ 445.68	$ 458.66	$ 288.88
Clothing	$ 897.34	$ 866.34	$ 866.42	$ 844.24	$ 627.11	$ 644.22	$ 983.65	$ 648.44	$ 893.24	$ 542.98	$ 877.95	$ 963.57
Electrical	$ 398.47	$ 624.12	$ 866.34	$ 783.54	$ 902.33	$ 783.24	$ 983.24	$ 842.56	$ 269.27	$ 865.22	$ 888.88	$ 893.24

Your Name   R2G

FIGURE 6-19: New York worksheet

R2G New York

Category	Jan	Feb	Mar	Apr	May	Jun	Jul	Aug	Sep	Oct	Nov	Dec
Luggage	$ 912.68	$ 869.54	$ 844.32	$ 951.55	$ 877.34	$ 865.32	$ 951.53	$ 782.54	$ 445.32	$ 951.55	$ 963.54	$ 511.37
Books	$ 782.51	$ 863.54	$ 458.35	$ 874.21	$ 125.68	$ 799.39	$ 117.36	$ 185.67	$ 136.24	$ 536.54	$ 959.77	$ 999.99
Clothing	$ 899.30	$ 951.35	$ 752.21	$ 453.21	$ 933.35	$ 231.55	$ 745.21	$ 526.68	$ 158.69	$ 752.36	$ 422.31	$ 231.58
Electrical	$ 793.21	$ 532.54	$ 785.34	$ 423.36	$ 744.35	$ 401.23	$ 455.62	$ 953.57	$ 855.47	$ 975.11	$ 999.99	$ 963.24

Your Name   R2G

Practice

Concepts Review

1. Which element do you click to organize open worksheet windows in a specific configuration?
2. Which element points to a ScreenTip for a hyperlink?
3. Which element points to a hyperlink?
4. Which element do you click to name and save a set of display and/or print settings?
5. Which element do you click to open another instance of the active worksheet in a separate window?
6. Which element do you click to view and change the way worksheet data is distributed on printed pages?
7. Which element do you click to move between instances of a workbook?

FIGURE 6-20

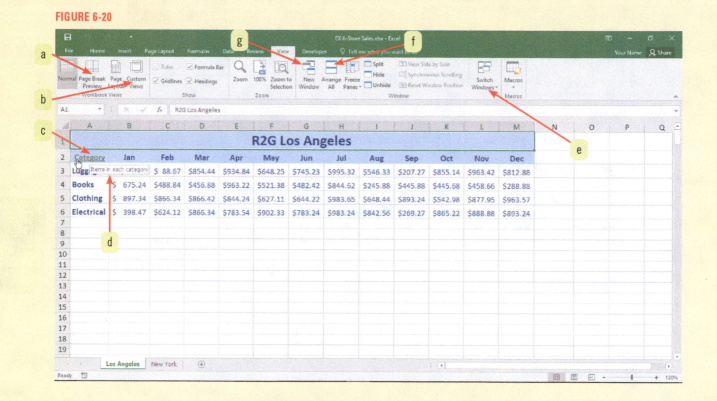

Match each term with the statement that best describes it.

8. Data entry area
9. Watermark
10. Hyperlink
11. Dynamic page breaks
12. HTML

a. Webpage format
b. Portion of a worksheet that can be changed
c. Translucent background design on a printed worksheet
d. An object that when clicked displays another worksheet or a webpage
e. Adjust automatically when rows and columns are inserted or deleted

Select the best answer from the list of choices.

13. You can group contiguous worksheets by clicking the first sheet, and then pressing and holding _____ while clicking the last sheet tab that you want to group.
    - **a.** [Alt]
    - **b.** [Spacebar]
    - **c.** [Shift]
    - **d.** [F6]

14. A _____ is a set of display and/or print settings that you can save and access later.
    - **a.** View
    - **b.** Property
    - **c.** Data area
    - **d.** Keyword

15. Which of the following formats means that users can view but not change data in a workbook?
    - **a.** Macro
    - **b.** Read-only
    - **c.** Webpage
    - **d.** Template

Skills Review

1. **View and arrange worksheets.**
   a. Start Excel, open EX 6-2.xlsx from the location where you store your Data Files, then save it as **EX 6-Tea**.
   b. Open another instance of the workbook in a new window.
   c. Activate the East sheet in the EX 6-Tea.xlsx:1 workbook. Activate the West sheet in the EX 6-Tea.xlsx:2 workbook.
   d. View the EX 6-Tea.xlsx:1 and EX 6-Tea.xlsx:2 workbooks tiled horizontally. View the workbooks in a vertical arrangement.
   e. Hide the EX 6-Tea.xlsx:2 instance, then unhide the instance. Close the EX 6-Tea.xlsx:2 instance, and maximize the EX 6-Tea.xlsx workbook.

2. **Protect worksheets and workbooks.**
   a. On the East sheet, unlock the expense data in the range B12:F19.
   b. Protect the sheet without using a password.
   c. To make sure the other cells are locked, attempt to make an entry in cell D4 and verify that you receive an error message.
   d. Change the first-quarter mortgage expense in cell B12 to 6000.
   e. Protect the workbook's structure without applying a password. Right-click the East and West sheet tabs to verify that you cannot insert, delete, rename, move, copy, hide, or unhide the sheets, or change their tab color.
   f. Unprotect the workbook. Unprotect the East worksheet.
   g. Save the workbook.

3. **Save custom views of a worksheet.**
   a. Using the East sheet, create a custom view of the entire worksheet called **Entire East Budget**.
   b. Hide rows 10 through 23, then create a new view called **Income** showing only the income data.
   c. Use the Custom Views dialog box to display all of the data on the East worksheet.
   d. Use the Custom Views dialog box to display only the income data on the East worksheet.
   e. Use the Custom Views dialog box to return to the Entire East Budget view.
   f. Save the workbook.

4. **Add a worksheet background.**
   a. Use EX 6-3.jpg as a worksheet background for the East sheet, then delete it.
   b. Add EX 6-3.jpg to the East header, then preview the sheet to verify that the background will print.
   c. Add your name to the center section of the East worksheet footer, then save the workbook.

Skills Review (continued)

5. Prepare a workbook for distribution.

  a. Inspect the workbook and remove any properties, personal data, and header and footer information.

  b. Use the file's Properties dialog box to add a title of **Quarterly Budget**, the keyword **campus**, and the category **tea**.

  c. Mark the workbook as final and verify that "[Read-Only]" appears in the title bar.

  d. Remove the final status, then save the workbook.

6. Insert hyperlinks.

  a. On the East worksheet, make cell A11 a hyperlink to the file **EX 6-Expenses.xlsx** in your Data Files folder.

  b. Test the link and verify that Sheet1 of the target file displays expense details.

  c. Return to the EX 6-Tea.xlsx workbook, edit the hyperlink in cell A11 to add a ScreenTip that reads **Expense Details**, then verify that the ScreenTip appears.

  d. On the West worksheet, enter the text **East Campus Budget** in cell A25.

  e. Make the text in cell A25 a hyperlink to cell A1 in the East worksheet. (*Hint*: Use the Place in This Document button and note the cell reference in the Type the cell reference text box.)

  f. Test the hyperlink. Remove the hyperlink in cell A25 of the West worksheet, remove the text in the cell, then save the workbook.

7. Save a workbook for distribution.

  a. Save the EX 6-Tea.xlsx workbook as an Excel 97-2003 workbook, and review the results of the Compatibility Checker.

  b. Close the EX 6-Tea.xls file, then reopen EX 6-Tea.xls in Compatibility Mode.

  c. Convert the .xls file to .xlsx format, resaving the file with the same name and replacing the previously saved file. This requires the workbook to be closed and reopened.

  d. Save the workbook.

8. Grouping worksheets.

  a. Group the East and West worksheet.

  b. Add your name to the center footer section of the worksheets. Add 1.25" custom margins to the top of both worksheets.

  c. Preview both sheets, verify the tea cup will not print (it was removed when the file was inspected), then ungroup the sheets.

  d. Save the workbook, comparing your worksheets to **FIGURE 6-21**.

  e. Submit EX 6-Tea.xlsx and EX 6-Expenses (the linked file) to your instructor, close all open files, then exit Excel.

FIGURE 6-21

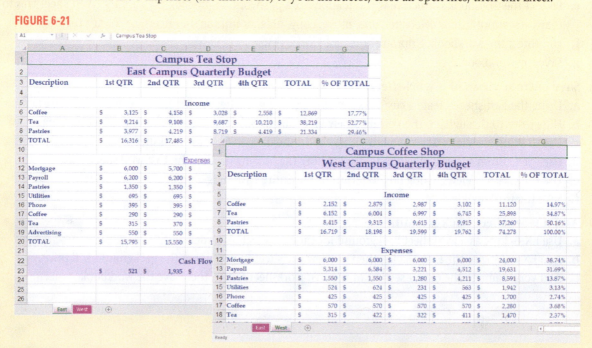

Independent Challenge 1

You manage American Pools, a pool supplier for the Florida home market. You are organizing your first-quarter sales in an Excel worksheet. Because the sheet for the month of January includes the same type of information you need for February and March, you decide to enter the headings for all of the first-quarter months at the same time. You use a separate worksheet for each month and create data for 3 months.

a. Start Excel, then save a new workbook as **EX 6-Pools.xlsx** in the location where you store your Data Files.

b. Name the first sheet **January**, name the second sheet **February**, and name the third sheet **March**.

c. Group the worksheets.

d. With the worksheets grouped, add the title **American Pools** centered across cells A1 and B1. Enter the labels **Type** in cell A2 and **Sales** in cell B2. Enter pool type labels in column A beginning in cell A3 and ending in cell A9. Use the following pool types in the range A3:A9: **Prefab**, **Masonry**, **Concrete**, **Vinyl**, **Gunite**, **Fiberglass**, and **Package**. Add the label **Total** in cell A10. Enter the formula to sum the Sales column in cell B10.

e. Ungroup the worksheets, and enter your own sales data for each of the sales categories in the range B3:B9 in the January, February, and March sheets.

f. Display each worksheet in its own window, then arrange the three sheets vertically.

g. Hide the window displaying the March sheet. Unhide the March sheet window.

h. Split the March window into two panes: the upper pane displaying rows 1 through 5, and the lower pane displaying rows 6 through 10. Scroll through the data in each pane, then remove the split. (*Hint*: Select row 6, click the View tab, then click Split in the Window group. Clicking Split again will remove the split.)

i. Close the windows displaying EX 6-Pools.xlsx:2 and EX 6-Pools.xlsx:3, then maximize the EX 6-Pools.xlsx workbook.

j. Add the keywords **pools custom** to your workbook, using the tags textbox in the Info place.

k. Group the worksheets again.

l. Add headers to all three worksheets that include your name in the left section and the sheet name in the center section. (*Hint*: You can add the sheet name to a header by clicking the Sheet Name button in the Header and Footer Elements group of the Header & Footer Tools Design tab.)

m. With the worksheets still grouped, format the worksheets using the fill and color buttons on the Home tab appropriately.

n. Ungroup the worksheets, then mark the workbook status as final. Close the workbook, reopen the workbook, and enable editing.

o. Save the workbook, submit the workbook to your instructor, then exit Excel.

Independent Challenge 2

As the payroll manager at National Solutions, a communications firm, you decide to organize the weekly timecard data using Excel worksheets. You use a separate worksheet for each week and track the hours for employees with different job classifications. A hyperlink in the worksheet provides pay rates for each classification, and custom views limit the information that is displayed.

a. Start Excel, open EX 6-4.xlsx from the location where you store your Data Files, then save it as **EX 6-Timecards**.

b. Compare the data in the workbook by arranging the Week 1, Week 2, and Week 3 sheets horizontally.

c. Maximize the Week 1 window. Unlock the hours data in the Week 1 sheet and protect the worksheet. Verify that the employee names, numbers, and classifications cannot be changed. Verify that the total hours data can be changed, but do not change the data.

d. Unprotect the Week 1 sheet, and create a custom view called **Complete Worksheet** that displays all the data.

Independent Challenge 2 (continued)

e. Hide column E and create a custom view of the data in the range A1:D22. Name the view **Employee Classifications**. Display each view, then return to the Complete Worksheet view.

f. Add a page break between columns D and E so that the Total Hours data prints on a second page. Preview the worksheet, then remove the page break. (*Hint*: Use the Breaks button on the Page Layout tab.)

g. Add a hyperlink to the Classification heading in cell D1 that links to the file EX 6-Classifications.xlsx. Add a ScreenTip that reads Pay Rates, then test the hyperlink. Compare your screen to FIGURE 6-22.

h. Save the EX 6-Classifications workbook as an Excel 97-2003 workbook, reviewing the Compatibility Checker information. Close the EX 6-Classifications.xls file.

i. Group the three worksheets in the EX 6-Timecards.xlsx workbook, and add your name to the center footer section.

j. Save the workbook, then preview the grouped worksheets.

k. Ungroup the worksheets, and add 2-inch top and left margins to the Week 1 worksheet.

l. Hide the Week 2 and Week 3 worksheets, inspect the file and remove all document properties, personal information, and hidden worksheets. Do not remove header and footer information.

m. Add the keyword **hours** to the workbook, save the workbook, then mark it as final.

n. Close the workbook, submit the workbook to your instructor, then exit Excel.

FIGURE 6-22

	A	B
1	National Solutions	
2	Classifications	Pay Rate
3	Project Manager	$70
4	Senior Project Manager	$85
5	Account Representative	$65
6	Senior Account Representative	$85
7		

Independent Challenge 3

One of your responsibilities as the office manager at South High School is to track supplies for the office. You decide to create a spreadsheet to track these orders, placing each month's orders on its own sheet. You create custom views that will focus on the categories of supplies. A hyperlink will provide a supplier's contact information.

a. Start Excel, open EX 6-5.xlsx from the location where you store your Data Files, then save it as **EX 6-South High**.

b. Arrange the sheets for the 3 months horizontally to compare expenses, then close the extra workbook windows and maximize the remaining window.

c. Create a custom view of the entire January worksheet named **All Supplies**. Hide the paper, pens, and miscellaneous supply data, and create a custom view displaying only the equipment supplies. Call the view **Equipment**.

d. Display the All Supplies view, group the worksheets, and create a total for the total costs in cell D32 on each month's sheet. If necessary, use the Format Painter to copy the format from cell D31 to cell D32.

e. With the sheets grouped, add the sheet name to the center section of all the sheets' headers and your name to the center section of all the sheets' footers.

f. Ungroup the sheets and use the Compatibility Checker to view the features that are unsupported in earlier Excel formats. (*Hint*: Click the File tab, on the Info tab, click the Check for Issues button, then click Check Compatibility.)

g. Add a hyperlink in cell A5 of the January sheet that opens the file EX 6-Equipment.xlsx. Add a ScreenTip of **Equipment Supplier**. Test the link, viewing the ScreenTip, then return to the EX 6-South High.xlsx workbook without closing the EX 6-Equipment.xlsx workbook. Save the EX 6-South High.xlsx workbook.

h. Hide the EX 6-Equipment.xlsx workbook, then unhide it.

Independent Challenge 3 (continued)

i. Freeze worksheet rows one through three on the January Sheet of the EX 6-South High.xlsx workbook. (*Hint*: Select row 4, click the View tab, click the Freeze Panes button in the Window group, then click Freeze Panes.) Scroll down in the worksheet to verify the top three rows remain visible.

j. Unfreeze rows one through three. (*Hint*: Click the View tab, click Freeze panes, then click Unfreeze Panes.)

k. Close both the EX 6-Equipment.xlsx and the EX 6-South High.xlsx workbooks.

l. Submit the workbooks to your instructor, then exit Excel.

Independent Challenge 4: Explore

As the assistant to the owner of an appliance store, you review the nonpayroll expense sheets submitted by employees for each job. You decide to create a spreadsheet to track these contract expenses.

a. Start Excel, open EX 6-6.xlsx from the location where you store your Data Files, then save it as **EX 6-Invoice** in the location where you store your Data Files.

b. Freeze rows 1 through 5 in the worksheet. Scroll vertically to verify rows 1 through 5 are visible at the top of the worksheet.

c. Research the steps necessary to hide a formula in the Formula Bar of a worksheet. Add a worksheet to the workbook. Record these steps in cell A1 on the new sheet of the workbook, then hide the display of the formula for cell B34 on Sheet1. Check the Formula Bar to verify the formula is hidden. Compare your worksheet to **FIGURE 6-23**.

d. Save your workbook to your OneDrive folder. If you don't have a Microsoft account, research the steps for creating an account.

e. Share your workbook with a classmate. Give your classmate permission to edit the workbook. Enter the message **Please review and make necessary changes**.

f. Unprotect Sheet1. (Your formula will be displayed.) Add a header that includes your name on the left side of the worksheet (this will unfreeze rows 1 through 5). Using the Page Layout tab, scale Sheet1 to fit vertically on one page. Save the workbook, then preview the worksheet.

g. Save the workbook as a pdf file.

h. Close the pdf file, then close the workbook.

i. Submit the workbook and pdf file to your instructor, then exit Excel.

FIGURE 6-23

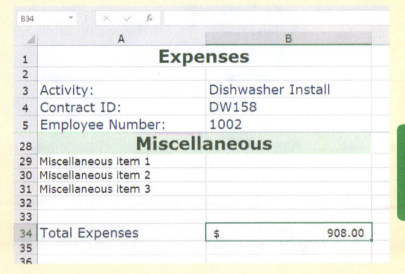

Visual Workshop

Start Excel, open EX 6-7.xlsx from the location where you store your Data Files, then save it as **EX 6-Listings**. Make your worksheet look like the one shown in FIGURE 6-24. The text in cell A4 is a hyperlink to the EX 6-Information workbook. The worksheet background is the Data File EX 6-8.jpg. Enter your name in the footer, save the workbook, submit the workbook to your instructor, close the workbook, then exit Excel.

FIGURE 6-24

	A	B	C	D	E	F
1	Ocean Side Realty					
2	Home Listings					
3	Listing Number	Location	Type	Bed	Bath	Garage
4	100	Waterfront	Condominium	2	1	No
5	12	[Price Information] erfront	Condominium	3	2	No
6	1597	1 block from water	House	4	2	Yes
7	1784	1 mile from water	House	5	3	No
8	2102	Waterfront	Condominium	4	2	No
9	2214	Village	House	2	1	No
10	2268	Waterfront	House	3	1	Yes
11	2784	Village	Condominium	3	2	No
12	3148	1 block from water	House	4	2	Yes
13	3364	1 mile from water	Condominium	2	2	No
14	3754	Waterfront	House	4	2	No
15	3977	Village	House	2	1	No
16	4102	Village	Condominium	2	1	No
17	4158	1 block from water	House	2	2	Yes
18						

Channong Inthasaro/Shutterstock.com

Managing Data Using Tables

CASE Reason2Go uses tables to analyze project data. The vice president of sales and marketing, Mary Watson, asks you to help her build and manage a table of information about 2017 conservation projects. You will help by planning and creating a table; adding, changing, finding, and deleting table information; sorting table data; and performing calculations with table data.

Module Objectives

After completing this module, you will be able to:

- Plan a table
- Create and format a table
- Add table data
- Find and replace table data

- Delete table data
- Sort table data
- Use formulas in a table
- Print a table

Files You Will Need

EX 7-1.xlsx   EX 7-4.xlsx

EX 7-2.xlsx   EX 7-5.xlsx

EX 7-3.xlsx   EX 7-6.xlsx

Plan a Table

Learning
Outcomes
• Plan the data
organization for
a table
• Plan the data
elements for
a table

In addition to using Excel spreadsheet features, you can analyze and manipulate data in a table structure. An Excel **table** is an organized collection of rows and columns of similarly structured worksheet data. Tables are a convenient way to understand and manage large amounts of information. When planning a table, consider what information you want your table to contain and how you want to work with the data, now and in the future. As you plan a table, you should understand its most important components. A table is organized into rows called records. A **record** is a table row that contains data about an object, person, or other items. Records are composed of fields. **Fields** are columns in the table; each field describes one element of the record, such as a customer's last name or street address. Each field has a **field name**, which is a column label, such as "Address," that describes its contents. Tables usually have a **header row** as the first row, which contains the field names. To plan your table, use the guidelines below. **CASE** *Mary asks you to compile a table of the 2017 conservation projects. Before entering the project data into an Excel worksheet, you plan the table contents.*

DETAILS

As you plan your table, use the following guidelines:

- **Identify the purpose of the table**

  The purpose of the table determines the kind of information the table should contain. You want to use the conservation projects table to find all departure dates for a particular project and to display the projects in order of departure date. You also want to quickly calculate the number of available places for a project.

- **Plan the structure of the table**

  In designing your table's structure, determine the fields (the table columns) you need to achieve the table's purpose. You have worked with the sales department to learn the type of information they need for each project. **FIGURE 7-1** shows a layout sketch for the table. Each row will contain one project record. The columns represent fields that contain pieces of descriptive information you will enter for each project, such as the name, departure date, and duration.

- **Plan your row and column structure**

  You can create a table from any contiguous range of cells on your worksheet. Plan and design your table so that all rows have similar types of information in the same column. A table should not have any blank rows or columns. Instead of using blank rows to separate table headings from data, use a table style, which will use formatting to make column labels stand out from your table data. **FIGURE 7-2** shows a table, populated with data that has been formatted using a table style.

- **Document the table design**

  In addition to your table sketch, you should make a list of the field names to document the type of data and any special number formatting required for each field. Field names should be as short as possible while still accurately describing the column information. When naming fields it is important to use text rather than numbers because Excel could interpret numbers as parts of formulas. Your field names should be unique and not easily confused with cell addresses, such as the name D2. You want your table to contain eight field names, each one corresponding to the major characteristics of the 2017 conservation projects. **TABLE 7-1** shows the documentation of the field names in your table.

FIGURE 7-1: Table layout sketch

Project	Depart Date	Number of Days	Project Capacity	Places Reserved	Price	Air Included	Insurance Included

Each project will be placed in a table row

Header row will contain field names

FIGURE 7-2: Formatted table with data

Header row contains field names

Records for each project, organized by field name

	A	B	C	D	E	F	G	H
1	Project	Depart Date	Number of Days	Project Capacity	Places Reserved	Price	Air Included	Insurance Included
2	Elephant	12/20/2017	12	10	0	$ 4,100	Yes	Yes
3	Dolphin	1/28/2017	14	10	0	$ 3,200	Yes	Yes
4	Coral Reef	7/25/2017	18	10	0	$ 3,100	Yes	No
5	Dolphin	8/11/2017	14	10	1	$ 4,600	Yes	No
6	Dolphin	9/14/2017	14	10	1	$ 2,105	No	No
7	Sumatran Orangutan	5/27/2017	17	10	1	$ 1,890	No	No
8	Sumatran Orangutan	12/18/2017	17	8	1	$ 2,204	No	Yes
9	Elephant	12/31/2017	12	10	2	$ 2,100	No	No
10	Great White Shark	8/20/2017	14	8	2	$ 3,922	Yes	Yes
11	Cheetah	7/12/2017	15	9	2	$ 2,100	No	No
12	Cheetah	9/20/2017	15	9	2	$ 3,902	Yes	Yes
13	Rhino	12/18/2017	15	8	2	$ 2,204	No	Yes
14	African Wild Dog	7/27/2017	18	10	2	$ 1,890	No	No
15	Elephant	9/23/2017	12	9	3	$ 2,110	No	No
16	Dolphin	6/9/2017	14	8	3	$ 4,200	Yes	Yes
17	Sumatran Orangutan	8/12/2017	17	10	3	$ 1,970	No	Yes
18	Great White Shark	5/20/2017	14	9	4	$ 2,663	No	Yes
19	Rhino	5/23/2017	15	9	4	$ 4,635	Yes	No

Practice   2017 Projects

Ready

TABLE 7-1: Table documentation

field name	type of data	description of data
Project	Text	Name of project
Depart Date	Date	Date project departs
Number of Days	Number with 0 decimal places	Duration of the project
Project Capacity	Number with 0 decimal places	Maximum number of people the project can accommodate
Places Reserved	Number with 0 decimal places	Number of reservations for the project
Price	Accounting with 0 decimal places and $ symbol	Project price (This price is not guaranteed until a 30% deposit is received)
Air Included	Text	Yes: Airfare is included in the price No: Airfare is not included in the price
Insurance Included	Text	Yes: Insurance is included in the price No: Insurance is not included in the price

Create and Format a Table

Learning Outcomes
• Create a table
• Format a table

Once you have planned the table structure, the sequence of fields, and appropriate data types, you are ready to create the table in Excel. After you create a table, a Table Tools Design tab appears, containing a gallery of table styles. **Table styles** allow you to easily add formatting to your table by using preset formatting combinations of fill color, borders, type style, and type color. **CASE** *Mary asks you to build a table with the 2017 conservation project data. You begin by entering the field names. Then you enter the project data that corresponds to each field name, create the table, and format the data using a table style.*

STEPS

1. **Start Excel, open EX 7-1.xlsx from the location where you store your Data Files, then save it as EX 7-Conservation Projects**

2. **Beginning in cell A1 of the Practice sheet, enter each field name in a separate column, as shown in the first row of FIGURE 7-3**
   Field names are usually in the first row of the table.

3. **Enter the information shown in FIGURE 7-3 in the rows immediately below the field names, leaving no blank rows**
   The data appears in columns organized by field name.

4. **Select the range A1:H4, click the Format button in the Cells group, click AutoFit Column Width, then click cell A1**
   Resizing the column widths this way is faster than double-clicking the column divider lines.

5. **With cell A1 selected, click the Insert tab, click the Table button in the Tables group, in the Create Table dialog box verify that your table data is in the range $A$1:$H$4, make sure My table has headers is checked as shown in FIGURE 7-4, then click OK**
   The data range is now defined as a table. **Filter list arrows**, which let you display portions of your data, now appear next to each column header. When you create a table, Excel automatically applies a table style. The default table style has a dark blue header row and alternating light and dark blue data rows. The Table Tools Design tab appears, and the Table Styles group displays a gallery of table formatting options. You decide to choose a different table style from the gallery.

6. **Click the Table Styles More button ⤓, scroll to view all of the table styles, then move the mouse pointer over several styles without clicking**
   The Table Styles gallery on the Table Tools Design tab has three style categories: Light, Medium, and Dark. Each category has numerous design types; for example, in some of the designs, the header row and total row are darker and the rows alternate colors. The available table designs use the current workbook theme colors so the table coordinates with your existing workbook content. If you select a different workbook theme and color scheme in the Themes group on the Page Layout tab, the Table Styles gallery uses those colors. As you point to each table style, Live Preview shows you what your table will look like with the style applied. However, you only see a preview of each style; you need to click a style to apply it.

7. **Click Table Style Medium 23 to apply it to your table, then click cell A1**
   Compare your table to FIGURE 7-5.

FIGURE 7-3: Field names and three records entered in worksheet

	A	B	C	D	E	F	G	H
1	Project	Depart Date	Number of Days	Project Capacity	Places Reserved	Price	Air Included	Insurance Included
2	Elephant	42747	12	10	5	4255	Yes	No
3	Rhino	42748	15	8	8	1984	No	No
4	Cheetah	42754	15	10	8	1966	No	Yes
5								

FIGURE 7-4: Create Table dialog box

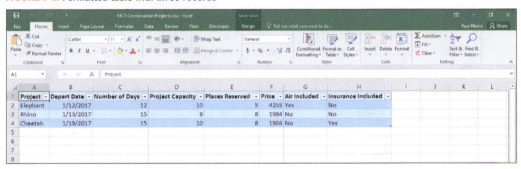

Table range

Verify that this box is checked

FIGURE 7-5: Formatted table with three records

Excel 2016

Changing table style options

You can change a table's appearance by using the check boxes in the Table Style Options group on the Table Tools Design tab, shown in **FIGURE 7-6**. For example, you can turn on or turn off the following options: Header Row, which displays or hides the header row; Total Row, which calculates totals for each column; **banding**, which creates different formatting for adjacent rows and columns; and special formatting for first and last columns. Use these options to modify a table's appearance either before or after applying a table style.

You can also create your own table style by clicking the Table Styles More button, then at the bottom of the Table Styles Gallery, clicking New Table Style. In the New Table Style dialog box, name the style in the Name text box, click a table element, then format selected table elements by clicking Format. You can also set a custom style as the default style for your tables by checking the Set as default table quick style for this document check box. You can click Clear at the bottom of the Table Styles gallery if you want to delete a table style from the currently selected table.

FIGURE 7-6: Table Style Options

Table Tools Design tab

Table Style Options group

Banded rows

Add Table Data

Learning Outcomes
- Add fields to a table
- Add records to a table

You can add records to a table by typing data directly below the last row of the table. After you press [Enter], the new row becomes part of the table and the table formatting extends to the new data. When the active cell is the last cell of a table, you can add a new row by pressing [Tab]. You can also insert rows in any table location. If you decide you need additional data fields, you can add new columns to a table. You can also expand a table by dragging the sizing handle in a table's lower-right corner; drag down to add rows and drag to the right to add columns. **CASE** *After entering all of the 2017 project data, Mary decides to offer two additional projects. She also wants the table to display the number of available places for each project and whether visas are required for the destination.*

STEPS

1. **Click the 2017 Projects sheet tab**

   The 2017 sheet containing the 2017 project data becomes active.

2. **Scroll down to the last table row, click cell A65, enter the data for the new Coral Reef project, as shown below, then press [Enter]**

Coral Reef	7/25/2017	18	10	0	$ 3,100	Yes	No

   As you scroll down, notice that the table headers are visible at the top of the table as long as the active cell is inside the table. The new Coral Reef project is now part of the table. You want to enter a record about a new January project above row 6.

3. **Scroll up to and click the inside left edge of cell A6 to select the table row data as shown in FIGURE 7-7, click the Insert list arrow in the Cells group, then click Insert Table Rows Above**

   Clicking the left edge of the first cell in a table row selects the entire table row, rather than the entire worksheet row. A new blank row 6 is available for the new record.

4. **Click cell A6, then enter the Dolphin record shown below**

Dolphin	1/28/2017	14	10	0	$ 3,200	Yes	Yes

   The new Dolphin project is part of the table. You want to add a new field that displays the number of available places for each project.

5. **Click cell I1, type the field name Places Available, then press [Enter]**

   The new field becomes part of the table, and the header formatting extends to the new field, as shown in FIGURE 7-8. The AutoCorrect menu allows you to undo or stop the automatic table expansion, but in this case you decide to leave this feature on. You want to add another new field to the table to display projects that require visas, but this time you will add the new field by resizing the table.

6. **Scroll down until cell I66 is visible, then drag the sizing handle in the table's lower-right corner one column to the right to add column J to the table, as shown in FIGURE 7-9**

   The table range is now A1:J66, and the new field name is Column1.

7. **Scroll up to and click cell J1, type Visa Required, then press [Enter]**

8. **Click the Insert tab, click the Header & Footer button in the Text group, enter your name in the center header text box, click cell A1, click the Normal button ▦ on the status bar, then save the workbook**

FIGURE 7-7: Table row 6 selected

	Project	Depart Date	Number of Days	Project Capacity	Places Reserved	Price	Air Included	Insurance Included
2	Elephant	1/12/2017	12	10	5	$ 4,255	Yes	No
3	Rhino	1/13/2017	15	8	8	$ 1,984	No	No
4	Cheetah	1/19/2017	15	10	8	$ 1,966	No	Yes
5	African Wild Dog	1/21/2017	18	7	7	$ 3,850	Yes	Yes
6	Dolphin	2/22/2017	14	10	10	$ 2,134	No	No
7	Orangutan	2/28/2017	17	8	4	$ 4,812	Yes	No
8	Great White Shark	3/13/2017	14	10	5	$ 4,350	Yes	No
9	Coral Reef	3/19/2017	18	6	5	$ 2,110	No	Yes
10	Orangutan	3/20/2017	17	10	8	$ 1,755	No	Yes
11	African Wild Dog	3/23/2017	18	8	7	$ 2,450	No	No
12	Rhino	4/8/2017	15	10	10	$ 3,115	Yes	Yes
13	Elephant	4/11/2017	12	10	5	$ 4,255	Yes	No

Clicking here selects the entire worksheet row

Clicking here selects the table row

Row 6 of table selected

FIGURE 7-8: New table column

	Project	Depart Date	Number of Days	Project Capacity	Places Reserved	Price	Air Included	Insurance Included	Places Available
2	Elephant	1/12/2017	12	10	5	$ 4,255	Yes	No	
3	Rhino	1/13/2017	15	8	8	$ 1,984	No	No	
4	Cheetah	1/19/2017	15	10	8	$ 1,966	No	Yes	
5	African Wild Dog	1/21/2017	18	7	7	$ 3,850	Yes	Yes	
6	Dolphin	1/28/2017	14	10	0	$ 3,200	Yes	Yes	
7	Dolphin	2/22/2017	14	10	10	$ 2,134	No	No	
8	Orangutan	2/28/2017	17	8	4	$ 4,812	Yes	No	
9	Great White Shark	3/13/2017	14	10	5	$ 4,350	Yes	No	
10	Coral Reef	3/19/2017	18	6	5	$ 2,110	No	Yes	

New table column will show available places for each project

New record in row 6

FIGURE 7-9: Resizing a table using the resizing handle

	Project	Depart Dat	Number of	Project Cap	Places Reser	Price	Air Include	Insurance In	Places Ava
55	African Wild Dog	10/29/2017	18	10	6	$ 4,200	Yes	Yes	
56	Great White Shark	10/31/2017	14	9	8	$ 1,900	No	No	
57	African Wild Dog	10/31/2017	18	9	5	$ 3,908	Yes	No	
58	Great White Shark	11/18/2017	14	10	5	$ 2,200	No	Yes	
59	Rhino	12/18/2017	15	8	2	$ 2,204	No	Yes	
60	Orangutan	12/18/2017	17	8	1	$ 2,204	No	Yes	
61	Elephant	12/20/2017	12	10	0	$ 4,100	Yes	Yes	
62	Dolphin	12/20/2017	14	10	5	$ 2,100	No	Yes	
63	African Wild Dog	12/21/2017	18	9	8	$ 2,105	No	No	
64	Cheetah	12/30/2017	15	9	5	$ 3,922	Yes	Yes	
65	Elephant	12/31/2017	12	10	2	$ 2,100	No	No	
66	Coral Reef	7/25/2017	18	10	0	$ 3,100	Yes	No	
67									
68									

Drag sizing handle to add column J

Selecting table elements

When working with tables you often need to select rows, columns, and even the entire table. Clicking to the right of a row number, inside column A, selects the entire table row. You can select a table column by clicking the top edge of the header. Be careful not to click a column letter or row number, however, because this selects the entire worksheet row or column. You can select the table data by clicking the upper-left corner of the first table cell. When selecting a column or a table, the first click selects only the data in the column or table. If you click a second time, you add the headers to the selection.

Find and Replace Table Data

Learning Outcomes
• Find data in a table
• Replace data in a table

From time to time, you need to locate specific records in your table. You can use the Excel Find feature to search your table for the information you need. You can also use the Replace feature to locate and replace existing entries or portions of entries with information you specify. If you don't know the exact spelling of the text you are searching for, you can use wildcards to help locate the records. **Wildcards** are special symbols that substitute for unknown characters. **CASE** ▶ *Because the Sumatran Orangutans are critically endangered, Mary wants you to replace "Orangutan" with "Sumatran Orangutan" to avoid confusion with last year's Borneo projects. She also wants to know how many Cheetah projects are scheduled for the year. You begin by searching for records with the text "Cheetah".*

STEPS

1. **Click cell A1 if necessary, click the Home tab, click the Find & Select button in the Editing group, then click Find**

   The Find and Replace dialog box opens, as shown in **FIGURE 7-10**. In the Find what text box, you enter criteria that specify the records you want to find. You want to search for records whose Project field contains the label "Cheetah".

2. **Type Cheetah in the Find what text box, then click Find Next**

   A4 is the active cell because it is the first instance of Cheetah in the table.

3. **Click Find Next and examine the record for each Cheetah project found until no more matching cells are found in the table and the active cell is A4 again, then click Close**

   There are seven Cheetah projects.

4. **Return to cell A1, click the Find & Select button in the Editing group, then click Replace**

   The Find and Replace dialog box opens with the Replace tab selected and "Cheetah" in the Find what text box, as shown in **FIGURE 7-11**. You will search for entries containing "Orangutan" and replace them with "Sumatran Orangutan". To save time, you will use the asterisk (*) wildcard to help you locate the records containing Orangutan.

QUICK TIP
You can also use the question mark (?) wildcard to represent any single character. For example, using "to?" as your search text would only find 3-letter words beginning with "to", such as "top" and "tot"; it would not find "tone" or "topography".

5. **Delete the text in the Find what text box, type Or* in the Find what text box, click the Replace with text box, then type Sumatran Orangutan**

   The asterisk (*) wildcard stands for one or more characters, meaning that the search text "Or*" will find words such as "orange", "cord", and "for". Because you notice that there are other table entries containing the text "or" with a lowercase "o" (Coral Reef), you need to make sure that only capitalized instances of the letter "O" are replaced.

6. **Click Options >>, click the Match case check box to select it, click Options <<, then click Find Next**

   Excel moves the cell pointer to the cell containing the first occurrence of "Orangutan".

7. **Click Replace All, click OK, then click Close**

   The dialog box closes. Excel made ten replacements. The Coral Reef projects remain unchanged because the "or" in "Coral" is lowercase.

8. **Save the workbook**

FIGURE 7-10: Find and Replace dialog box

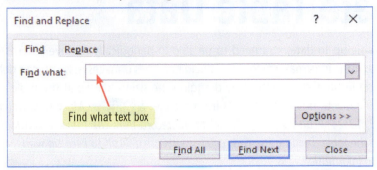

Find what text box

FIGURE 7-11: The Replace tab in the Find and Replace dialog box

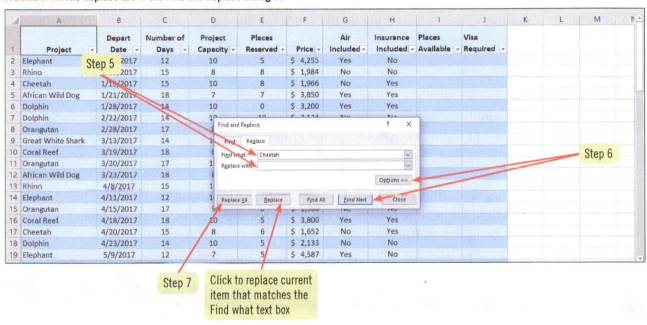

Step 5

Step 6

Step 7

Click to replace current item that matches the Find what text box

Using Find and Select features

You can also use the Find feature to navigate to a specific place in a workbook by clicking the Find & Select button in the Editing group on the Home tab, clicking Go To, typing a cell address, then clicking OK. Clicking the Find & Select button also allows you to find comments and conditional formatting in a worksheet. You can use the Go to Special dialog box to select cells that contain different types of formulas or objects. Some Go to Special commands also appear on the Find & Select menu. Using this menu, you can also change the mouse pointer shape to the Select Objects pointer ⬚ so you can quickly select drawing objects when necessary. To return to the standard Excel pointer ✛, press [Esc].

Delete Table Data

Learning Outcomes
• Delete a table field
• Delete a table row
• Remove duplicate data from a table

To keep a table up to date, you need to be able to periodically remove records. You may even need to remove fields if the information stored in a field becomes unnecessary. You can delete table data using the Delete button in the Cells group or by dragging the sizing handle at the table's lower-right corner. You can also easily delete duplicate records from a table. **CASE** *Mary is canceling the Rhino project that departs on 1/13/2017 and asks you to delete the record from the table. You will also remove any duplicate records from the table. Because the visa requirements are difficult to keep up with, Mary asks you to delete the field with visa information.*

STEPS

1. **Click the inside left edge of cell A3 to select the table row, click the Delete list arrow in the Cells group, then click Delete Table Rows**

   The Rhino project is deleted, and the Cheetah project moves up to row 3, as shown in **FIGURE 7-12**. You can also delete a table row or a column using the Resize Table button in the Properties group of the Table Tools Design tab, or by right-clicking the row or column, pointing to Delete on the shortcut menu, then clicking Table Columns or Table Rows. You decide to check the table for duplicate records.

   QUICK TIP
   You can also remove duplicates from worksheet data by clicking the Data tab, then clicking the Remove Duplicates button in the Data Tools group.

2. **Click the Table Tools Design tab, then click the Remove Duplicates button in the Tools group**

   The Remove Duplicates dialog box opens, as shown in **FIGURE 7-13**. You need to select the columns that will be used to evaluate duplicates. Because you don't want to delete projects with the same destination but different departure dates, you will look for duplicate data in those columns.

3. **Make sure that the My data has headers check box is checked, remove the selection from all of the check boxes except the Project and Depart Date fields, then click OK**

   One duplicate record is found and removed, leaving 63 records of data and a total of 64 rows in the table, including the header row. You want to remove the last column, which contains space for visa information.

4. **Click OK, scroll down until cell J64 is visible, then drag the sizing handle of the table's lower-right corner one column to the left to remove column J from the table**

   The table range is now A1:I64, and the Visa Required field no longer appears in the table.

5. **Delete the contents of cell J1, return to cell A1, then save the workbook**

FIGURE 7-12: Table with row deleted

Project	Depart Date	Number of Days	Project Capacity	Places Reserved	Price	Air Included	Insurance Included	Places Available	Visa Required
Elephant	1/12/2017	12	10	5	$ 4,255	Yes	No		
Cheetah	1/19/2017	15	10	8	$ 1,966	No	Yes		
African Wild Dog	1/21/2017	18	7	7	$ 3,850	Yes	Yes		
Dolphin	1/28/2017	14	10	0	$ 3,200	Yes	Yes		
Dolphin	2/22/2017	14	10	10	$ 2,134	No	No		
Sumatran Orangutan	2/28/2017	17	8	4	$ 4,812	Yes	No		
Great White Shark	3/13/2017	14	10	5	$ 4,350	Yes	No		
Coral Reef	3/19/2017	18	6	5	$ 2,110	No	Yes		
Sumatran Orangutan	3/20/2017	17	10	8	$ 1,755	No	Yes		
African Wild Dog	3/23/2017	18	8	7	$ 2,450	No	No		
Rhino	4/8/2017	15	10	10	$ 3,115	Yes	Yes		
Elephant	4/11/2017	12	10	5	$ 4,255	Yes	No		
Sumatran Orangutan	4/15/2017	17	9	8	$ 1,900	No	No		
Coral Reef	4/18/2017	18	10	5	$ 3,800	Yes	Yes		
Cheetah	4/20/2017	15	8	6	$ 1,652	No	Yes		
Dolphin	4/23/2017	14	10	5	$ 2,133	No	No		
	/2017	12	7	5	$ 4,587	Yes	No		

Row is deleted and rows below move up by one

FIGURE 7-13: Remove Duplicates dialog box

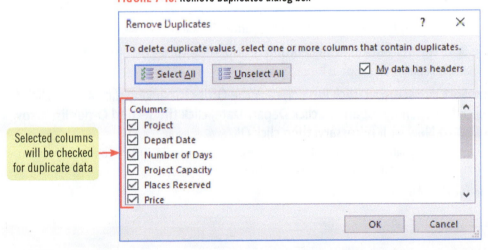

Selected columns will be checked for duplicate data

Sort Table Data

Usually, you enter table records in the order in which you receive information, rather than in alphabetical or numerical order. When you add records to a table, you usually enter them at the end of the table. You can change the order of the records any time using the Excel **sort** feature. Because the data is structured as a table, Excel changes the order of the records while keeping each record, or row of information, together. You can sort a table in ascending or descending order on one field using the filter list arrows next to the field name. In **ascending order**, the lowest value (the beginning of the alphabet or the earliest date) appears at the top of the table. In a field containing labels and numbers, numbers appear first in the sorted list. In **descending order**, the highest value (the end of the alphabet or the latest date) appears at the top of the table. In a field containing labels and numbers, labels appear first. TABLE 7-2 provides examples of ascending and descending sorts. **CASE** *Mary wants the project data sorted by departure date, displaying projects that depart the soonest at the top of the table.*

STEPS

1. **Click the** Depart Date filter list arrow, **then click** Sort Oldest to Newest

   Excel rearranges the records in ascending order by departure date, as shown in FIGURE 7-14. The Depart Date filter list arrow has an upward pointing arrow indicating the ascending sort in the field. You can also sort the table on one field using the Sort & Filter button.

2. **Click the** Home tab, **click any** cell **in the Price column, click the** Sort & Filter button **in the Editing group, then click** Sort Largest to Smallest

   Excel sorts the table, placing records with higher prices at the top. The Price filter list arrow now has a downward pointing arrow next to the filter list arrow, indicating the descending sort order. You can also rearrange the table data using a **multilevel sort**. This type of sort rearranges the table data using more than one field, where each field is a different level, based on its importance in the sort. If you use two sort levels, the data is sorted by the first field, and the second field is sorted within each grouping of the first field. Since you have many groups of projects with different departure dates, you want to use a multilevel sort to arrange the table data first by projects and then by departure dates within each project.

3. **Click the** Sort & Filter button **in the Editing group, then click** Custom Sort

   The Sort dialog box opens, as shown in FIGURE 7-15.

4. **Click the** Sort by list arrow, **click** Project, **click the** Order list arrow, **click** A to Z, **click** Add Level, **click the** Then by list arrow, **click** Depart Date, **click the second** Order list arrow, **click** Oldest to Newest **if necessary, then click** OK

   FIGURE 7-16 shows the table sorted alphabetically in ascending order (A–Z) by Project and, within each project grouping, in ascending order by the Depart Date.

5. **Save the workbook**

Sorting conditionally formatted data

If conditional formats have been applied to a table, you can sort the table using conditional formatting to arrange the rows. For example, if cells are conditionally formatted with color, you can sort a field on Cell Color, using the color with the order of On Top or On Bottom in the Sort dialog box. If the data is not in a table, you can select a cell in the column of conditionally formatted data you want to sort by, or select the range of cells to be sorted, right-click the selection, point to Sort, then select the font color, highlighted color, or icon that you want to appear on top.

FIGURE 7-14: Table sorted by departure date

Records are sorted by departure date in ascending order

Up arrow indicates ascending sort in the field

	Project	Depart Date	Number of Days	Project Capacity	Places Reserved	Price	Air Included	Insurance Included	Places Available
2	Elephant	1/12/2017	12	10	5	4,255	Yes	No	
3	Cheetah	1/19/2017	15	10		,966	No	Yes	
4	African Wild Dog	1/21/2017	18	7		,850	Yes	Yes	
5	Dolphin	1/28/2017	14	10		,200	Yes	Yes	
6	Dolphin	2/22/2017	14	10		,134	No	No	
7	Sumatran Orangutan	2/28/2017	17	8	4	$ 4,812	Yes	No	
8	Great White Shark	3/13/2017	14	10	5	$ 4,350	Yes	No	
9	Coral Reef	3/19/2017	18	6	5	$ 2,110	No	Yes	
10	Sumatran Orangutan	3/20/2017	17	10	8	$ 1,755	No	Yes	
11	African Wild Dog	3/23/2017	18	8	7	$ 2,450	No	No	
12	Rhino	4/8/2017	15	10	10	$ 3,115	Yes	Yes	
13	Elephant	4/11/2017	12	10	5	$ 4,255	Yes	No	
14	Sumatran Orangutan	4/15/2017	17	9	8	$ 1,900	No	No	
15	Coral Reef	4/18/2017	18	10	5	$ 3,800	Yes	Yes	
16	Cheetah	4/20/2017	15	8	6	$ 1,652	No	Yes	
17	Dolphin	4/23/2017	14	10	5	$ 2,133	No	No	
18	Elephant	5/9/2017	12	7	5	$ 4,587	Yes	No	

FIGURE 7-15: Sort dialog box

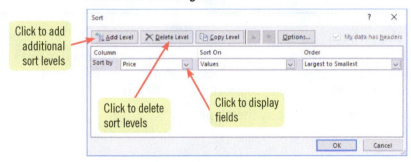

Click to add additional sort levels

Click to delete sort levels

Click to display fields

FIGURE 7-16: Table sorted using two levels

	Project	Depart Date	Number of Days	Project Capacity	Places Reserved	Price	Air Included	Insurance Included	Places Available
2	African Wild Dog	1/21/2017	18	7	7	$ 3,850	Yes	Yes	
3	African Wild Dog	3/23/2017	18	8	7	$ 2,450	No	No	
4	African Wild Dog	5/18/2017	18	7	5	$ 4,638	Yes	Yes	
5	African Wild Dog	6/10/2017	18	10	5	$ 2,190	No	No	
6	African Wild Dog	6/27/2017	18	10	7	$ 1,944	No	No	
7	African Wild Dog	7/27/2017	18	10	2	$ 1,890	No	No	
8	African Wild Dog	8/23/2017	18	7			No	No	
9	African Wild Dog	9/18/2017	18	10			Yes	Yes	
10	African Wild Dog	10/29/2017	18	10			Yes	Yes	
11	African Wild Dog	10/31/2017	18	9			Yes	No	
12	African Wild Dog	12/21/2017	18	9			No	No	
13	Cheetah	1/19/2017	15	10	8	$ 1,966	No	Yes	
14	Cheetah				6	$ 1,652	No	Yes	
15	Cheetah				8	$ 4,600	Yes	No	
16	Cheetah				2	$ 2,100	No	No	
17	Cheetah	9/20/2017	15	9	2	$ 3,902	Yes	Yes	

Second-level sort arranges records by departure date within each project grouping

First-level sort on project arranges records by project name

TABLE 7-2: Sort order options and examples

option	alphabetic	numeric	date	alphanumeric
Ascending	A, B, C	7, 8, 9	1/1, 2/1, 3/1	12A, 99B, DX8, QT7
Descending	C, B, A	9, 8, 7	3/1, 2/1, 1/1	QT7, DX8, 99B, 12A

Specifying a custom sort order

You can identify a custom sort order for the field selected in the Sort by box. Click the Order list arrow in the Sort dialog box, click Custom List, then click the desired custom order. Commonly used custom sort orders are days of the week (Sun, Mon, Tues, Wed, etc.) and months (Jan, Feb, Mar, etc.); alphabetic sorts do not sort these items properly.

Use Formulas in a Table

Many tables are large, making it difficult to know from viewing them the "story" the table tells. The Excel table calculation features help you summarize table data so you can see important patterns and trends. After you enter a single formula into a table cell, the **calculated columns** feature fills in the remaining cells with the formula's results. The column continues to fill with the formula results as you enter rows in the table. This makes it easy to update your formulas because you only need to edit the formula once, and the change will fill in to the other column cells. The **structured reference** feature allows your formulas to refer to table columns by names that are automatically generated when you create the table. These names adjust as you add or delete table fields. An example of a table reference is =[Sales]–[Costs], where Sales and Costs are field names in the table. Tables also have a specific area at the bottom called the **table total row** for calculations using the data in the table columns. The cells in this row contain a dropdown list of functions that can be used for the column calculation. The table total row adapts to any changes in the table size. **CASE** *Mary asks you to calculate the number of available places for each project. You will also add summary information to the end of the table.*

STEPS

1. **Click cell I2, then type =[**
   A list of the table field names appears, as shown in **FIGURE 7-17**. Structured referencing allows you to use the names that Excel created when you defined your table to reference fields in a formula. You can choose a field by clicking it and pressing [Tab] or by double-clicking the field name.

2. **Click [Project Capacity], press [Tab], then type]**
   Excel begins the formula, placing [Project Capacity] in the cell in blue and framing the Project Capacity data in a blue border.

3. **Type -[, double-click [Places Reserved], then type]**
   Excel places [Places Reserved] in the cell in red and outlines the Places Reserved data in a red border.

4. **Press [Enter]**
   The formula result, 0, is displayed in cell I2. The table column also fills with the formula, displaying the number of available places for each project.

5. **Click the AutoCorrect Options list arrow [img] to view options for the column**
   Because the calculated columns option saves time, you decide to leave the feature on. You want to display the total number of available places on all of the projects.

6. **Press [Esc] to close the menu, click the Table Tools Design tab, then click the Total Row check box in the Table Style Options group to select it**
   A total row appears at the bottom of the table, and the sum of the available places, 268, is displayed in cell I65. You can include other formulas in the total row.

7. **Click cell C65 (the Number of Days column), then click the cell list arrow on the right side of the cell**
   The list of available functions appears, as shown in **FIGURE 7-18**. You want to find the average project length.

8. **Click Average, then save your workbook**
   The average project length, 15 days, appears in cell C65.

FIGURE 7-17: Table field names

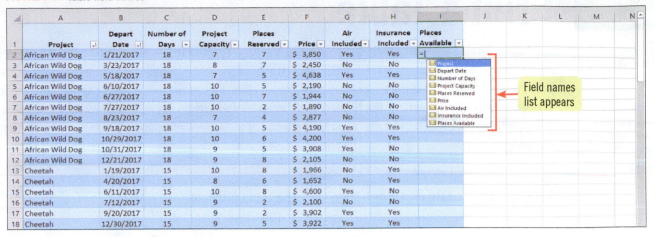

FIGURE 7-18: Functions in the Total row

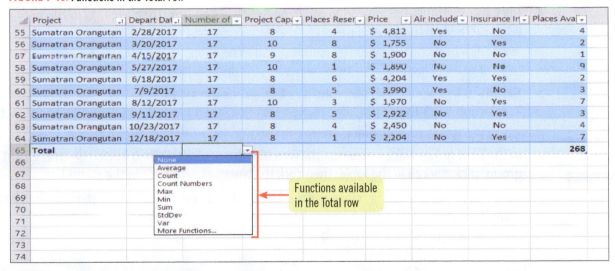

Excel 2016

Print a Table

Learning Outcomes
- Preview a table
- Add print titles to a table

You can determine the way a table will print using the Page Layout tab. Because tables often have more rows than can fit on a page, you can define the first row of the table (containing the field names) as the **print title**, which prints at the top of every page. If your table does not include any descriptive information above the field names, you can use headers and footers to add identifying text, such as the table title or the report date. **CASE** ▶ *Mary asks you for a printout of the project information. You begin by previewing the table.*

STEPS

1. **Click the File tab, click Print, then view the table preview**

   Below the table you see 1 of 2, which indicates you are viewing page 1 of a 2-page document.

2. **In the Preview window, click the Next Page button ▶ in the Preview area to view the second page**

   All of the field names in the table fit across the width of page 1. Because the records on page 2 appear without column headings, you want to set up the first row of the table, which contains the field names, as a print title.

QUICK TIP

You can hide or print headings and grid-lines using the check boxes in the Sheet Options group on the Page Layout tab.

3. **Return to the worksheet, click the Page Layout tab, click the Print Titles button in the Page Setup group, click inside the Rows to repeat at top text box under Print titles, in the worksheet scroll up to row 1 if necessary, click any cell in row 1 on the table, then compare your Page Setup dialog box to FIGURE 7-19**

   When you select row 1 as a print title, Excel automatically inserts an absolute reference to the row that will repeat at the top of each page.

4. **Click the Print Preview button in the Page Setup dialog box, then click ▶ in the preview window to view the second page**

   Setting up a print title to repeat row 1 causes the field names to appear at the top of each printed page. The printout would be more informative with a header to identify the table information.

QUICK TIP

You can also add a header or a footer by clicking the Page Layout button in the status bar and click-ing in the header or footer area.

5. **Return to the worksheet, click the Insert tab, click the Header & Footer button in the Text group, click the left header section text box, then type 2017 Conservation Projects**

6. **Select the left header section text, click the Home tab, click the Increase Font Size button A˄ in the Font group twice to change the font size to 14, click the Bold button B in the Font group, click any cell in the table, then click the Normal button ▦ in the status bar**

7. **Save the table, preview it, close the workbook, exit Excel, then submit the workbook to your instructor**

   Compare your printed table with FIGURE 7-20.

FIGURE 7-19: Page Setup dialog box

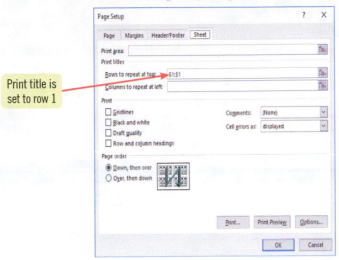

Print title is set to row 1

FIGURE 7-20: Printed table

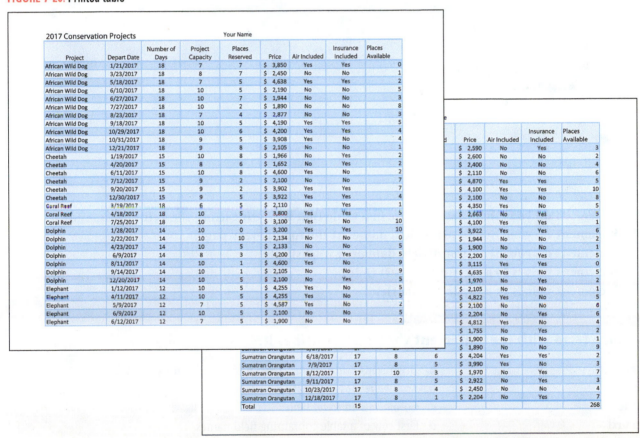

Excel 2016

Setting a print area

Sometimes you will want to print only part of a worksheet. To do this, select any worksheet range, click the File tab, click Print, click the Print Active Sheets list arrow, then click Print Selection. If you want to print a selected area repeatedly, it's best to define a **print area**, the area of the worksheet that previews and prints when you use the Print command in Backstage view. To set a print area, select the range of data on the worksheet that you want to print, click the Page Layout tab, click the Print Area button in the Page Setup group, then click Set Print Area. You can add to the print area by selecting a range, clicking the Print Area button, then clicking Add to Print Area. A print area can consist of one contiguous range of cells, or multiple areas in different parts of a worksheet.

Practice

Concepts Review

FIGURE 7-21

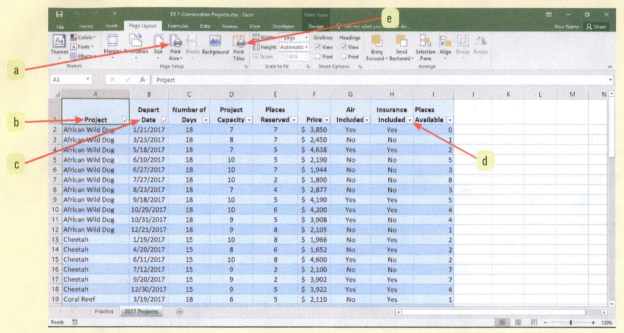

1. Which element do you click to set a range in a table that will print using the Print command?
2. Which element do you click to print field names at the top of every page?
3. Which element do you click to sort field data on a worksheet?
4. Which element points to a second-level sort field?
5. Which element points to a top-level sort field?

Match each term with the statement that best describes it.

6. Sort
7. Field
8. Table
9. Record
10. Header row

a. Organized collection of related information in Excel
b. Arrange records in a particular sequence
c. Column in an Excel table
d. First row of a table containing field names
e. Row in an Excel table

Select the best answer from the list of choices.

11. Which of the following series appears in descending order?
   a. 8, 6, 4, C, B, A
   b. 4, 5, 6, A, B, C
   c. 8, 7, 6, 5, 6, 7
   d. C, B, A, 6, 5, 4

12. **Which of the following Excel options do you use to sort a table of employee names in order from Z to A?**
    a. Ascending
    b. Absolute
    c. Alphabetic
    d. Descending

13. **When printing a table on multiple pages, you can define a print title to:**
    a. Include the sheet name in table reports.
    b. Include field names at the top of each printed page.
    c. Exclude from the printout all rows under the first row.
    d. Include gridlines in the printout.

14. **You can easily add formatting to a table by using:**
    a. Table styles.
    b. Print titles.
    c. Print areas.
    d. Calculated columns.

Skills Review

1. **Create and format a table.**
   a. Start Excel, open EX 7-2.xlsx from the location where you store your Data Files, then save it as **EX 7-Employees**.
   b. Using the Practice sheet, enter the field names in the first row and the first two records in rows two and three, as shown in the table below, adjusting column widths as necessary to fit the text entries.

Last Name	First Name	Years Employed	Department	Full/Part Time	Training Completed
Diamond	Irene	4	Support	P	Y
Mendez	Darryl	3	Sales	F	N

   c. Define the data you entered as a table, then add a table style of Medium 9.
   d. On the Staff sheet, define the cells containing data as a table with a header row. Adjust the column widths, if necessary, to display the field names. Enter your name in the center section of the worksheet footer, return to Normal view if necessary, then save the workbook.
   e. Apply a table style of Light 19 to the table.
   f. Enter your name in the center section of the worksheet footer, return to Normal view if necessary, then save the workbook.

2. **Add table data.**
   a. Add a new record in row seven for **Holly Wallace**, a 5-year employee in the Support department. Holly works part time and has completed training. Adjust the height of the new row to match the other table rows.
   b. Insert a table row above Julie Kosby's record, and add a new record for **Sally Alden**. Sally works full time, has worked at the company for 2 years in Sales, and has not completed training. Adjust the table formatting if necessary.
   c. Insert a new data field in cell G1 with a label **Weeks Vacation**. Wrap the label in the cell to display the field name with **Weeks** above **Vacation**, and then widen the column as necessary to see both words. (*Hint*: Use the Wrap Text button in the Alignment group on the Home tab.)
   d. Add a new column to the table by dragging the table's sizing handle, and give the new field a label of **Employee #**. Widen the column to fit the label.
   e. Save the file.

3. **Find and replace table data.**
   a. Return to cell A1.
   b. Open the Find and Replace dialog box and, then if necessary uncheck the Match case option. Find the first record that contains the text **Support**.
   c. Find the second and third records that contain the text **Support**.
   d. Replace all **Support** text in the table with **Service**, then save the file.

4. Delete table data.

    a. Go to cell A1.

    b. Delete the record for Irene Diamond.

    c. Use the Remove Duplicates button to confirm that the table does not have any duplicate records.

    d. Delete the Employee # table column, then delete its column header, if necessary.

    e. Save the file.

5. Sort table data.

    a. Sort the table by Years Employed in largest to smallest order.

    b. Sort the table by Last Name in A to Z order.

    c. Perform a multilevel sort: Sort the table first by Full/Part Time in A to Z order and then by Last Name in A to Z order.

    d. Check the table to make sure the records appear in the correct order.

    e. Save the file.

6. Use formulas in a table.

    a. In cell G2, enter the formula that calculates an employee's vacation time; base the formula on the company policy that employees working at the company less than 4 years have 2 weeks of vacation. At 4 years of employment and longer, an employee has 3 weeks of vacation time. Use the table's field names where appropriate. (*Hint*: The formula is: **=IF([Years Employed]<4,2,3).**)

    b. Check the table to make sure the formula filled into the cells in column G and that the correct vacation time is calculated for all cells in the column.

    c. Add a Total Row to display the total number of vacation weeks.

    d. Change the function in the Total Row to display the maximum number of vacation weeks. Change the entry in cell A8 from Total to **Maximum**.

    e. Compare your table to FIGURE 7-22, then save the workbook.

FIGURE 7-22

	A	B	C	D	E	F	G
1	Last Name	First Name	Years Employed	Department	Full/Part Time	Training Completed	Weeks Vacation
2	Alden	Sally	2	Sales	F	N	2
3	Green	Jane	1	Service	F	N	2
4	Kosby	Julie	4	Sales	F	Y	3
5	Mendez	Darryl	3	Sales	F	N	2
6	Ropes	Mark	1	Sales	P	Y	2
7	Wallace	Holly	5	Service	P	Y	3
8	**Maximum**						3

7. Print a table.

    a. Add a header that reads **Employees** in the left section, then format the header in bold with a font size of **16**.

    b. Add column A as a print title that repeats at the left of each printed page.

    c. Preview your table to check that the last names appear on both pages.

    d. Change the page orientation to landscape, preview the worksheet, then save the workbook.

    e. Submit your workbook to your instructor. Close the workbook, then exit Excel.

Independent Challenge 1

You are the clinical coordinator for an acupuncture clinic. Your administrative assistant created an Excel worksheet with client data including the results of a survey. You will create a table using the client data, and analyze the survey results to help focus the clinic's expenses in the most successful areas.

    a. Start Excel, open EX 7-3.xlsx from the location where you store your Data Files, then save it as **EX 7-Clients**.

    b. Create a table from the worksheet data, and apply Table Style Light 10.

Independent Challenge 1 (continued)

c. Add the two records shown in the table below:

Last Name	First Name	Street Address	City	State	Zip	Area Code	Ad Source
Ross	Kim	4 Ridge Rd.	San Francisco	CA	94177	415	Health Center
Jones	Kathy	512 17th St.	Seattle	WA	98001	206	Radio

d. Find the record for Mike Rondo, then delete it.

e. Click cell A1 and replace all instances of **TV** with **Social Media**.

f. Remove duplicate records where all fields are identical.

g. Sort the list by Last Name in A to Z order.

h. Sort the list again by Area Code in Smallest to Largest order.

i. Sort the table first by Survey Source in A to Z order, then by State in A to Z order. Compare your table to **FIGURE 7-23**.

FIGURE 7-23

	A	B	C	D	E	F	G	H	I
1	Last Name	First Name	Street Address	City	State	Zip	Area Code	Survey Source	
2	Graham	Shelley	989 26th St.	Chicago	IL	60611	773	Education Website	
3	Hogan	Andy	32 William St.	Concord	MA	01742	508	Education Website	
4	Kelly	Shawn	22 Kendall St.	Cambridge	MA	02138	617	Education Website	
5	Masters	Latrice	88 Las Puntas Rd.	Boston	MA	02205	617	Education Website	
6	Nelson	Michael	229 Rally Rd.	Kansas City	MO	64105	816	Education Website	
7	Dickenson	Tonia	883 E. 34th St.	New York	NY	10044	212	Education Website	
8	Gonzales	Fred	5532 West St.	Houston	TX	77098	281	Education Website	
9	Chelly	Yvonne	900 Sola St.	San Diego	CA	92106	619	Health Center	
10	Worthen	Sally	2120 Central St.	San Francisco	CA	93772	415	Health Center	
11	Malone	Kris	1 South St.	San Francisco	CA	94177	415	Health Center	
12	Ross	Kim	4 Ridge Rd.	San Francisco	CA	94177	415	Health Center	
13	Roberts	Bob	56 Water St	Chicago	IL	60618	771	Health Center	
14	Kim	Janie	9 First St.	San Francisco	CA	94177	415	Health Website	
15	Oren	Scott	72 Yankee St.	Brookfield	CT	06830	203	Health Website	
16	Duran	Maria	Galvin St.	Chicago	IL	60614	773	Health Website	
17	Smith	Carolyn	921 Lopez St.	San Diego	CA	92104	619	Newspaper	
18	Herbert	Greg	1192 Dome St.	San Diego	CA	93303	619	Newspaper	
19	Kelly	Janie	9 First St.	San Francisco	CA	94177	415	Newspaper	
20	Roberts	Bob	56 Water St	Chicago	IL	60614	312	Newspaper	
21	Miller	Hope	111 Stratton St.	Chicago	IL	60614	773	Newspaper	
22	Warner	Salvatore	100 Westside St.	Chicago	IL	60620	312	Newspaper	

j. Enter your name in the center section of the worksheet footer.

k. Add a centered header that reads **Client Survey** in bold with a font size of 16.

l. Add print titles to repeat the first row at the top of each printed page.

m. Save the workbook, preview it, then submit the workbook to your instructor.

n. Close the workbook, then exit Excel.

Independent Challenge 2

You manage Illuminate, a store that sells LED bulbs in bulk online. Your customers purchase items in quantities of 10 or more. You decide to plan and build a table that tracks recent sales, and includes customer information and transaction details.

a. Prepare a plan for a table that includes details about sales transactions, including the customer's name and what they purchased.

b. Sketch a sample table on a piece of paper, indicating how the table should be built. Create a table documenting the table design including the field names, type of data, and description of the data. Some examples of items are 60W Soft White, 65W Soft White, 60W Daylight, 65W Daylight, and 100W Daylight.

Independent Challenge 2 (continued)

c. Start Excel, create a new workbook, then save it as **EX 7-LED** in the location where you store your Data Files. Enter the field names shown in the table below in the designated cells:

cell	field name
A1	Customer Last
B1	Customer First
C1	Item
D1	Quantity
E1	Cost

d. Enter eight data records using your own data.

e. Define the data as a table using the data in the range A1:E9. Adjust the column widths as necessary.

f. Apply the Table Style Light 7 to the table.

g. Add a field named **Total** in cell F1.

h. Enter a formula in cell F2 that calculates the total by multiplying the Quantity field by the Cost field. Check that the formula was filled down in the column.

i. Format the Cost and Total columns using the Accounting number format. Adjust the column widths as necessary.

j. Add a new record to your table in row 10. Add another record above row 4.

k. Sort the table in ascending order by Cost.

l. Enter your name in the worksheet footer, then save the workbook.

m. Preview the worksheet, then submit your workbook to your instructor.

n. Close the workbook, then exit Excel.

Independent Challenge 3

You are a sales manager at a consulting firm. You are managing your accounts using an Excel worksheet and have decided that a table will provide additional features to help you keep track of the accounts. You will use the table sorting features and table formulas to analyze your account data.

a. Start Excel, open EX 7-4.xlsx from the location where you store your Data Files, then save it as **EX 7-Accounts**.

b. Create a table with the worksheet data, and apply a table style of your choice. Adjust the column widths as necessary.

c. Sort the table on the Budget field using the Smallest to Largest order.

d. Sort the table using two fields, first by Contact in A to Z order, then by Budget in Smallest to Largest order.

e. Add the new field label **Balance** in cell G1, and adjust the column width as necessary.

f. Enter a formula in cell G2 that uses structured references to table fields to calculate the balance on an account as the Budget minus the Expenses.

g. Add a new record with an account number of **4113** with a type of **Inside**, a code of **I5**, a budget of **$550,000**, expenses of **$400,000**, and a contact of **Maureen Smith**.

h. Verify that the formula accurately calculated the balance for the new record.

i. Replace all of the Maureen Smith data with **Maureen Lang**.

j. Find the record for the 2188 account number and delete it.

k. Delete the Type and code fields from the table.

Independent Challenge 3 (continued)

l. Add a total row to the table and display the totals for appropriate columns. Adjust the column widths as necessary. Compare your table to FIGURE 7-24. (Your table style may differ.)

FIGURE 7-24

	A	B	C	D	E
1	Account Number ▾	Budget ▾↓	Expenses ▾	Contact ▾↓	Balance ▾
2	1084	$ 275,000	$ 215,000	Cindy Boil	$ 60,000
3	5431	$ 375,000	$ 250,000	Cindy Boil	$ 125,000
4	9624	$ 650,000	$ 550,000	Cindy Boil	$ 100,000
5	2117	$ 550,000	$ 525,000	Kathy Jenkins	$ 25,000
6	5647	$ 750,000	$ 600,000	Kathy Jenkins	$ 150,000
7	6671	$ 175,000	$ 150,000	Maureen Lang	$ 25,000
8	1097	$ 250,000	$ 210,000	Maureen Lang	$ 40,000
9	4301	$ 350,000	$ 210,000	Maureen Lang	$ 140,000
10	7814	$ 410,000	$ 320,000	Maureen Lang	$ 90,000
11	4113	$ 550,000	$ 400,000	Maureen Lang	$ 150,000
12	Total	$ 4,335,000	$ 3,430,000		$ 905,000
13					
14					

m. Enter your name in the center section of the worksheet footer, add a center section header of **Accounts** using formatting of your choice, change the page orientation to landscape, then save the workbook.

n. Preview your workbook, submit the workbook to your instructor, close the workbook, then exit Excel.

Independent Challenge 4: Explore

As the sales manager at a environmental supply firm, you track the sales data of the associates in the department using a table in Excel. You decide to highlight associates that have met the annual sales targets for the annual meeting.

a. Start Excel, open EX 7-5.xlsx from the location where you store your Data Files, then save it as **EX 7-Sales**.

b. Create a table that includes all the worksheet data, and apply the table style of your choice. Adjust the column widths as necessary.

c. Sort the table on the Balance field using the Largest to Smallest order.

d. Use conditional formatting to format the cells of the table containing positive balances with a light red fill.

e. Sort the table using the Balance field using the order of No Fill on top.

f. Format the table to emphasize the Balance column, and turn off the banded rows. (*Hint*: Use the Table Style Options on the Table Tools Design tab.)

g. Research how to print nonadjacent areas on a single page. (Excel prints nonadjacent areas of a worksheet on separate pages by default.) Add a new sheet to the workbook, then enter the result of your research on Sheet2 of the workbook.

h. Return to Sheet1 and create a print area that prints only the Employee Number, Associate, and Balance columns of the table on one page.

FIGURE 7-25

	A	B	E
1	Employee Number ▾	Associate ▾	Balance ▾↓
2	6547	Larry Makay	$ (5,000)
3	2984	George Well	$ (10,000)
4	4874	George Well	$ (73,126)
5	6647	Kris Lowe	$ (95,000)
6	5512	Nancy Alden	$ 108,357
7	3004	Lou Colby	$ 95,000
8	4257	Bob Allen	$ 50,000
9	9821	Joe Wood	$ 45,000
10	8624	Judy Smith	$ 25,000
11	1005	Janet Casey	$ 17,790

i. Compare your table with FIGURE 7-25. Save the workbook.

j. Preview your print area to make sure it will print on a single page.

k. Enter your name in the worksheet footer, then save the workbook.

l. Submit the workbook to your instructor, close the workbook, then exit Excel.

Visual Workshop

Start Excel, open EX 7-6.xlsx from the location where you store your Data Files, then save it as **EX 7-Technicians**. Create a table and sort the data as shown in FIGURE 7-26. (*Hint*: The table is formatted using Table Style Medium 13.) Add a worksheet header with the sheet name in the center section that is formatted in bold with a size of 14. Enter your name in the center section of the worksheet footer. Save the workbook, preview the table, close the workbook, submit the workbook to your instructor, then exit Excel.

FIGURE 7-26

	A	B	C	D	E
1	Job Number	Employee Number	Amount Billed	Location	Technician Name
2	2257	69741	$ 109.88	Main	Eric Mallon
3	1032	65418	$ 158.32	Satellite	Eric Mallon
4	1587	10057	$ 986.34	Main	Jerry Thomas
5	1533	66997	$ 112.98	Satellite	Jerry Thomas
6	2187	58814	$ 521.77	Satellite	Jerry Thomas
7	2588	69784	$ 630.55	Main	Joan Rand
8	2001	48779	$ 478.24	Satellite	Joan Rand
9	1251	69847	$ 324.87	Main	Kathy Green
10	2113	36697	$ 163.88	Main	Kathy Green
11	2357	10087	$ 268.24	Main	Mark Eaton
12	1111	13987	$ 658.30	Satellite	Mark Eaton
13					

Analyzing Table Data

CASE The vice president of sales and marketing, Mary Watson, asks you to display information from a table of scheduled projects to help the sales representatives with customer inquiries. She also asks you to summarize the project sales for a presentation at the international sales meeting. You will prepare these using various filters, subtotals, and Excel functions.

Module Objectives

After completing this module, you will be able to:

- Filter a table
- Create a custom filter
- Filter a table with the Advanced Filter
- Extract table data
- Look up values in a table
- Summarize table data
- Validate table data
- Create subtotals

Files You Will Need

EX 8-1.xlsx	EX 8-5.xlsx
EX 8-2.xlsx	EX 8-6.xlsx
EX 8-3.xlsx	EX 8-7.xlsx
EX 8-4.xlsx	

Filter a Table

An Excel table lets you easily manipulate large amounts of data to view only the data you want, using a feature called **AutoFilter**. When you create a table, arrows automatically appear next to each column header. These arrows are called **filter list arrows**, **AutoFilter list arrows**, or **list arrows**, and you can use them to **filter** a table to display only the records that meet criteria you specify, temporarily hiding records that do not meet those criteria. For example, you can use the filter list arrow next to the Project field header to display only records that contain Cheetah in the Project field. Once you filter data, you can copy, chart, and print the displayed records. You can easily clear a filter to redisplay all the records. **CASE** Mary asks you to display only the records for the Cheetah projects. She also asks for information about the projects that have the most reservations and the projects that depart in March.

STEPS

1. **Start Excel, open EX 8-1.xlsx from where you store your Data Files, then save it as EX 8-Projects**

2. **Click the Project list arrow**

   Sort options appear at the top of the menu, advanced filtering options appear in the middle, and at the bottom is a list of the project data from column A, as shown in **FIGURE 8-1**. Because you want to display data for only the Cheetah projects, your **search criterion** (the text you are searching for) is Cheetah. You can select one of the Project data options in the menu, which acts as your search criterion.

3. **In the list of projects for the Project field, click Select All to clear the check marks from the projects, scroll down the list of projects, click Cheetah, then click OK**

   Only those records containing "Cheetah" in the Project field appear, as shown in **FIGURE 8-2**. The row numbers for the matching records change to blue, and the list arrow for the filtered field has a filter icon 🔽 . Both indicate that there is a filter in effect and that some of the records are temporarily hidden.

4. **Move the pointer over the Project list arrow**

   The ScreenTip Project: Equals "Cheetah" describes the filter for the field, meaning that only the Cheetah records appear. You decide to remove the filter to redisplay all of the table data.

5. **Click the Project list arrow, then click Clear Filter From "Project"**

   You have cleared the Cheetah filter, and all the records reappear. You want to display the most popular projects, those that are in the top five percent of seats reserved.

6. **Click the Places Reserved list arrow, point to Number Filters, click Top 10, select 10 in the middle box, type 5, click the Items list arrow, click Percent, then click OK**

   Excel displays the records for the top five percent in the number of Places Reserved field, as shown in **FIGURE 8-3**. You decide to clear the filter to redisplay all the records.

7. **On the Home tab, click the Sort & Filter button in the Editing group, then click Clear**

   You have cleared the filter and all the records reappear. You can clear a filter using either the AutoFilter menu command or the Sort & Filter button on the Home tab. The Sort & Filter button is convenient for clearing multiple filters at once. You want to find all of the projects that depart in March.

8. **Click the Depart Date list arrow, point to Date Filters, point to All Dates in the Period, then click March**

   Excel displays the records for only the projects that leave in March. You decide to clear the filter and display all of the records.

9. **Click the Sort & Filter button in the Editing group, click Clear, then save the workbook**

FIGURE 8-1: Worksheet showing AutoFilter options

Project AutoFilter list arrow

Sort Options

Advanced filtering options

List of projects

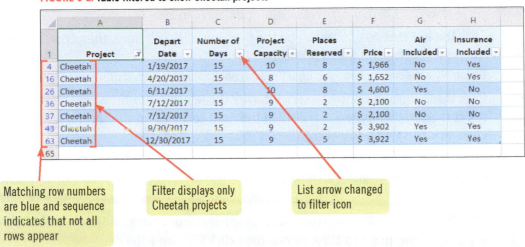

FIGURE 8-2: Table filtered to show Cheetah projects

	A	B	C	D	E	F	G	H
1	Project	Depart Date	Number of Days	Project Capacity	Places Reserved	Price	Air Included	Insurance Included
4	Cheetah	1/19/2017	15	10	8	$ 1,966	No	Yes
16	Cheetah	4/20/2017	15	8	6	$ 1,652	No	Yes
26	Cheetah	6/11/2017	15	10	8	$ 4,600	Yes	No
36	Cheetah	7/12/2017	15	9	2	$ 2,100	No	No
37	Cheetah	7/12/2017	15	9	2	$ 2,100	No	No
49	Cheetah	9/20/2017	15	9	2	$ 3,902	Yes	Yes
63	Cheetah	12/30/2017	15	9	5	$ 3,922	Yes	Yes
65								

Matching row numbers are blue and sequence indicates that not all rows appear

Filter displays only Cheetah projects

List arrow changed to filter icon

FIGURE 8-3: Table filtered with top 5% of Places Reserved

	A	B	C	D	E	F	G	H	I	J	K	L
1	Project	Depart Date	Number of Days	Project Capacity	Places Reserved	Price	Air Included	Insurance Included				
6	Dolphin	2/22/2017	14	10	10	$ 2,134	No	No				
12	Rhino	4/8/2017	15	10	10	$ 3,115	Yes	Yes				
32	Great White Shark	7/2/2017	14	10	9	$ 4,100	Yes	Yes				
65												
66												
67												

Table filtered with top 5% in this field

Excel 2016

Create a Custom Filter

Learning Outcomes
- Filter records with multiple criteria
- Determine when to use AND and OR logical conditions

While AutoFilter lists can display records that are equal to certain amounts, you often need more detailed filters, which you can create with the help of options in the Custom AutoFilter dialog box. For example, your criteria can contain comparison operators such as "greater than" or "less than" that let you display values above or below a certain amount. You can also use **logical conditions** like And and Or to narrow a search even further. You can have Excel display records that meet a criterion in a field *and* another criterion in that same field. This is often used to find records between two values. For example, by specifying an **And logical condition**, you can display records for customers with incomes that are above $40,000 *and* below $70,000. You can also have Excel display records that meet either criterion in a field by specifying an Or condition. The **Or logical condition** is used to find records that satisfy either of two values. For example, in a table of book data you can use the Or condition to find records that contain either Beginning *or* Introduction in the title name. **CASE** *Mary wants to locate projects for customers who want to participate in the winter months. She also wants to find projects that depart between February 15, 2017 and April 15, 2017. She asks you to create custom filters to find the projects satisfying these criteria.*

STEPS

1. **Click the Depart Date list arrow, point to Date Filters, then click Custom Filter**

   The Custom AutoFilter dialog box opens. You enter your criteria in the text boxes. The left text box on the first line currently displays "equals." Because you want to find all projects that occur in the winter months, you decide to search for tours starting before March 1 and after December 1.

2. **Click the left text box list arrow on the first line, click is before, then type 3/1/2017 in the right text box on the first line**

   To complete the custom filter, you need to add a condition for projects starting after December 1.

QUICK TIP

When specifying criteria in the Custom Filter dialog box, you can use the (?) wildcard to represent any single character and the (*) wildcard to represent any series of characters.

3. **Click the Or option button to select it, click the left text box list arrow on the second line, select is after, then type 12/1/2017 in the right text box on the second line**

   Your completed Custom AutoFilter dialog box should match **FIGURE 8-4**.

4. **Click OK**

   The dialog box closes, and only those records having departing before 3/1 or after 12/1 appear in the worksheet. You want to find all projects that depart between February 15, 2017 and April 15, 2017.

5. **Click the Depart Date list arrow, click Clear Filter From "Depart Date", click the Depart Date list arrow, point to Date Filters, then click Custom Filter**

   You want to find the departure dates that are between February 15, 2017 and April 15, 2017 (that is, after February 15 *and* before April 15).

6. **Click the left text box list arrow on the first line, click is after, then type 2/15/2017 in the right text box on the first line**

   The And condition is selected, which is correct.

7. **Click the left text box list arrow on the second line, select is before, type 4/15/2017 in the right text box on the second line, then click OK**

   The records displayed have departure dates between February 15, 2017 and April 15, 2017. Compare your records to those shown in **FIGURE 8-5**.

8. **Click the Depart Date list arrow, click Clear Filter From "Depart Date", then add your name to the center section of the footer**

   You have cleared the filter, and all the project records reappear.

FIGURE 8-4: Custom AutoFilter dialog box

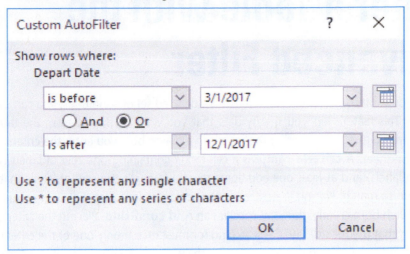

FIGURE 8-5: Results of custom filter

	A	B	C	D	E	F	G	H
1	Project	Depart Date	Number of Days	Project Capacity	Places Reserved	Price	Air Included	Insurance Included
6	Dolphin	2/22/2017	14	10	10	$ 2,134	No	No
7	Orangutan	2/28/2017	17	8	4	$ 4,812	Yes	No
8	Great White Shark	3/13/2017	14	10	5	$ 4,350	Yes	No
9	Coral Reef	3/19/2017	18	6	5	$ 2,110	No	Yes
10	Orangutan	3/20/2017	17	10	8	$ 1,755	No	Yes
11	African Wild Dog	3/23/2017	18	8	7	$ 2,450	No	No
12	Rhino	4/8/2017	15	10	10	$ 3,115	Yes	Yes
13	Elephant	4/11/2017	12	10	5	$ 4,255	Yes	No
65								
66								

Departure dates are between 2/15 and 4/15

Using more than one rule when conditionally formatting data

You can apply conditional formatting to table cells in the same way that you can format a range of worksheet data. You can add multiple rules by clicking the Home tab, clicking the Conditional Formatting button in the Styles group, then clicking New Rule for each additional rule that you want to apply. You can also add rules using the Conditional Formatting Rules Manager, which displays all of the rules for a data range. To use the Rules Manager, click the Home tab, click the

Conditional Formatting button in the Styles group, click Manage Rules, then click New Rule for each rule that you want to apply to the data range. You can also use a function to conditionally format cells. For example, if you have a column of invoice dates and you want to format the dates that are overdue, open the Rules Manager, click Use a formula in the Select a Rule Type section, and then edit the rule description add a formula such as "<TODAY()."

Filter a Table with the Advanced Filter

When you want to see table data that meets a detailed set of conditions, you can use the Advanced Filter feature. This feature lets you specify data that you want to display from the table using And and Or conditions. Rather than entering the criteria in a dialog box, you enter the criteria in a criteria range on your worksheet. A **criteria range** is a cell range containing one row of labels (usually a copy of the column labels) and at least one additional row underneath the row of labels that contains the criteria you want to match. Placing the criteria in the same row indicates that the records you are searching for must match both criteria; that is, it specifies an **And condition**. Placing the criteria in the different rows indicates that the records you are searching for must match only one of the criterion; that is, it specifies an **Or condition**. With the criteria range on the worksheet, you can easily see the criteria by which your table is sorted. Another advantage of the Advanced Filter is that you can move filtered table data to a different area of the worksheet or to a new worksheet, as you will see in the next lesson. **CASE** *Mary wants to identify projects that depart after 6/1/2017 and that cost less than $2,000. She asks you to use the Advanced Filter to retrieve these records. You begin by defining the criteria range.*

STEPS

1. **Select table rows 1 through 6, then click the Insert list arrow in the Cells group**
   Six blank rows are added above the table.

2. **Click Insert Sheet Rows; click cell A1, type Criteria Range, then click the Enter button ✓ on the formula bar**
   Excel does not require the label "Criteria Range", but it is useful to see the column labels as you organize the worksheet and use filters.

3. **Select the range A7:H7, click the Copy button in the Clipboard group, click cell A2, click the Paste button in the Clipboard group, then press [Esc]**
   Next, you want to insert criteria that will display records for only those projects that depart after June 1, 2017 and that cost under $2,000.

4. **Click cell B3, type >6/1/2017, click cell F3, type <2000, then click ✓**
   You have entered the criteria in the cells directly beneath the Criteria Range labels, as shown in **FIGURE 8-6**.

5. **Click any cell in the table, click the Data tab, then click the Advanced button in the Sort & Filter group**
   The Advanced Filter dialog box opens, with the table (list) range already entered. The default setting under Action is to filter the table in its current location ("in-place") rather than copy it to another location.

6. **Click the Criteria range text box, select the range A2:H3 in the worksheet, then click OK**
   You have specified the criteria range and used the filter. The filtered table contains seven records that match both criteria—the departure date is after 6/1/2017 and the price is less than $2,000, as shown in **FIGURE 8-7**. You'll filter this table even further in the next lesson.

FIGURE 8-6: Criteria in the same row indicating an and condition

	Project	Depart Date	Number of Days	Project Capacity	Places Reserved	Price	Air Included	Insurance Included
1	Criteria Range							
2								
3		>6/1/2017				<2000		
4								
5								
6								
7	Project	Date	Days	Capacity	Reserved	Price	Included	Included
8	Elephant	1/12/2017	12	10	5	$ 4,255	Yes	No
9	Rhino	1/13/2017	15	8	8	$ 1,984	No	No

Filtered records will match these criteria

FIGURE 8-7: Filtered table

	Project	Depart Date	Number of Days	Project Capacity	Places Reserved	Price	Air Included	Insurance Included
1	Criteria Range							
2								
3		>6/1/2017				<2000		
4								
5								
6								
7	Project	Depart Date	Number of Days	Project Capacity	Places Reserved	Price	Air Included	Insurance Included
33	Elephant	6/12/2017	12	7	5	$ 1,900	No	No
34	Rhino	6/12/2017	15	8	6	$ 1,970	No	Yes
37	African Wild Dog	6/27/2017	18	10	7	$ 1,944	No	No
44	African Wild Dog	7/27/2017	18	10	2	$ 1,890	No	No
46	Orangutan	8/12/2017	17	10	3	$ 1,970	No	Yes
49	Great White Shark	8/27/2017	14	10	8	$ 1,944	No	No
61	Great White Shark	10/31/2017	14	9	8	$ 1,900	No	No
71								
72								

Depart dates are after 6/1/2017

Prices are less than $2000

Saving time with conditional formatting

You can emphasize top- or bottom-ranked values in a field using conditional formatting. To highlight the top or bottom values in a field, select the field data, click the Conditional Formatting button in the Styles group on the Home tab, point to Top/ Bottom Rules, select a Top or Bottom rule, if necessary enter the percentage or number of cells in the selected range that you want to format, select the format for the cells that meet the top or bottom criteria, then click OK. You can also format your worksheet or table data using icon sets and color scales based on the cell values. A **color scale** uses a set of two, three, or four fill colors to convey relative values. For example, red could fill cells to indicate they have higher values and green could signify lower values. To add a color scale, select a data range, click the Home tab, click the Conditional Formatting button in the Styles group, then point to Color Scales. On the submenu, you can select preformatted color sets or click More Rules to create your own color sets. **Icon sets** let you visually communicate relative cell values by adding icons to cells based on the values they contain. An upward-pointing green arrow might represent the highest values, and downward-pointing red arrows could represent lower values. To add an icon set to a data range, select a data range, click the Conditional Formatting button in the Styles group, then point to Icon Sets. You can customize the values that are used as thresholds for color scales and icon sets by clicking the Conditional Formatting button in the Styles group, clicking Manage Rules, clicking the rule in the Conditional Formatting Rules Manager dialog box, then clicking Edit Rule.

Extract Table Data

Learning Outcomes
• Extract filtered records to another worksheet location
• Clear filtered records

Whenever you take the time to specify a complicated set of search criteria, it's a good idea to extract the matching records, rather than filtering it in place. When you **extract** data, you place a copy of a filtered table in a range that you specify in the Advanced Filter dialog box. This way, you won't accidentally clear the filter or lose track of the records you spent time compiling. To extract data, you use an Advanced Filter and enter the criteria beneath the copied field names, as you did in the previous lesson. You then specify the location where you want the extracted data to appear. **CASE** *Mary needs to filter the table one step further to reflect only African Wild Dog or Great White Shark projects in the current filtered table. She asks you to complete this filter by specifying an Or condition, which you will do by entering two sets of criteria in two separate rows. You decide to save the filtered records by extracting them to a different location in the worksheet.*

STEPS

1. **In cell A3 enter African Wild Dog, then in cell A4 enter Great White Shark**

   The new sets of criteria need to appear in two separate rows, so you need to copy the previous filter criteria to the second row.

2. **Copy the criteria in cells B3:F3 to B4:F4**

   The criteria are shown in **FIGURE 8-8**. When you use the Advanced Filter this time, you indicate that you want to copy the filtered table to a range beginning in cell A75, so that Mary can easily refer to the data, even if you use more filters later.

3. **If necessary, click the Data tab, then click Advanced in the Sort & Filter group**

4. **Under Action, click the Copy to another location option button to select it, click the Copy to text box, then type A75**

   The last time you filtered the table, the criteria range included only rows 2 and 3. Now you have criteria in row 4, so you need to adjust the criteria range.

5. **Edit the contents of the Criteria range text box to show the range $A$2:$H$4, click OK, then if necessary scroll down until row 75 is visible**

   The matching records appear in the range beginning in cell A75, as shown in **FIGURE 8-9**. The original table, starting in cell A7, contains the records filtered in the previous lesson.

6. **Press [Ctrl][Home], then click the Clear button in the Sort & Filter group**

   The original table is displayed starting in cell A7, and the extracted table remains in A75:H79.

7. **Save the workbook**

FIGURE 8-8: Criteria in separate rows

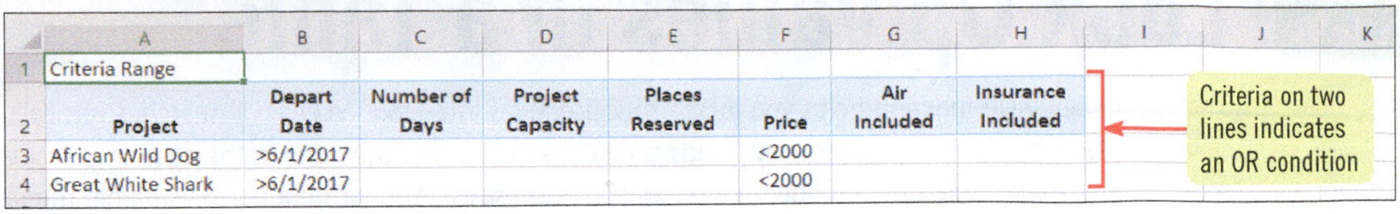

	A	B	C	D	E	F	G	H	I	J	K
1	Criteria Range										
2	Project	Depart Date	Number of Days	Project Capacity	Places Reserved	Price	Air Included	Insurance Included			
3	African Wild Dog	>6/1/2017				<2000					
4	Great White Shark	>6/1/2017				<2000					

Criteria on two lines indicates an OR condition

FIGURE 8-9: Extracted data records

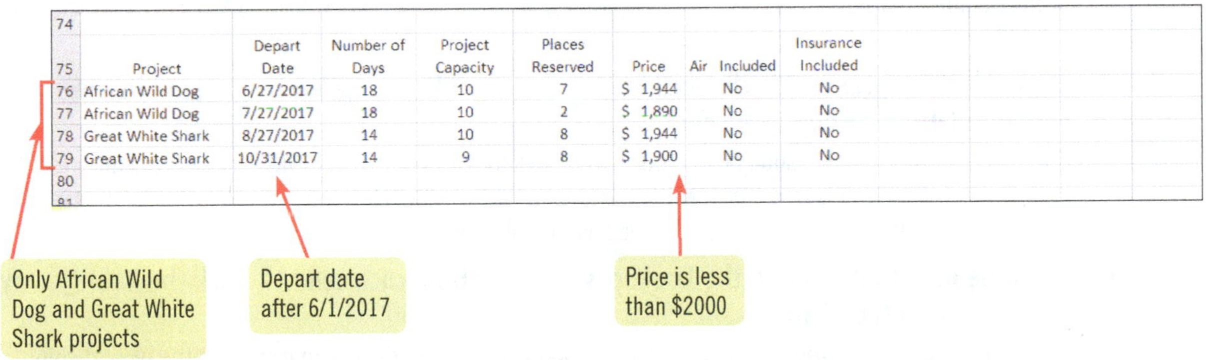

	Project	Depart Date	Number of Days	Project Capacity	Places Reserved	Price	Air Included	Insurance Included			
74											
75	Project	Depart Date	Number of Days	Project Capacity	Places Reserved	Price	Air Included	Insurance Included			
76	African Wild Dog	6/27/2017	18	10	7	$ 1,944	No	No			
77	African Wild Dog	7/27/2017	18	10	2	$ 1,890	No	No			
78	Great White Shark	8/27/2017	14	10	8	$ 1,944	No	No			
79	Great White Shark	10/31/2017	14	9	8	$ 1,900	No	No			
80											

Only African Wild Dog and Great White Shark projects

Depart date after 6/1/2017

Price is less than $2000

Understanding the criteria range and the copy-to location

When you define the criteria range and the copy-to location in the Advanced Filter dialog box, Excel automatically creates the range names Criteria and Extract for these ranges in the worksheet. The Criteria range includes the field names and any criteria rows underneath them. The Extract range includes just the field names above the extracted table. You can select these ranges by clicking the Name box list arrow, then clicking the range name. If you click the Name Manager button in the Defined Names group on the Formulas tab, you will see these new names and the ranges associated with each one.

Look Up Values in a Table

Learning Outcomes
- Use table references in a VLOOKUP formula
- Find table information using VLOOKUP

The Excel VLOOKUP function helps you locate specific values in a table. VLOOKUP searches vertically (V) down the far left column of a table, then reads across the row to find the value in the column you specify, much as you might look up a number in a name and address list: You locate a person's name, then read across the row to find the phone number you want. **CASE** ▶ *Mary wants to be able to find a project by entering the project code. You will use the VLOOKUP function to accomplish this task. You begin by viewing the table name so you can refer to it in a lookup function.*

STEPS

1. **Click the Lookup sheet tab, click the Formulas tab in the Ribbon, then click the Name Manager button in the Defined Names group**

   The named ranges for the workbook appear in the Name Manager dialog box, as shown in **FIGURE 8-10**. The Criteria and Extract ranges appear at the top of the range name list. At the bottom of the list is information about the three tables in the workbook. Table1 refers to the table on the 2017 Projects sheet, Table2 refers to the table on the Lookup sheet, and Table3 refers to the table on the Subtotals worksheet. The Excel structured reference feature automatically created these table names when the tables were created.

2. **Click Close**

   You want to find the project represented by the code 754Q. The VLOOKUP function lets you find the project name for any project code. You will enter a project code in cell M1 and a VLOOKUP function in cell M2.

3. **Click cell M1, enter 754Q, click cell M2, click the Lookup & Reference button in the Function Library group, then click VLOOKUP**

   The Function Arguments dialog box opens, with boxes for each of the VLOOKUP arguments. Because the value you want to find is in cell M1, M1 is the Lookup_value. The table you want to search is the table on the Lookup sheet, so its assigned name, Table2, is the Table_array.

4. **With the insertion point in the Lookup_value text box, click cell M1, click the Table_array text box, then type Table2**

   The column containing the information that you want to find and display in cell M2 is the second column from the left in the table range, so the Col_index_num is 2. Because you want to find an exact match for the value in cell M1, the Range_lookup argument is FALSE.

5. **Click the Col_index_num text box, type 2, click the Range_lookup text box, then enter FALSE**

   Your completed Function Arguments dialog box should match **FIGURE 8-11**.

6. **Click OK**

   Excel searches down the far-left column of the table until it finds a project code that matches the one in cell M1. It then looks in column 2 of the table range and finds the project for that record, Dolphin, and displays it in cell M2. You use this function to determine the project for one other project code.

7. **Click cell M1, type 335P, then click the Enter button ✓ on the formula bar**

   The VLOOKUP function returns the value of Elephant in cell M2.

8. **Press [Ctrl][Home], then save the workbook**

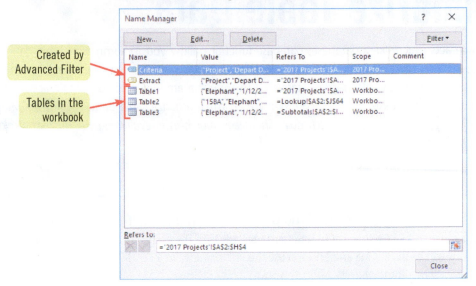

FIGURE 8-10: Named ranges in the workbook

Created by Advanced Filter

Tables in the workbook

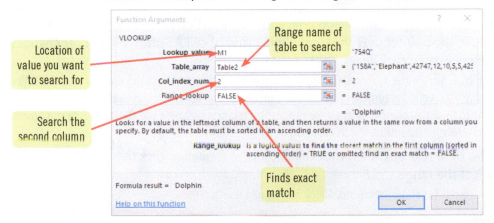

FIGURE 8-11: Completed Function Arguments dialog box for VLOOKUP

Range name of table to search

Location of value you want to search for

Search the second column

Finds exact match

Using other LOOKUP functions

When your data is arranged horizontally in rows instead of vertically in columns, use the HLOOKUP (Horizontal Lookup) function. HLOOKUP searches horizontally across the upper row of a table until it finds the matching value, then looks down the number of rows you specify. The arguments are identical to those for the VLOOKUP function, except that instead of a Col_index_number, HLOOKUP uses a Row_index_number, which indicates the location of the row you want to search. You can use the MATCH function when you want the position of an item in a range. The MATCH function uses the syntax: MATCH (lookup_value,lookup_array,match_ type) where the lookup_value is the value you want to match in the lookup_ array range. The match_type can be 0 for an exact match,

1 for matching the largest value that is less than or equal to lookup_value, or –1 for matching the smallest value that is greater than or equal to the lookup_value. The Transpose function is a LOOKUP function that can be used to rearrange a range of cells, which is also called an array. For example, a vertical range of cells will be arranged horizontally or vice versa. The Transpose array function is entered using the syntax: =TRANSPOSE(range array).

The LOOKUP function is used to locate information in a table. The syntax for the LOOKUP formula is LOOKUP(lookup_value, array). The lookup_value is the value that will be used in the search, the array is the range of cells that will be searched for the lookup_value.

Excel 2016

Summarize Table Data

Learning Outcomes
- Summarize table data using DSUM
- Summarize table data using DCOUNT or DCOUNTA

Because a table acts much like a database, database functions allow you to summarize table data in a variety of ways. When working with a sales activity table, for example, you can use Excel to count the number of client contacts by sales representative or to total the amount sold to specific accounts by month. **TABLE 8-1** lists database functions commonly used to summarize table data. **CASE** ▶ *Mary is considering adding projects for the 2017 schedule. She needs your help in evaluating the number of places available for scheduled projects.*

STEPS

1. **Review the criteria range for the Rhino project in the range L5:L6**

   The criteria range in L5:L6 tells Excel to summarize records with the entry "Rhino" in the Project column. The functions will be in cells M8 and M9. You use this criteria range in a DSUM function to sum the places available for only the Rhino projects.

2. **Click cell M8, click the Insert Function button in the Function Library group, in the Search for a function text box type database, click Go, scroll to and click DSUM under Select a function, then click OK**

   The first argument of the DSUM function is the table, or database.

   > **QUICK TIP**
   > Because the DSUM formula uses the column headings to locate and sum the table data, you need to include the header row in the database range.

3. **In the Function Arguments dialog box, with the insertion point in the Database text box, move the pointer over the upper-left corner of cell A1 until the pointer changes to ↘, click once, then click again**

   The first click selects the table's data range, and the second click selects the entire table, including the header row. The second argument of the DSUM function is the label for the column that you want to sum. You want to total the number of available places. The last argument for the DSUM function is the criteria that will be used to determine which values to total.

   > **QUICK TIP**
   > You can move the Function Arguments dialog box if it overlaps a cell or range that you need to click. You can also click the Collapse Dialog Box button 🔳, select the cell or range, then click the Expand Dialog Box button 🔳 to return to the Function Arguments dialog box.

4. **Click the Field text box, then click cell G1, Places Available; click the Criteria text box and select the range L5:L6**

   Your completed Function Arguments dialog box should match **FIGURE 8-12**.

5. **Click OK**

   The result in cell M8 is 25. Excel totaled the information in the Places Available column for those records that meet the criterion of Project equals Rhino. The DCOUNT and the DCOUNTA functions can help you determine the number of records meeting specified criteria in a database field. DCOUNTA counts the number of nonblank cells. You will use DCOUNTA to determine the number of projects scheduled.

6. **Click cell M9, click the Insert Function button 🖍 on the formula bar, in the Search for a function text box type database, click Go, then double-click DCOUNTA in the Select a function list**

7. **With the insertion point in the Database text box, move the pointer over the upper-left corner of cell A1 until the pointer changes to ↘, click once, click again to include the header row, click the Field text box, click cell B1, click the Criteria text box and select the range L5:L6, then click OK**

   The result in cell M9 is 8, and it indicates that there are eight Rhino projects scheduled for the year. You also want to display the number of places available for the Dolphin projects.

8. **Click cell L6, type Dolphin, then click the Enter button ✅ on the formula bar**

   The formulas in cells M8 and M9 are updated to reflect the new criteria. **FIGURE 8-13** shows that 33 places are available in the six scheduled Dolphin projects.

FIGURE 8-12: Completed Function Arguments dialog box for DSUM

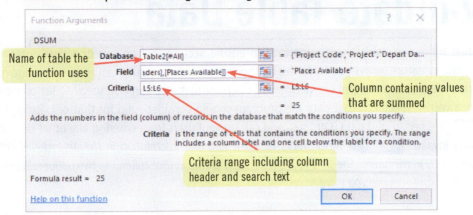

Name of table the function uses → Database Table2[#All] = {"Project Code","Project","Depart Da...

Field iders],[Places Available]] = "Places Available"

Criteria L5:L6 = L5:L6

= 25

Adds the numbers in the field (column) of records in the database that match the conditions you specify.

Criteria is the range of cells that contains the conditions you specify. The range includes a column label and one cell below the label for a condition.

Column containing values that are summed

Criteria range including column header and search text

Formula result = 25

Help on this function

OK   Cancel

FIGURE 8-13: Result generated by database functions

	E	F	G	H	I	J	K	L	M
1	Project Capacity	Places Reserved	Places Available	Price	Air Included	Insurance Included		Project Code	335P
2	10	5	5	$ 4,255	Yes	No		Project	Elephant
3	8	8	0	$ 1,984	No	No		Project Information	
4	10	8	2	$ 1,966	No	Yes			
5	7	7	0	$ 3,850	Yes	Yes		Project	
6	10	10	0	$ 2,134	No	No		Dolphin	
7	8	4	4	$ 4,812	Yes	No			
8	10	5	5	$ 4,350	Yes	No		Places Available	33
9	6	5	1	$ 2,110	No	Yes		Number of projects scheduled	6
10	10	8	2	$ 1,755	No	Yes			
11	8	7	1	$ 2,450	No	No			
12	10	10	0	$ 3,115	Yes	Yes			
13	10	5	5	$ 4,255	Yes	No			
14	9	8	1	$ 1,900	No	No			

Information for Dolphin projects

TABLE 8-1: Common database functions

function	result
DGET	Extracts a single record from a table that matches criteria you specify
DSUM	Totals numbers in a given table column that match criteria you specify
DAVERAGE	Averages numbers in a given table column that match criteria you specify
DCOUNT	Counts the cells that contain numbers in a given table column that match criteria you specify
DCOUNTA	Counts the cells that contain nonblank data in a given table column that match criteria you specify

Analyzing Table Data

Validate Table Data

Learning Outcomes
• Use data validation to restrict data entry to specified values
• Insert table data using data validation

When setting up tables, you want to help ensure accuracy when you or others enter data. The Data Validation feature allows you to do this by specifying what data users can enter in a range of cells. You can restrict data to whole numbers, decimal numbers, or text. You can also specify a list of acceptable entries. Once you've specified what data the program should consider valid for that cell, Excel displays an error message when invalid data is entered and can prevent users from entering any other data that it considers to be invalid. **CASE** Mary wants to make sure that information in the Air Included column is entered consistently in the future. She asks you to restrict the entries in that column to two options: Yes and No. First, you select the table column you want to restrict.

STEPS

1. **Click the top edge of the Air Included column header**
   The column data is selected.

2. **Click the Data tab, click the Data Validation button in the Data Tools group, in the Data Validation dialog box click the Settings tab if necessary, click the Allow list arrow, then click List**
   Selecting the List option lets you type a list of specific options.

   QUICK TIP
   To specify a long list of valid entries, type the list in a column or row elsewhere in the worksheet, then type the list range in the Source text box.

3. **Click the Source text box, then type Yes, No**
   You have entered the list of acceptable entries, separated by commas, as shown in **FIGURE 8-14**. You want the data entry person to be able to select a valid entry from a drop-down list.

4. **Verify that the In-cell dropdown check box contains a check mark, then click OK**
   The dialog box closes, and you return to the worksheet.

   TROUBLE
   If you get an invalid data error, make sure that cell I1 is not included in the selection. If I1 is included, open the Data Validation dialog box, click Clear All, click OK, then begin with Step 1 again.

5. **Click the Home tab, click any cell in the last table row, click the Insert list arrow in the Cells group, click Insert Table Row Below, click the Air Included cell in this row, then click its list arrow**
   A list of valid list entries opens, as shown in **FIGURE 8-15**. You could click an item in the list to enter in the cell, but you want to test the data restriction by entering an invalid entry.

6. **Click the list arrow to close the list, type Maybe, then press [Enter]**
   A warning dialog box appears and prevents you from entering the invalid data, as shown in **FIGURE 8-16**.

7. **Click Cancel, click the list arrow, then click Yes**
   The cell accepts the valid entry. The data restriction ensures that records contain only one of the two correct entries in the Air Included column. The table is ready for future data entry.

8. **Delete the last table row, add your name to the center section of the footer, then save the workbook**

Restricting cell values and data length

In addition to providing an in-cell drop-down list for data entry, you can use data validation to restrict the values that are entered into cells. For example, you might want to restrict cells in a selected range to values less than a certain number, date, or time. To do so, click the Data tab, click the Data Validation button in the Data Tools group, on the Settings tab click the Allow list arrow, select Whole number, Decimal, Date, or Time, click the Data list arrow, select less than, then in the bottom text box, enter the maximum value. You can also limit the length of data entered into cells by choosing Text length in the Allow list, clicking the Data list arrow and selecting less than, then entering the maximum length in the Maximum text box.

FIGURE 8-14: Creating data restrictions

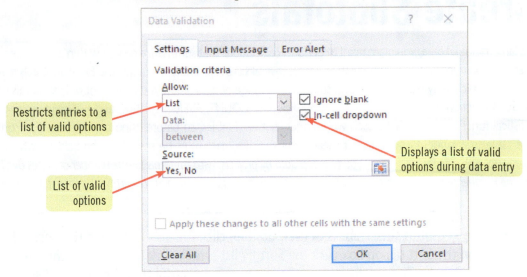

Restricts entries to a list of valid options

List of valid options

Displays a list of valid options during data entry

FIGURE 8-15: Entering data in restricted cells

59	621R	Orangutan	12/18/2017	17	8	1	7	$ 2,204	No	Yes
60	592D	Elephant	12/20/2017	12	10	0	10	$ 4,100	Yes	Yes
61	793T	Dolphin	12/20/2017	14	10	5	5	$ 2,100	No	Yes
62	307R	African Wild Dog	12/21/2017	18	9	8	1	$ 2,105	No	No
63	927F	Cheetah	12/30/2017	15	9	5	4	$ 3,922	Yes	Yes
64	448G	Elephant	12/31/2017	12	10	2	8	$ 2,100	No	No
65							0			
66										
67										
68										

Dropdown list → Yes / No

FIGURE 8-16: Invalid data warning

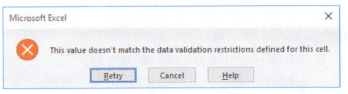

Microsoft Excel

This value doesn't match the data validation restrictions defined for this cell.

Retry   Cancel   Help

Adding input messages and error alerts

You can customize the way data validation works by using the two other tabs in the Data Validation dialog box: Input Message and Error Alert. The Input Message tab lets you set a message that appears when the user selects that cell. For example, the message might contain instructions about what type of data to enter. On the Input Message tab, enter a message title and message, then click OK. The Error Alert tab lets you set one of three alert styles if a user enters invalid data. The Information style displays your message with the information icon but allows the user to proceed with data entry. The Warning style displays your information with the warning icon and gives the user the option to proceed with data entry or not. The Stop style, which you used in this lesson, is the default; it displays your message and only lets the user retry or cancel data entry for that cell.

Create Subtotals

Learning Outcomes
• Summarize worksheet data using subtotals
• Use outline symbols
• Convert a table to a range

In a large range of data, you often need to perform calculations that summarize groups within a set of data. For example, you might need to subtotal the sales for several sales reps listed in a table. The Excel Subtotals feature provides a quick, easy way to group and summarize a range of data. It lets you create not only subtotals using the SUM function, but other statistics as well, including COUNT, AVERAGE, MAX, and MIN. However, these statistical functions can only be used with ranges, not with tables, so before using one you need to convert your table to a range. In order to get meaningful statistics, data must be sorted on the field on which you will group. **CASE** ▶ *Mary wants you to group data by projects, with subtotals for the number of places available and the number of places reserved. You begin by first sorting the table and then converting the table to a range.*

STEPS

1. **Click the** Subtotals **sheet tab, click the** Data tab, **click the** Sort button **in the Sort & Filter group, in the Sort dialog box click the** Sort by list arrow, **click** Project, **click the** Add Level button, **click the** Then by list arrow, **click** Depart Date, **verify that the order is** Oldest to Newest, **then click** OK

   You have sorted the table in ascending order, first by project, then by departure date within each project grouping.

2. **Click any cell in the table, click the** Table Tools Design tab, **click the** Convert to Range button **in the Tools group, then click** Yes

   The filter list arrows and the Table Tools Design tab no longer appear.

3. **Click the** Data tab **if necessary, click any cell in the data range if necessary, then click the** Subtotal button **in the Outline group**

   The Subtotal dialog box opens. Here you specify the items you want subtotaled, the function you want to apply to the values, and the fields you want to summarize.

4. **Click the** At each change in list arrow, **click** Project **if necessary, click the** Use function list arrow, **click** Sum; **in the "Add subtotal to" list click the** Places Reserved **and** Places Available check boxes **to select them if necessary, then click the** Insurance Included check box **to deselect it**

5. **If necessary, click the** Replace current subtotals **and** Summary below data check boxes **to select them**

   Your completed Subtotal dialog box should match **FIGURE 8-17**.

6. **Click** OK, **then scroll down so you can see row 73**

   The subtotaled data appears after each project grouping, showing the calculated subtotals and grand total in columns E and F. Excel displays an outline to the left of the worksheet, with outline buttons to control the level of detail that appears. The button number corresponds to the detail level that is displayed. You want to show the second level of detail, the subtotals and the grand total.

7. **Click the** outline symbol 2

   Only the subtotals and the grand total appear. Your subtotals and grand total should match **FIGURE 8-18**.

8. **Add your name to the center section of the footer, preview the worksheet, then save the workbook**

9. **Close the workbook, exit Excel, then submit the workbook to your instructor**

FIGURE 8-17: Completed Subtotal dialog box

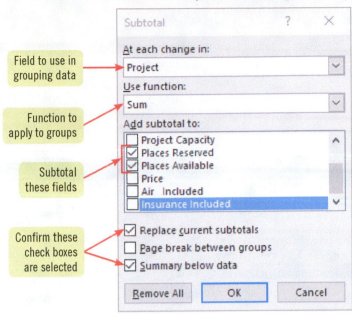

Field to use in grouping data

Function to apply to groups

Subtotal these fields

Confirm these check boxes are selected

FIGURE 8-18: Data with subtotals and grand total

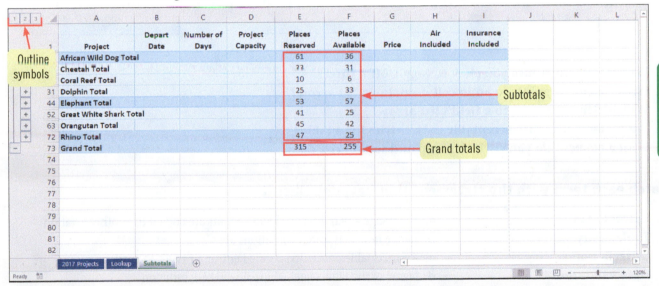

Outline symbols

Subtotals

Grand totals

Excel 2016

Practice

Concepts Review

FIGURE 8-19

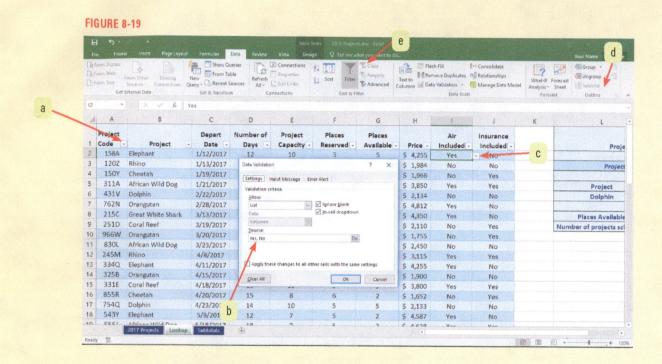

1. Which element would you click to toggle off a filter?
2. Which element points to an in-cell drop-down list arrow?
3. Which element points to a field's list arrow?
4. Where do you specify acceptable data entries for a table?
5. Which element do you click to group and summarize data?

Match each term with the statement that best describes it.

6. **Extracted table**
7. **Table_array**
8. **Criteria range**
9. **Data validation**
10. **DSUM**

   a. Cell range when Advanced Filter results are copied to another location
   b. Range in which search conditions are set
   c. Restricts table entries to specified entries or types of entries
   d. Name of the table searched in a VLOOKUP function
   e. Function used to total table values that meet specified criteria

Select the best answer from the list of choices.

11. **What does it mean when you select the Or option when creating a custom filter?**
   a. Both criteria must be true to find a match.
   b. Neither criterion has to be 100% true.
   c. Either criterion can be true to find a match.
   d. A custom filter requires a criteria range.

12. **The _____ logical condition finds records matching both listed criteria.**
   a. True
   b. Or
   c. And
   d. False

13. **Which function finds the position of an item in a table?**
   a. VLOOKUP   **c.** DGET
   b. MATCH   **d.** HLOOKUP

14. **What must a data range have before subtotals can be inserted?**
   a. Enough records to show multiple subtotals   **c.** Formatted cells
   b. Sorted data   **d.** Grand totals

Skills Review

1. **Filter a table.**
   a. Start Excel, open EX 8-2.xlsx from where you store your Data Files, then save it as **EX 8-HR**.
   b. With the Compensation sheet active, filter the table to list only records for employees in the Dallas branch.
   c. Clear the filter, then add a filter that displays the records for employees in the Dallas and LA branches.
   d. Redisplay all employees, then use a filter to show the three employees with the highest annual salary.
   e. Redisplay all the records.

2. **Create a custom filter.**
   a. Create a custom filter showing employees hired before 1/1/2015 or after 12/31/2016.
   b. Create a custom filter showing employees hired between 1/1/2014 and 12/31/2015.
   c. Enter your name in the worksheet footer, then preview the filtered worksheet.
   d. Redisplay all records.
   e. Save the workbook.

3. **Filter and extract a table with the Advanced Filter.**
   a. Retrieve a list of employees who were hired before 1/1/2017 and who have an annual salary of more than $75,000 a year. Define a criteria range by inserting six new rows above the table on the worksheet and copying the field names into the first row.
   b. In cell D2, enter the criterion **<1/1/2017**, then in cell G2 enter **>75000**.
   c. Click any cell in the table.
   d. Open the Advanced Filter dialog box.
   e. Indicate that you want to copy to another location, enter the criteria range **A1:J2**, verify that the List range is $A$7:$J$17, then indicate that you want to place the extracted list in the range starting at cell **A20**.
   f. Confirm that the retrieved list meets the criteria as shown in FIGURE 8-20.
   g. Save the workbook, then preview the worksheet.

FIGURE 8-20

	Employee Number	First Name	Last Name	Hire Date	Branch	Monthly Salary	Annual Salary	Annual Bonus	Benefits Dollars	Annual Compensation	K
1	Employee Number	First Name	Last Name	Hire Date	Branch	Monthly Salary	Annual Salary	Annual Bonus	Benefits Dollars	Annual Compensation	
2				<1/1/2017			>75000				
3											
4											
5											
6											
7	Employee Number	First Name	Last Name	Hire Date	Branch	Monthly Salary	Annual Salary	Annual Bonus	Benefits Dollars	Annual Compensation	
8	1005	Molly	Lake	2/12/2015	LA	$ 4,850	$ 58,200	$ 1,470	$ 13,386	$ 73,056	
9	1778	Lynn	Waters	4/1/2016	Chicago	$ 5,170	$ 62,040	$ 5,125	$ 14,269	$ 81,434	
10	1469	Donna	Davie	5/6/2016	Dallas	$ 6,550	$ 78,600	$ 6,725	$ 18,078	$ 103,403	
11	1734	Martha	Mele	12/10/2016	Dallas	$ 7,450	$ 89,400	$ 5,550	$ 20,562	$ 115,512	
12	1578	Hank	Gole	2/15/2014	Chicago	$ 4,950	$ 59,400	$ 1,680	$ 13,662	$ 74,742	
13	1499	Peter	East	3/25/2015	LA	$ 1,750	$ 21,000	$ 1,630	$ 4,830	$ 27,460	
14	1080	Emily	Malone	6/23/2014	Chicago	$ 4,225	$ 50,700	$ 2,320	$ 11,661	$ 64,681	
15	1998	Mike	Magee	8/3/2017	Chicago	$ 5,750	$ 69,000	$ 5,900	$ 15,870	$ 90,770	
16	1662	Ted	Reily	9/29/2016	LA	$ 7,500	$ 90,000	$ 3,002	$ 20,700	$ 113,702	
17	1322	Jason	Round	5/12/2016	Dallas	$ 4,750	$ 57,000	$ 995	$ 13,110	$ 71,105	
18											
19											
20	Employee Number	First Name	Last Name	Hire Date	Branch	Monthly Salary	Annual Salary	Annual Bonus	Benefits Dollars	Annual Compensation	
21	1469	Donna	Davie	5/6/2016	Dallas	$ 6,550	$ 78,600	$ 6,725	$ 18,078	$ 103,403	
22	1734	Martha	Mele	12/10/2016	Dallas	$ 7,450	$ 89,400	$ 5,550	$ 20,562	$ 115,512	
23	1662	Ted	Reily	9/29/2016	LA	$ 7,500	$ 90,000	$ 3,002	$ 20,700	$ 113,702	
24											

Skills Review (continued)

4. Look up values in a table.

a. Click the Summary sheet tab. Use the Name Manager to view the table names in the workbook, then close the dialog box.

b. Prepare to use a lookup function to locate an employee's annual compensation; enter the Employee Number **1578** in cell A18.

c. In cell B18, use the VLOOKUP function and enter **A18** as the Lookup_value, **Table2** as the Table_array, **10** as the Col_index_num, and **FALSE** as the Range_lookup; observe the compensation displayed for that employee number, then check it against the table to make sure it is correct.

d. Replace the existing Employee Number in cell A18 with **1998**, and view the annual compensation for that employee.

e. Format cell B18 with the Accounting format with the $ symbol and no decimal places.

f. Save the workbook.

5. Summarize table data.

a. Prepare to enter a database function to average the annual salaries by branch, using the LA branch as the initial criterion. In cell E18, use the DAVERAGE function, and click the upper-left corner of cell A1 twice to select the table and its header row as the Database, select cell G1 for the Field, and select the range D17:D18 for the Criteria. Verify that the average LA salary is 56400.

b. Test the function further by entering the text **Dallas** in cell D18. When the criterion is entered, cell E18 should display 75000.

c. Format cell E18 in Accounting format with the $ symbol and no decimal places.

d. Save the workbook.

6. Validate table data.

a. Select the data in column E of the table, and set a validation criterion specifying that you want to allow a list of valid options.

b. Enter a list of valid options that restricts the entries to **LA**, **Chicago**, and **Dallas**. Remember to use a comma between each item in the list.

c. Indicate that you want the options to appear in an in-cell drop-down list, then close the dialog box.

d. Add a row to the table. Go to cell E12, then select Chicago in the drop-down list.

e. Complete the new record by adding an Employee Number of **1119**, a First Name of **Cate**, a Last Name of **Smith**, a Hire Date of **10/1/2017**, a monthly salary of **$5000**, and an Annual Bonus of **$5000**. Format the range F12:J12 as Accounting with no decimal places and using the $ symbol. Compare your screen to FIGURE 8-21.

f. Add your name to the center section of the footer, save the worksheet, then preview the worksheet.

FIGURE 8-21

	A	B	C	D	E	F	G	H	I	J	K
1	Employee Number	First Name	Last Name	Hire Date	Branch	Monthly Salary	Annual Salary	Annual Bonus	Benefits Dollars	Annual Compensation	
2	1005	Molly	Lake	2/12/2015	LA	$ 4,850	$ 58,200	$ 1,470	$ 13,386	$ 73,056	
3	1778	Lynn	Waters	4/1/2016	Chicago	$ 5,170	$ 62,040	$ 5,125	$ 14,269	$ 81,434	
4	1469	Donna	Davie	5/6/2016	Dallas	$ 6,550	$ 78,600	$ 6,725	$ 18,078	$ 103,403	
5	1734	Martha	Mele	12/10/2016	Dallas	$ 7,450	$ 89,400	$ 5,550	$ 20,562	$ 115,512	
6	1578	Hank	Gole	2/15/2014	Chicago	$ 4,950	$ 59,400	$ 1,680	$ 13,662	$ 74,742	
7	1499	Peter	East	3/25/2015	LA	$ 1,750	$ 21,000	$ 1,630	$ 4,830	$ 27,460	
8	1080	Emily	Malone	6/23/2014	Chicago	$ 4,225	$ 50,700	$ 2,320	$ 11,661	$ 64,681	
9	1998	Mike	Magee	8/3/2017	Chicago	$ 5,750	$ 69,000	$ 5,900	$ 15,870	$ 90,770	
10	1662	Ted	Reily	9/29/2016	LA	$ 7,500	$ 90,000	$ 3,002	$ 20,700	$ 113,702	
11	1322	Jason	Round	5/12/2016	Dallas	$ 4,750	$ 57,000	$ 995	$ 13,110	$ 71,105	
12	1119	Cate	Smith	10/1/2017	Chicago	$ 5,000	$ 60,000	$ 5,000	$ 13,800	$ 78,800	
13											
14											
15											
16											
17	Employee Number	Annual Compensation			Branch	Average Annual Salary					
18	1998	$ 90,770			Dallas	$ 75,000					
19											
20											

Skills Review (continued)

7. Create subtotals.

    a. Click the Subtotals sheet tab.

    b. Use the Branch field list arrow to sort the table in ascending order by branch.

    c. Convert the table to a range.

    d. Group and create subtotals of the Annual Compensation data by branch, using the SUM function.

    e. Click the 2 outline button on the outline to display only the subtotals and the grand total. Compare your screen to **FIGURE 8-22**.

    f. Enter your name in the worksheet footer, save the workbook, then preview the worksheet.

    g. Save the workbook, close the workbook, exit Excel, then submit your workbook to your instructor.

FIGURE 8-22

		A	B	C	D	E	F	G	H	I	J
1		Employee Number	First Name	Last Name	Hire Date	Branch	Monthly Salary	Annual Salary	Annual Bonus	Benefits Dollars	Annual Compensation
6						Chicago Total					$ 311,627
10						Dallas Total					$ 290,020
14						LA Total					$ 214,218
15						Grand Total					$ 815,865
16											
17											
18											

Independent Challenge 1

As the manager of Tampa Medical, a diagnostic supply company, you spend a lot of time managing your inventory. To help with this task, you have created an Excel table that you can extract information from using filters. You also need to add data validation and summary information to the table.

    a. Start Excel, open EX 8-3.xlsx from where you store your Data Files, then save it as **EX 8-Diagnostic**.

    b. Using the table data on the Inventory sheet, create a filter to display information about only the pulse monitors. Clear the filter.

    c. Use a Custom Filter to generate a list of products with a quantity greater than 15. Clear the filter.

    d. Copy the labels in cells A1:E1 into A16:E16. Type **Stethoscope** in cell A17, and type **<$275.00** in cell C17. Use the Advanced Filter with a criteria range of A16:E17 to extract a table of stethoscopes priced less than $275.00 to the range of cells beginning in cell A20. Enter your name in the worksheet footer, save the workbook, then preview the worksheet.

    e. On the Summary sheet, select the table data in column B. Open the Data Validation dialog box, then indicate you want to use a validation list with the acceptable entries of **Lee**, **Rand**, **Barry**. Make sure the In-cell dropdown check box is selected.

    f. Test the data validation by trying to change any cell in column B of the table to **Lane**.

    g. Using **FIGURE 8-23** as a guide, enter a function in cell E18 that calculates the total quantity of Stethoscopes available in your inventory. Enter your name in the worksheet footer, preview the worksheet, then save the workbook.

    h. On the Subtotals sheet, sort the table in ascending order by product. Convert the table to a range. Insert subtotals by product using the Sum function, then select Quantity in the "Add Subtotal to" box. Remove the check box for the Total field, if necessary. Use the appropriate button on the outline to display only the subtotals and grand total. Save the workbook, then preview the worksheet.

    i. Submit the workbook to your instructor. Close the workbook, then exit Excel.

FIGURE 8-23

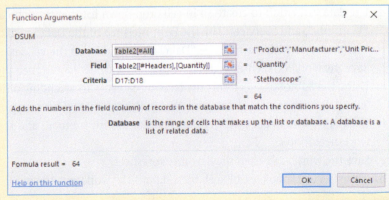

Independent Challenge 2

As the senior accountant at Miami Plumbing Supply, you are adding new features to the company's accounts receivables workbook. The business supplies both residential and commercial plumbers. You have put together an invoice table to track sales for the month of June. Now that you have this table, you would like to manipulate it in several ways. First, you want to filter the table to show only invoices over a certain amount with certain order dates. You also want to subtotal the total column by residential and commercial supplies. To prevent data entry errors you will restrict entries in the Order Date column. Finally, you would like to add database and lookup functions to your worksheet to efficiently retrieve data from the table.

a. Start Excel, open EX 8-4.xlsx from where you store your Data Files, then save it as **EX 8-Invoices**.

b. Use the Advanced Filter to show invoices with amounts more than $300.00 ordered before 6/15/2017, using cells A27:B28 to enter your criteria and extracting the results to cell A33. (*Hint*: You don't need to specify an entire row as the criteria range.) Enter your name in the worksheet footer.

c. Use the Data Validation dialog box to restrict entries to those with order dates between 6/1/2017 and 6/30/2017. Test the data restrictions by attempting to enter an invalid date in cell B25.

d. Enter **23706** in cell G28. Enter a VLOOKUP function in cell H28 to retrieve the total based on the invoice number entered in cell G28. Make sure you have an exact match with the invoice number. Test the function with the invoice number 23699.

e. Enter the date **6/1/2017** in cell J28. Use the database function, DCOUNT, in cell K28 to count the number of invoices for the date in cell J28. Save the workbook, then preview the worksheet.

f. On the Subtotals worksheet, sort the table in ascending order by Type, then convert the table to a range. Create subtotals showing the totals for commercial and residential invoices. Display only the subtotals for the commercial and residential accounts, along with the grand total.

g. Save the workbook, preview the worksheet, close the workbook, then exit Excel. Submit the workbook to your instructor.

Independent Challenge 3

You are the manager of Fitness Now, a service company for fitness equipment. You have created an Excel table that contains your invoice data, along with the totals for each invoice. You would like to manipulate this table to display service categories and invoices meeting specific criteria. You would also like to add subtotals to the table and add database functions to total categories of invoices. Finally, you want to restrict entries in the Category column.

a. Start Excel, open EX 8-5.xlsx from where you store your Data Files, then save it as **EX 8-Equipment**.

b. On the Invoice sheet, use the headings in row 37 to create an advanced filter that extracts records with the following criteria to cell A42: totals greater than $1500 having dates either before 9/10/2017 or after 9/19/2017. (*Hint*: Recall that when you want records to meet one criterion or another, you need to place the criteria on separate lines.)

c. Use the DSUM function in cell G2 to let worksheet users find the total amount for the category entered in cell F2. Format the cell containing the total using the Accounting format with the $ symbol and no decimals. Verify the warranty category total is $8,228. Preview the worksheet.

d. Use data validation to create an in-cell drop-down list that restricts category entries to "Preventative Maintenance", "Warranty", and "Service". Use the Error Alert tab of the Data Validation dialog box to set the alert style to the Warning style with the message "Data is not valid." Test the validation in the table with valid and invalid entries. Save the workbook, enter your name in the worksheet footer, then preview the worksheet.

e. Using the Subtotals sheet, sort the table by category in ascending order. Convert the table to a range, and add Subtotals to the totals by category. Widen the columns, if necessary.

f. Use the outline to display only category names with subtotals and the grand total. Enter your name in the worksheet footer.

g. Save the workbook, then preview the worksheet.

h. Close the workbook, exit Excel, then submit the workbook to your instructor.

Independent Challenge 4: Explore

You are an inventory manager at East Coast Medical, a medical equipment distributor. You track your inventory of equipment in an Excel worksheet. You would like to use conditional formatting in your worksheet to help track the products that need to be reordered as well as your inventory expenses. You would also like to prevent data entry errors. Finally, you would like to add an area to quickly look up prices and quantities for customers.

a. Start Excel, open EX 8-6.xlsx from where you store your Data Files, then save it as **EX 8-East Coast Medical**.

b. Using FIGURE 8-24 as a guide, use conditional formatting to add icons to the quantity column using the following criteria: format quantities greater than or equal to 300 with a green circle, quantities greater than or equal to 100 but less than 300 with a yellow circle, and quantities less than 100 with a red circle. (*Hint*: You may need to click in the top Value text box for the correct value to display for the red circle.)

c. Conditionally format the Total data using Top/Bottom Rules to emphasize the cells containing the top 30 percent with red text.

d. Add another rule to format the bottom 20 percent in the Total column with purple text from the standard colors palette.

e. Restrict the Wholesale Price field entries to decimal values between 0 and 10000. Add an input message of **Prices must be less than $10,000**. Add an Information level error message of **Please check price**. Test the validation entering a price of $10,100 in cell C3 and allow the new price to be entered.

FIGURE 8-24

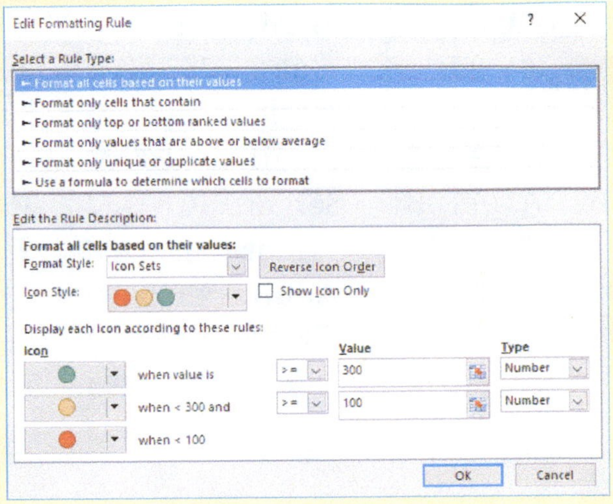

f. Below the table, create a product lookup area with the following labels in adjacent cells: **Product Number**, **Wholesale Price**, **Quantity**. Right align these labels in the cells.

g. Using the Table Tools Design tab, name the table "Inventory".

h. Enter 1445 under the label Product Number in your products lookup area.

i. In the product lookup area, enter lookup functions to locate the wholesale price and quantity information for the product number that you entered in the previous step. Use the assigned table name of Inventory and make sure you match the product number exactly. Format the wholesale price with the Accounting format and two decimal places.

j. Enter your name in the center section of the worksheet header, save the workbook, then preview the worksheet comparing it to FIGURE 8-25.

k. Close the workbook, exit Excel, then submit the workbook to your instructor.

FIGURE 8-25

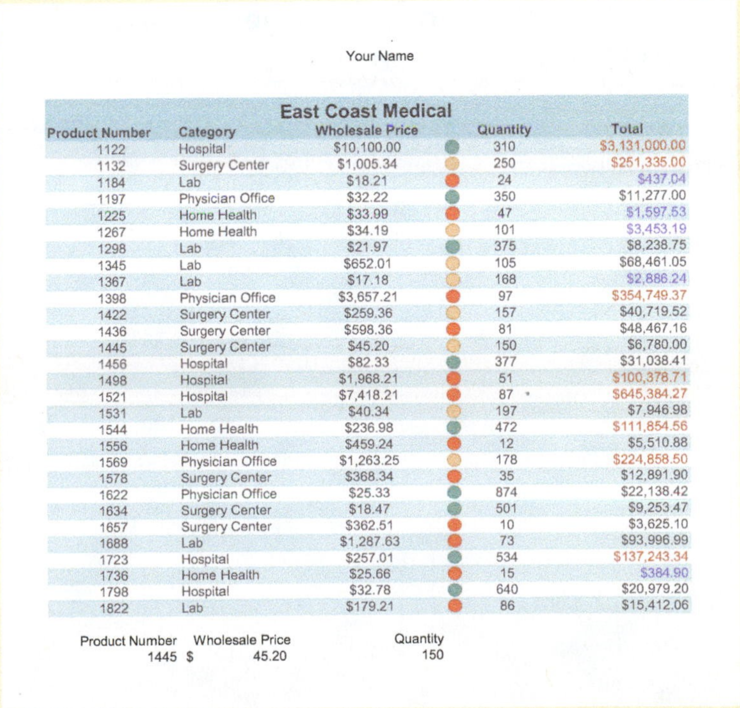

Your Name

East Coast Medical

Product Number	Category	Wholesale Price	Quantity	Total
1122	Hospital	$10,100.00	310	$3,131,000.00
1132	Surgery Center	$1,005.34	250	$251,335.00
1184	Lab	$18.21	24	$437.04
1197	Physician Office	$32.22	350	$11,277.00
1225	Home Health	$33.99	47	$1,597.53
1267	Home Health	$34.19	101	$3,453.19
1298	Lab	$21.97	375	$8,238.75
1345	Lab	$652.01	105	$68,461.05
1367	Lab	$17.18	168	$2,886.24
1398	Physician Office	$3,657.21	97	$354,749.37
1422	Surgery Center	$259.36	157	$40,719.52
1436	Surgery Center	$598.36	81	$48,467.16
1445	Surgery Center	$45.20	150	$6,780.00
1456	Hospital	$82.33	377	$31,038.41
1498	Hospital	$1,968.21	51	$100,378.71
1521	Hospital	$7,418.21	87	$645,384.27
1531	Lab	$40.34	197	$7,946.98
1544	Home Health	$236.98	472	$111,854.56
1556	Home Health	$459.24	12	$5,510.88
1569	Physician Office	$1,263.25	178	$224,858.50
1578	Surgery Center	$368.34	35	$12,891.90
1622	Physician Office	$25.33	874	$22,138.42
1634	Surgery Center	$18.47	501	$9,253.47
1657	Surgery Center	$362.51	10	$3,625.10
1688	Lab	$1,287.63	73	$93,996.99
1723	Hospital	$257.01	534	$137,243.34
1736	Home Health	$25.66	15	$384.90
1798	Hospital	$32.78	640	$20,979.20
1822	Lab	$179.21	86	$15,412.06

Product Number	Wholesale Price	Quantity
1445	$ 45.20	150

Excel 2016

Visual Workshop

Open EX 8-7.xlsx from where you store your Data Files, then save it as **EX 8-Therapy**. Complete the worksheet as shown in FIGURE 8-26. An in-cell drop-down list has been added to the data entered in the Pool field. The range A18:F21 is extracted from the table using the criteria in cells A15:A16. Add your name to the worksheet footer, save the workbook, preview the worksheet, then submit the workbook to your instructor.

FIGURE 8-26

	A	B	C	D	E	F
1				**Aquatic Therapy Schedule**		
2						
3	**Code**	**Group**	**Time**	**Day**	**Pool**	**Instructor**
4	AQA100	Baby	10:30 AM	Thursday	Teaching Pool	Malone
5	AQA101	Child	8:00 AM	Tuesday	Teaching Pool	Grey
6	AQA102	Adult	9:00 AM	Wednesday	Lap Pool	Malone
7	AQA103	Senior	10:00 AM	Monday	Lap Pool	Brent
8	AQA104	Senior	11:00 AM	Friday	Lap Pool	Paulson
9	AQA105	Adult	12:00 PM	Saturday	Lap Pool	Grey
10	AQA106	Child	12:00 PM	Tuesday	Teaching Pool	Rand
11	AQA107	Senior	2:00 PM	Monday	Lap Pool	Walton
12	AQA108	Adult	4:00 PM	Tuesday	Lap Pool	Malone
13					Please select Teaching Pool or Lap Pool.	
14						
15	**Group**					
16	Senior					
17						
18	**Code**	**Group**	**Time**	**Day**	**Pool**	**Instructor**
19	AQA103	Senior	10:00 AM	Monday	Lap Pool	Brent
20	AQA104	Senior	11:00 AM	Friday	Lap Pool	Paulson
21	AQA107	Senior	2:00 PM	Monday	Lap Pool	Walton
22						

Glossary

3-D reference A worksheet reference that uses values on other sheets or workbooks, effectively creating another dimension to a workbook.

Absolute cell reference In a formula, a cell address that refers to a specific cell and does not change when you copy the formula; indicated by a dollar sign before the column letter and/or row number. *See also* Relative cell reference.

Active The currently available document, program, or object; on the taskbar, when more than one program is open, the button for the active program appears slightly lighter.

Active cell The cell in which you are currently working.

Add-in Software that works with an installed app to extend its features.

Alignment The placement of cell contents in relation to a cell's edges; for example, left-aligned, centered, or right-aligned.

And logical condition A filtering feature that searches for records by specifying that all entered criteria must be matched.

Animation emphasis effect In Sway, a special effect you can apply to an object to animate it.

Argument Information necessary for a formula or function to calculate an answer.

Arithmetic operators In a formula, symbols that perform mathematical calculations, such as addition (+), subtraction (–), multiplication (*), division (/), or exponentiation (^).

Ascending order In sorting an Excel field (column), the lowest value (the beginning of the alphabet, or the earliest date) appears at the beginning of the sorted data.

AutoFill Feature activated by dragging the fill handle; copies a cell's contents or continues a series of entries into adjacent cells.

AutoFill Options button Button that appears after using the fill handle to copy cell contents; enables you to choose to fill cells with specific elements (such as formatting) of the copied cell if desired.

AutoFilter A table feature that lets you click a list arrow and select criteria by which to display certain types of records; *also called* filter.

AutoFilter list arrows *See* Filter List arrows.

AutoFit A feature that automatically adjusts the width of a column or the height of a row to accommodate its widest or tallest entry.

Backstage view View that appears when the File tab is clicked. The navigation bar on the left side contains commands to perform actions common to most Office programs, such as opening a file, saving a file, and closing the file.

Backward-compatible Software feature that enables documents saved in an older version of a program to be opened in a newer version of the program.

Banding Worksheet formatting in which adjacent rows and columns are formatted differently.

Business Intelligence tools Excel features for gathering and analyzing data to answer sophisticated business questions.

Calculated columns In a table, a column that automatically fills in cells with formula results, using a formula entered in only one other cell in the same column.

Calculation operators Symbols in a formula that indicate what type of calculation to perform on the cells, ranges, or values.

Card A section for a particular type of content in a Sway presentation.

Category axis Horizontal axis in a chart, usually containing the names of data categories; in a 2-dimensional chart, also known as the x-axis.

Cell The intersection of a column and a row in a worksheet or table.

Cell address The location of a cell, expressed by cell coordinates; for example, the cell address of the cell in column A, row 1 is A1.

Cell pointer Dark rectangle that outlines the active cell.

Cell styles Predesigned combinations of formats based on themes that can be applied to selected cells to enhance the look of a worksheet.

Chart sheet A separate sheet in a workbook that contains only a chart, which is linked to the workbook data.

Charts Pictorial representations of worksheet data that make it easier to see patterns, trends, and relationships; *also called* graphs.

Clip A media file, such as a graphic, sound, animation, or movie; also, a short segment of audio or video.

Clip art A graphic image, such as a corporate logo, a picture, or a photo, that can be inserted into a document.

Clipboard A temporary Windows storage area that holds the selections you copy or cut.

Cloud computing Work done in a virtual environment using data, applications, and resources stored on servers and accessed over the Internet or a company's internal network rather than on users' computers.

Color scale In conditional formatting, a formatting scheme that uses a set of two, three, or four fill colors to convey relative values of data.

Column heading Box that appears above each column in a worksheet; identifies the column letter, such as A, B, etc.

Combination chart Two charts in one, such as a column chart combined with a line chart, that together graph related but dissimilar data.

Comparison operators In a formula, symbols that compare values for the purpose of true/false results.

Compatibility The ability of different programs to work together and exchange data.

Complex formula A formula that uses more than one arithmetic operator.

Conditional formatting A type of cell formatting that changes based on the cell's value or the outcome of a formula.

Consolidate To combine data on multiple worksheets and display the result on another worksheet.

Contextual tab A tab that is displayed only when a specific task can be performed; appears in an accent color.

Cortana The Microsoft Windows virtual assistant that integrates with Microsoft Edge to find and provide information.

Creative Commons license A public copyright license that allows the free distribution of an otherwise copyrighted work.

Criteria range In advanced filtering, a cell range containing one row of labels and at least one additional row underneath it that contains the criteria you want to match.

D
Data entry area The unlocked portion of a worksheet where users are able to enter and change data.

Data marker A graphical representation of a data point in a chart, such as a bar or column.

Data point Individual piece of data plotted in a chart.

Data series The selected range in a worksheet whose related data points Excel converts into a chart.

Delimiter A separator such as a space, comma, or semicolon between elements in imported data.

Descending order In sorting an Excel field (column), the order that begins with the letter Z, the highest number, or the latest date of the values in a field.

Dialog box launcher An icon you can click to open a dialog box or task pane from which to choose related commands.

Docs.com A Microsoft website designed for sharing Sway sites.

Document window Most of the screen in any given program, where you create a document, slide, or worksheet.

Drawing canvas In OneNote, a container for shapes and lines.

Dynamic page breaks In a larger workbook, horizontal or vertical dashed lines that represent the place where pages print separately. They also adjust automatically when you insert or delete rows or columns, or change column widths or row heights.

E
Edit To make a change to the contents of an active cell.

Electronic spreadsheet A computer program used to perform calculations and analyze and present numeric data.

Embedded chart A chart displayed as an object in a worksheet.

Exploding Visually pulling a slice of a pie chart away from the whole pie chart in order to add emphasis to the pie slice.

External reference indicator The exclamation point (!) used in a formula to indicate that a referenced cell is outside the active sheet.

Extract To place a copy of a filtered table in a range you specify in the Advanced Filter dialog box.

F
Field In a table (an Excel database), a column that describes a characteristic about records, such as first name or city.

Field name A column label that describes a field.

File A stored collection of data.

Filter list arrows List arrows that appear next to field names in an Excel table; used to display portions of your data. *Also called* AutoFilter list arrows.

Flash Fill An Excel feature that automatically fills in column or row data based on calculations you enter.

Font The typeface or design of a set of characters (letters, numbers, symbols, and punctuation marks).

Font size The size of characters, measured in units called points.

Font style Format such as bold, italic, and underlining that can be applied to change the way characters look in a worksheet or chart.

Format The appearance of a cell and its contents, including font, font styles, font color, fill color, borders, and shading. *See also* Number format.

Formula A set of instructions used to perform one or more numeric calculations, such as adding, multiplying, or averaging, on values or cells.

Formula bar The area above the worksheet grid where you enter or edit data in the active cell.

Formula prefix An arithmetic symbol, such as the equal sign (=), used to start a formula.

Free response quiz A type of Office Mix quiz containing questions that require short answers.

Freeze To hold in place selected columns or rows when scrolling in a worksheet that is divided in panes. *See also* Panes.

Function A predefined formula that provides a shortcut for a common or complex calculation, such as SUM (for calculating a sum) or FV (for calculating the future value of an investment).

G
Gallery A visual collection of choices you can browse through to make a selection. Often available with Live Preview.

Gridlines Evenly spaced horizontal and/or vertical lines used in a worksheet or chart to make it easier to read.

Groups Each tab on the Ribbon is arranged into groups to make features easy to find.

H
Header row In an Excel table, the first row; it contains field (column) names.

HTML (Hypertext Markup Language) The coding format used for web documents.

Hub A pane in Microsoft Edge that provides access to favorite websites, a reading list, browsing history, and downloaded files.

Hyperlink An object (a filename, a word, a phrase, or a graphic) in a worksheet that, when you click it, displays another worksheet or a Webpage called the target. *See also* Target.

Icon sets In conditional formatting, groups of images used to visually communicate relative cell values based on the values they contain.

Ink to Math tool The OneNote tool that converts handwritten mathematical formulas to formatted equations or expressions.

Ink to Text tool The OneNote tool that converts inked handwriting to typed text.

Inked handwriting In OneNote, writing produced when using a pen tool to enter text.

Inking toolbar In Microsoft Edge, a collection of tools for annotating a webpage.

Insertion point A blinking vertical line that appears when you click in the formula bar or in an active cell; indicates where new text will be inserted.

Instance A worksheet in its own workbook window.

Integrate To incorporate a document and parts of a document created in one program into another program; for example, to incorporate an Excel chart into a PowerPoint slide, or an Access table into a Word document.

Interface The look and feel of a program; for example, the appearance of commands and the way they are organized in the program window.

Intranet An internal network site used by a group of people who work together.

Keywords Terms added to a workbook's Document Properties that help locate the file in a search.

Labels Descriptive text or other information that identifies data in rows, columns, or charts, but is not included in calculations.

Landscape Page orientation in which the contents of a page span the length of a page rather than its width, making the page wider than it is tall.

Launch To open or start a program on your computer.

Legend In a chart, information that identifies how data is represented by colors or patterns.

Linking The dynamic referencing of data in the same or in other workbooks, so that when data in the other location is changed, the references in the current location are automatically updated.

List arrows *See* AutoFilter list arrows.

Live Preview A feature that lets you point to a choice in a gallery or palette and see the results in the document without actually clicking the choice.

Lock To secure a row, column, or sheet so that data in that location cannot be changed.

Logical conditions Using the operators And and Or to narrow a custom filter criteria.

Logical formula A formula with calculations that are based on stated conditions.

Logical test The first part of an IF function; if the logical test is true, then the second part of the function is applied; if it is false, then the third part of the function is applied.

Macros Programmed instructions that perform tasks in a workbook.

Major gridlines In a chart, the gridlines that represent the values at the tick marks on the value axis.

Metadata Information that describes data and is used in Microsoft Windows document searches.

Microsoft OneNote Mobile app The lightweight version of Microsoft OneNote designed for phones, tablets, and other mobile devices.

Minor gridlines In a chart, the gridlines that represent the values between the tick marks on the value axis.

Mixed reference Cell reference that combines both absolute and relative cell addressing.

Mode indicator An area on the left end of the status bar that indicates the program's status. For example, when you are changing the contents of a cell, the word 'Edit' appears in the mode indicator.

Multilevel sort A reordering of table data using more than one column (field) at a time.

Name box Box to the left of the formula bar that shows the cell reference or name of the active cell.

Navigate To move around in a worksheet; for example, you can use the arrow keys on the keyboard to navigate from cell to cell, or press [Page Up] or [Page Down] to move one screen at a time.

Normal view Default worksheet view that shows the worksheet without features such as headers and footers; ideal for creating and editing a worksheet, but may not be detailed enough when formatting a document.

Note In OneNote, a small window that contains text or other types of information.

Notebook In OneNote, the container for notes, drawings, and other content.

Number format A format applied to values to express numeric concepts, such as currency, date, and percentage.

Object Independent element on a worksheet (such as a chart or graphic) that is not located in a specific cell or range; can be moved and resized and displays handles when selected.

OneDrive An online storage and file sharing service; access to OneDrive is through a Microsoft account.

Online collaboration The ability to incorporate feedback or share information across the Internet or a company network or intranet.

Or logical condition A filtering feature that searches for records by specifying that only one entered criterion must be matched.

Order of precedence Rules that determine the order in which operations are performed within a formula containing more than one arithmetic operator.

Page In OneNote, a workspace for inserting notes and other content, similar to a page in a physical notebook.

Page Break Preview A view that displays a reduced view of each page in a worksheet, along with page break indicators that you can drag to include more or less information on a page.

Page Layout view Provides an accurate view of how a worksheet will look when printed, including headers and footers.

Panes Sections into which you can divide a worksheet when you want to work on separate parts of the worksheet at the same time; one pane freezes, or remains in place, while you scroll in another pane until you see the desired information.

Paste Options button Button that appears onscreen after pasting content; enables you to choose to paste only specific elements of the copied selection, such as the formatting or values, if desired.

Plot area In a chart, the area inside the horizontal and vertical axes.

Point A unit of measure used for font size and row height. One point is equal to 1/72nd of an inch.

Portrait Page orientation in which the contents of a page span the width of a page, so the page is taller than it is wide.

Previewing Prior to printing, seeing onscreen exactly how the printed document will look.

Print area A portion of a worksheet that you can define using the Print Area button on the Page Layout tab; after you select and define a print area, the Quick Print feature prints only that worksheet area.

Print title In a table that spans more than one page, the field names that print at the top of every printed page.

Properties File characteristics, such as the author's name, keywords, or the title, that help others understand, identify, and locate the file.

Publish To share Excel workbook data on a network or on the web so that others can access it using a web browser.

Quick Access toolbar A small toolbar on the left side of a Microsoft application program window's title bar, containing icons that you click to quickly perform common actions, such as saving a file.

Quick Analysis tool An icon that is displayed below and to the right of a range that lets you easily create charts and other elements.

Range A selection of two or more cells, such as B5:B14.

Read-only format Describes cells that display data but that cannot be changed in a protected worksheet.

Reading view In Microsoft Edge, the display of a webpage that removes ads and most graphics and uses a simple format for the text.

Record In a table, data concerning an object or a person.

Reference operators In a formula, symbols which enable you to use ranges in calculations.

Relative cell reference In a formula, a cell address that refers to a cell's location in relation to the cell containing the formula and that automatically changes to reflect the new location when the formula is copied or moved; default type of referencing used in Excel worksheets. *See also* Absolute cell reference.

Responsive design A way to provide content so that it adapts appropriately to the size of the display on any device.

Return In a function, to display a result.

Ribbon Appears beneath the title bar in every Office app window and displays likely commands for the current task.

Sandbox A computer security mechanism that helps to prevent attackers from gaining control of a computer.

Scope In a named cell or range, the worksheet(s) in which the name can be used.

Screen capture An electronic snapshot of your screen, which you can paste into a document.

Screen clipping In OneNote, an image copied from any part of a computer screen.

Screen recording In Office Mix, a video you create by capturing your desktop and any actions performed on it.

Screenshot An image of an open file that is pasted into an Excel document; you can move, copy, and edit the image.

Scroll bars Bars on the right edge (vertical scroll bar) and bottom edge (horizontal scroll bar) of a window that allow you to move around in a document that is too large to fit on the screen at once.

Search criterion In a workbook or table search, the text you are searching for.

Secondary axis In a combination chart, an additional axis that supplies the scale for one of the chart types used.

Section tab In OneNote, a divider for organizing a notebook.

Sheet tab scrolling buttons Allow you to navigate to additional sheet tabs when available; located to the left of the sheet tabs.

Sheet tabs Identify the sheets in a workbook and let you switch between sheets; located below the worksheet grid.

Single-file webpage Format that integrates all of the worksheets and graphical elements from a workbook into a single file, in the format MHTML, also known as MHT.

Sizing handles Small series of dots at the corners and edges of a chart indicating that the chart is selected; drag to resize the chart.

Slide Notes In Office Mix, the written and displayed version of notes typically used to recite narration while creating a slide recording.

Slide recording In Office Mix, a video you create by recording action with a webcam, a camera attached or built in to a computer.

SmartArt graphics Predesigned diagram types for specific types of data, including List, Process, Cycle, and Hierarchy.

Sparkline A quick, simple chart located within a cell that serves as a visual indicator of data trends.

Stated conditions In a logical formula, criteria you create.

Status bar Bar at the bottom of the Excel window that provides a brief description about the active command or task in progress.

Storyline In Sway, the workspace for assembling a presentation.

Structured reference Allows table formulas to refer to table columns by names that are automatically generated when the table is created.

Suite A group of programs that are bundled together and share a similar interface, making it easy to transfer skills and program content among them.

Sway site A website Sway creates to share and display a Sway presentation.

Sync In OneNote, to save a new or updated notebook so that all versions of the notebook, such as a notebook on OneDrive and a copy on a hard drive, have the same contents.

Table An organized collection of rows and columns of similarly structured data on a worksheet.

Table styles Predesigned formatting that can be applied to a range of cells or even to an entire worksheet; especially useful for those ranges with labels in the left column and top row, and totals in the bottom row or right column. *See also* Table.

Table total row A row you can add to the bottom of a table for calculations using the data in the table columns.

Tabs Organizational unit used for commands on the Ribbon. The tab names appear at the top of the Ribbon and the active tab appears in front.

Target The location that a hyperlink displays after you click it.

Template In Excel, a predesigned, formatted file that serves as the basis for a new workbook; in OneNote, a page design you can apply to new pages to provide an appealing background, a consistent layout, or elements suitable for certain types of notes, such as meeting notes or to-do lists.

Text annotations Labels added to a chart to draw attention to or describe a particular area.

Text concatenation operators In a formula, symbols used to join strings of text in different cells.

Theme A predefined set of colors, fonts, line and fill effects, and other formats that can be applied to an Excel worksheet and give it a consistent, professional look.

Tick marks Notations of a scale of measure on a chart axis.

Title bar Appears at the top of every Office program window; displays the document name and program name.

To Do tag In OneNote, an icon that helps you keep track of your assignments and other tasks; in Microsoft Edge, an annotation on a webpage.

User interface A term for all the ways you interact with an app.

Value axis In a chart, the axis that contains numerical values; in a 2-dimensional chart, also known as the y-axis.

Values Numbers, formulas, and functions used in calculations.

View A method of displaying a document window to show more or fewer details or a different combination of elements that makes it easier to complete certain tasks, such as formatting or reading text.

Watermark A translucent background design on a worksheet that is displayed when the worksheet is printed. A watermark is a graphic file that is inserted into the document header.

What-if analysis A decision-making tool in which data is changed and formulas are recalculated, in order to predict various possible outcomes.

Wildcard A special symbol that substitutes for unknown characters in defining search criteria in the Find and Replace dialog box. The most common types of wildcards are the question mark (?), which stands for any single character, and the asterisk (*), which represents any group of characters.

Workbook A collection of related worksheets contained within a single file which has the file extension xlsx.

Worksheet A single sheet within a workbook file; also, the entire area within an electronic spreadsheet that contains a grid of columns and rows.

Worksheet window Area of the program window that displays part of the current worksheet; the worksheet window displays only a small fraction of the worksheet, which can contain a total of 1,048,576 rows and 16,384 columns.

X-axis The horizontal axis in a chart; often shows data categories, such as months or locations.

XML Acronym that stands for eXtensible Markup Language, which is a language used to structure, store, and send information.

Y-axis The vertical axis in a chart; often shows numerical values.

Z-axis The third axis in a true 3-D chart, lets you compare data points across both categories and values.

Zooming in A feature that makes a document appear larger but shows less of it on screen at once; does not affect actual document size.

Zooming out A feature that shows more of a document on screen at once but at a reduced size; does not affect actual document size.

Index

C

X

Y

Z